Using Google App Engine

DATE DUE

D1469823

Using Google App Engine

Charles Severance

O'REILLY®
Beijing · Cambridge · Farnham · Köln · Sebastopol · Taipei · Tokyo

Using Google App Engine
by Charles Severance

Copyright © 2009 Charles Severance. All rights reserved.
Printed in the United States of America.

Published by O'Reilly Media, Inc., 1005 Gravenstein Highway North, Sebastopol, CA 95472.

O'Reilly books may be purchased for educational, business, or sales promotional use. Online editions are also available for most titles (*http://my.safaribooksonline.com*). For more information, contact our corporate/institutional sales department: (800) 998-9938 or *corporate@oreilly.com*.

Editor: Mike Loukides	**Indexer:** Fred Brown
Production Editor: Loranah Dimant	**Cover Designer:** Karen Montgomery
Copyeditor: Nancy Kotary	**Interior Designer:** David Futato
Proofreader: Nancy Reinhardt	**Illustrator:** Robert Romano

Printing History:

May 2009:	First Edition.

ISBN: 978-0-596-80069-7

[M]

1241457704

Table of Contents

Preface

The greatest single reason that the World Wide Web has been so widely used and adopted is because individuals are allowed to participate in the Web. People can produce web content and create a MySpace page or home pages provided by their school or organization and contribute their creativity and content to the Web. Free services like Blogger, Flickr, Google Sites, Google Groups, and others have given us all an outlet for our creativity and presence on the Web—at no charge.

For most of the life of the Web, if you wanted to have your own rich software-backed website with data storage, your only choice was to purchase hosting services from an Internet Service Provider (ISP) and learn database management and a programming language like PHP to build or run your software. Learning and paying for this much technology was just beyond the reach of most web users, who simply had to accept the limited features of MySpace, Blogger, or whatever system hosted their web content.

In April 2008, Google announced a product called App Engine. When you write a program for the Web that runs on App Engine, your software runs on the Google servers somewhere in the Google "cloud." It is as if you are a Google employee and you have access to the entire scalable Google infrastructure. App Engine captures much of Google's experience of building fast, reliable, and scalable websites, and through App Engine, Google is revealing many of the secrets about how its own applications scale to millions of users.

The most exciting part of the Google App Engine announcement is the fact that it is free for moderate levels of use. Every person with a Gmail account can have a number of free applications running on the Google infrastructure. If your application becomes extremely popular and your traffic goes above the allowed levels of the free account, you can pay to use more of Google's resources. As your application scales, Google engineers and operations staff take care of all the hardware, data storage, backup, and network provisioning for you.

The cost of purchasing resources from Google's cloud of servers is likely far less than purchasing/renting/maintaining the same amount of resources on your own. Google focuses on providing hardware and network; you focus on building your application and the user community around your application.

Maybe you could write the next Twitter, Craigslist, or del.icio.us. Maybe your idea will be the next big thing that will take off and you can "retire" on the revenue from Google AdWords. Or maybe you just want a site for your local off-road motorcycle club to publish its newsletter, share crash pictures, and maintain a mailing list.

Google App Engine removes the cost barrier from building and deploying software and data-backed websites and putting those sites into production. This book aims to make it easier for the average user to build and deploy basic websites using Google App Engine.

The hope is that literally millions of people from around the world will now be empowered to program on the Web. Who knows what creative applications will evolve in this new and exciting era?

Who Should Read This Book?

This book is aimed at anyone who wants to get started with Google App Engine. Perhaps you are a seasoned programmer with many other languages under your belt; perhaps you have played a bit with HTML and CSS, and you want to learn about software and data-backed websites by deploying your own site or application. It's written for anyone who wants to learn about this new and exciting capability previously reserved for the technical elite.

The book assumes no existing knowledge of programming or web technologies and is written in a way that is understandable to nonprogrammers. It starts from the beginning and covers all the necessary prerequisite technologies, including the Python programming language, HyperText Markup Language (HTML), Cascading Style Sheets (CSS), and the HyperText Transport Protocol (HTTP).

In fact, this book's secret plan is to transform someone from with no knowledge about web technologies into a fire-breathing web application developer in less than a week. By the end of this book, you will know at least enough about these web technologies to be dangerous to yourself and to others. You will have built and understood a fully working and deployed Google App Engine program that touches on all the major technical aspects of the App Engine environment, and you will be in an ideal position to extend your knowledge using Google's online materials or other books to dig more deeply into the subject.

What's in This Book?

This book uses a consistent example of a website with members and multiuser chat, which is built continuously throughout the book. The example is used to introduce topics from HTML and CSS all the way through using AJAX to update your pages dynamically without redrawing the entire screen.

Although I'll cover a lot of material, coverage is limited to include only the information that you need to know to build your application. Once you venture into building more sophisticated applications, you will need additional books and online resources on HTML, CSS, Python, jQuery, and JavaScript.

Chapters 1 through 4 cover the necessary background material in the web technologies that are brought together in the book. If you have experience with any of the topics in Chapters 1 through 4, you can safely skip those chapters (but they'll still be there in case you have a question or need a refresher).

Chapter 1, *Programming on the Web*
> Programming in Google's production environment is different from running your own server or using a hosting account on an ISP. Google takes care of everything related to running your application in production. The trade-off is that you need to follow Google's rules and be a good citizen in Google's community of other applications. This chapter provides a description of the cloud and how it is different from being responsible for your own servers, plus it helps to explain some of the nuances of the App Engine environment.

Chapter 2, *HTML and CSS*
> I assume that folks know the basics of HTML, but there are some important bits that must be covered so that your pages are nice and clean. In the last few years, the legacy browsers that did not support modern HTML and CSS have pretty much died out, so we can write simple and clean HTML and leave the formatting to CSS. I also explore how to validate your HTML and CSS and conform to the document type (DOCTYPE). I talk about page layout using CSS and introduce a bit of the CSS block model so that you can make pretty web pages with simple navigation. If you have been learning HTML by viewing the source code of other people's MySpace pages, you probably need a refresher on the "modern" way to design pages using HTML and CSS.

Chapter 3, *Python*
> This is a very quick introduction to Python that covers only the areas of Python that are necessary for reading the rest of the book. Because we are writing a web application and not a general-purpose application, you need to know only a subset of Python. Python is a great language for beginners, casual users, and power users because it is both simple and powerful. Many claim that Python is *the* language for people who actually use computers.

Chapter 4, *Sending Data to Your Application*
> This chapter sounds a little nerdy—and it is! I think that you actually need to know how the browser talks to a web server and exchanges data using HTTP. It is not all that complex, once you understand it—and it's worth learning. This chapter introduces the first simple App Engine program that we will use to explore how the HTTP request/response cycle works from both the browser and server perspectives.

Chapter 5, *The App Engine webapp Framework*

Properly written App Engine programs consist of a set of cooperating objects. The object-oriented design pattern is how we create and link these objects to get our work done. In this chapter, I teach the basics of object-oriented Python and then jump right into a sample App Engine program using the Google object-oriented web framework. Like the rest of the background chapters, I explain the basics of objects in Python by covering only what you need to know for App Engine.

Chapter 6, *Templates*

In this chapter, I introduce the first part of the Model-View-Controller pattern used in most web frameworks. Using templates, I separate the look and feel of the application (the View) from the rest of the logic of the application. Templates are files that contain HTML augmented using the Django template language to allow certain areas of the HTML to contain information that comes from your Python code (the Controller). You will learn about basic templates as well as inherited templates—where common material is kept in one file and reused across many files—object-oriented templates, as it were.

Chapter 7, *Cookies and Sessions*

In this chapter, I introduce the concept of a session. Sessions and cookies combine to allow the web server to work with multiple simultaneous users. Sessions associate bits of information, such as the name of the currently logged-in user, with one particular browser so that it can distinguish which incoming requests come from which browser.

Chapter 8, *App Engine Datastore*

Google App Engine does not provide you with a relational database. Experts in relational databases will likely feel a bit out of their element when they first look at the Google App Engine Models and Datastore. Readers who have never learned relational databases can be quite thankful that Models (as in Model-View-Controller) are much simpler to use than relational databases. Also, Google has learned through experience that relational databases simply cannot scale to levels beyond millions of users. The Google Datastore can be scaled well beyond a million users. Although you may never need to scale to several million users, you will like how using Models makes storage easier.

Chapter 9, *JavaScript, jQuery, and AJAX*

This chapter adds a little in-browser interactivity to our application via jQuery and AJAX to implement a simple multiuser chat. It also covers how you create multiple data models and link data objects together in the Google Datastore. I explain just enough JavaScript, jQuery, and AJAX to help you understand how your application works with these technologies.

Chapter 10, *Running Your Application on the Google Infrastructure*

This chapter covers how to run your application in the Google infrastructure cloud. You will learn how to get your free App Engine accounts and then upload your software into the cloud. You also learn about the administration interfaces that allow you to monitor and manage your application and data while you are in production.

Chapter 11, *Memory Cache*

The App Engine Memory Cache is a critical technology for making fast and scalable websites. Clever use of Memory Cache can dramatically reduce the load on a Datastore or the network and increase application responsiveness, particularly for material that is read over and over. In this chapter, we explore how the Memory Cache works and develop simple Session capability using the Memory Cache.

Teaching with This Book

This book came out of a University of Michigan School of Information course titled "Design of Complex Websites (SI539)." This course explores emerging web technologies, including ColdFusion, PHP, Ruby on Rails, and now Google Application Engine. The basic idea of the course was to teach in one semester students with very limited technical background enough about database-backed web development "to be dangerous to themselves and others." The course and book are aimed at introducing these concepts to a nontechnical audience.

The book is written at a beginning level; I think that it can be used to support a semester-long "Introduction to Web Programming" course from high school through graduate school. Because this book includes introductions to Python and to HTML and CSS, I hope that it can be used by itself or with supporting material.

For beginning students, you can have a series of assignments that are very similar to the examples in the book, with minor changes such as color or adding images to pages. The assignments can be made more difficult by having the students do a series of parallel, but different, projects that correspond roughly to the concepts in the book's running examples.

The book can also be used to support a one-day workshop in App Engine. It would probably be difficult to teach Python, HTML, CSS, and App Engine in a single day. But because the examples are a single evolving application and each example builds on the previous one, it is possible to skip steps in the interest of time. You might have one exercise where the students modify the *ae-08-login* example (login without session) to produce *ae-09-session* (login with session) and then skip ahead to modify the *ae-11-chat* (non-AJAX chat) to produce *ae-12-ajax* (AJAX-based chat). The chapters walk readers through the necessary changes from each version of the application to the next.

To help support the use of the book in a classroom setting, I provide freely reusable classroom materials that make it easier to use the book in other courses at my personal website (*http://www.dr-chuck.com*). I would love to hear from other teachers who use the book so that we can all share our experiences, assignments, tips, and lecture materials.

Conventions Used in This Book

The following typographical conventions are used in this book:

Italic
> Indicates new terms, URLs, email addresses, filenames, file extensions, pathnames, directories, and Unix utilities.

`Constant width`
> Indicates commands, options, switches, variables, attributes, keys, functions, types, classes, namespaces, methods, modules, properties, parameters, values, objects, events, event handlers, XML tags, HTML tags, macros, the contents of files, or the output from commands.

`Constant width bold`
> Shows commands or other text that should be typed literally by the user.

`Constant width italic`
> Shows text that should be replaced with user-supplied values.

 This icon signifies a tip, suggestion, or general note.

 This icon indicates a warning or caution.

Using Code Examples

This book is here to help you get your job done. In general, you may use the code in this book in your programs and documentation. You do not need to contact us for permission unless you're reproducing a significant portion of the code. For example, writing a program that uses several chunks of code from this book does not require permission. Selling or distributing a CD-ROM of examples from O'Reilly books *does* require permission. Answering a question by citing this book and quoting example code does not require permission. Incorporating a significant amount of example code from this book into your product's documentation *does* require permission.

We appreciate, but do not require, attribution. An attribution usually includes the title, author, publisher, and ISBN. For example: *"Using Google App Engine*, by Charles Severance. Copyright 2009 Charles Severance, 978-0-596-80069-7."

If you feel that your use of code examples falls outside fair use or the permission given above, feel free to contact us at *permissions@oreilly.com*.

Safari® Books Online

Safari When you see a Safari® Books Online icon on the cover of your favorite technology book, that means the book is available online through the O'Reilly Network Safari Bookshelf.

Safari offers a solution that's better than e-books. It's a virtual library that lets you easily search thousands of top tech books, cut and paste code samples, download chapters, and find quick answers when you need the most accurate, current information. Try it for free at *http://my.safaribooksonline.com*.

Comments and Questions

Please address comments and questions concerning this book to the publisher:

O'Reilly Media, Inc.
1005 Gravenstein Highway North
Sebastopol, CA 95472
800-998-9938 (in the United States or Canada)
707-829-0515 (international or local)
707-829-0104 (fax)

We have a web page for this book, where we list errata, examples, and any additional information. You can access this page at:

http://www.oreilly.com/catalog/9780596800697

To comment or ask technical questions about this book, send email to:

bookquestions@oreilly.com

For more information about our books, conferences, Resource Centers, and the O'Reilly Network, see our website at:

http://www.oreilly.com

Acknowledgments

Writing a book is always an engrossing experience for me. It tends to take over my life and spare time and consumes all my free energy until the book is done. By the time the book is completed, it is amazing how many other people have had a significant contribution to the quality of the resulting product. In a sense, although one person's name is on the front cover, this is truly the work of a wise crowd of great friends who have given me so much help and support.

This is my second book with Mike Loukides as my editor, and once again, it was a joy to work with him. Mike is so good at working with an author who is also a busy academic and is trying to juggle classes, travel, consulting, and research along with writing.

For this book, Judy Loukides was also a great help in getting the book together on time. Judy jumped in and helped at a very crucial moment when time was running out and her help is greatly appreciated.

I have two good friends, mentors, colleagues, and coauthors in Noah Botimer and Gonzalo Silverio. Gonzalo has always been my guide to learning CSS throughout the Sakai project and as I taught CSS in my courses at the University of Michigan. He taught me that CSS was really clean and straightforward. It is particularly straightforward if you can always run to Gonzalo when you run into a difficult bit. Noah has always been there to help me figure out the really difficult things. He is great at digging into how something really works and helping me understand it well enough to teach the material to my students and take all the credit.

The technical reviewers did a great job of making sure that the book was sound. Trek Glowaki, Nick Johnson, Steven Githens, Kirby Urner, and Matt Simmons all did a great job in a very short time frame. I also want to thank Pete Koomen of Google for his encouragement at the 2008 Google I/O conference and throughout the process.

Paul Resnick, Sean Munson, Jim Eng, Marc Alier, and Jordi Piguillem Poch took the risk of using the book in their courses even before it was published. I very much appreciate their feedback and guidance as well as the feedback I got from their students. I need to thank the students from the "Design of Complex Websites" course at the University of Michigan in Fall 2008, who showed amazing patience as I gave them the earliest versions of each chapter, often produced only a few hours before lecture. They read the chapters carefully, patiently pointed out places where the narrative "dropped the ball," and reread the revised versions of the chapters.

I certainly appreciate how my students, friends, and colleagues gave me the space and time to write the book.

And I want to thank my parents, Marcia and Russ, for setting high expectations and helping me to learn to always think outside the box and always be prepared for new experiences. I want to thank my wife, Teresa, and my children, Amanda and Brent, for being patient during those months where I pretty much had no time for anything else except "the book."

## CHAPTER 1

Programming on the Web

You probably have been using the Web now for many years to read news, shop, gather information, and communicate with your friends. You start your web browser (Internet Explorer, Firefox, Safari, Opera, Chrome, or another) and navigate around the Web. You may even have a MySpace page or a blog somewhere and have written a bit of HyperText Markup Language (HTML) to customize the look of your page. Some web pages are just flat content, where you see the exact same thing every time you visit that page, and other pages have highly dynamic content and display something very different based on your actions or what you type.

In this book, you will learn how to write applications that generate those dynamic web pages and how to run your applications on the Google App Engine infrastructure.

A perfect example of an interactive and dynamic page is Google Search (Figure 1-1).

Figure 1-1. Google Search

When you come to Google Search, you can type anything into the search box and click the Google Search button. Figure 1-2 shows search results for your request.

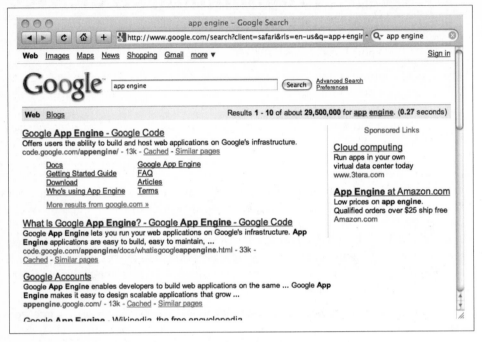

Figure 1-2. Google Search results

Google Search is a "web application"—it is software that runs on the Web. The Google Search application takes as its input many requests per second from web browsers around the world. When the Google Search application receives the request, it springs into action looking for web pages in its large datastore that match the search terms, sorts those pages based on relevance, and sends an HTML page back to your browser, which shows you the results of your search.

The Google Search engine is quite complex and makes use of a vast amount of data around the Web to make its decisions about what pages to show you and in what order to present your pages. The web applications that you write will generally be much simpler—but all the concepts will be the same. Your web applications will take incoming requests from browsers and your software will make decisions, use data, update data, and present a response to the user.

Because you will be writing a program, rather than just writing documents, the response that you give to the user can be as dynamic and as unique or customized for each user as you like. When a program is building your web pages, the sky is the limit.

The Request/Response Cycle

For you to be able to write your web applications, you must first know a few basic things about how the Web works. We must dig a little deeper into what happens when you click on a page and are shown a new page. You need to see how your web application is part of the cycle of requesting and displaying web pages. We call this the HyperText Transport Protocol (HTTP) request/response cycle.

The request/response cycle is pretty easy to understand. It starts when the user clicks on a web page or takes some other action and ends when the new page is displayed to the user. The cycle involves making a request and getting a response across the Internet by connecting to software and data stored in data centers connected to the Internet (Figure 1-3).

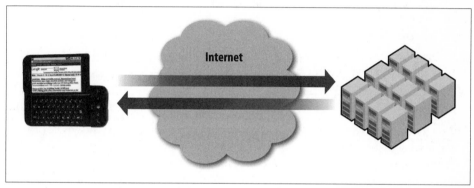

Figure 1-3. Connecting across the Internet

Although you probably have a general notion as to what is going on when you are using your web browser to surf the Web, before you can really develop web applications, you need to understand the process in more detail (Figure 1-4).

Your browser looks at the Uniform Resource Locator, or URL (i.e., *http://www.google .com/search*) that you clicked on. It then opens an Internet connection to the server in the URL (*http://www.google.com*) and requests the */search* document. It also sends any data that you have typed into form fields along with the request for the */search* document.

When your browser makes the connection, requests a document, and sends any input data that you have typed, it is called an "HTTP request" because your browser is requesting a new document to display.

The HTTP request information is routed across the Internet to the appropriate server. The server is usually one of hundreds or thousands of servers located in one of Google's many data centers around the world. When the server receives the request, it looks at the document that is being requested (*/search*), which user the request is coming from (in case you have previously logged in with this browser), and the data from any input

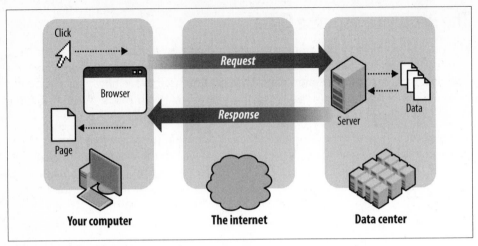

Figure 1-4. The request/response cycle

fields. The server application then pulls data from a database or other source of data, produces a new HTML document, and sends that document back to your web browser. When your web browser receives the new HTML document, it looks at the HTML markup and CSS (Cascading Style Sheets), formats the new page, and shows it to you.

Although there are many steps that take a few paragraphs to describe, the whole process from clicking on one page to the display of the next page usually happens in less than a second. Of course, if your network connection is down or very slow or the server is running slowly, the process happens in "slow motion," so the fact that there are several steps is a little more obvious as the progress bar crawls across your screen while your browser is waiting for the request to be sent and the response to be retrieved over your slow Internet connection.

If the page references images or other files in the HTML, your browser also makes separate requests for those documents. Many browsers will show a status bar as each of these requests/response cycles are processed by showing a running count on the browser's status bar as the files are retrieved:

```
Retrieving "http://www.appenginelearn.com/"-Completed 5 of 8 items.
```

This message simply means that to display the page you requested, your browser needs to retrieve eight documents instead of just one. And although it is making progress, so far it has received only five of the documents. A document can be an HTML page, CSS layout, image file, media file, or any number of different types of documents.

In a sense, the HTTP request/response cycle determines the overall layout of the book: to build a web application, you need to have a general understanding of all aspects of the request/response cycle and what is happening at both ends (browser and server) of the request/response cycle (Figure 1-5).

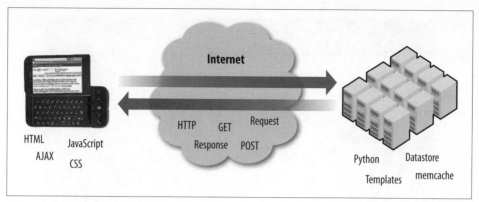

Figure 1-5. The technologies of the Web

You need to learn about how the browser operates using HTML and CSS so that you know how to properly format web pages for display in the browser. You also need to learn about how to add interactivity to web pages using JavaScript and AJAX (Asynchronous JavaScript and XML).

You need to understand the mechanics of how the browser makes its requests using the HTTP protocol—in particular, the different types of requests (GET or POST) and how to handle incoming data entered by the user on forms or files to be uploaded as part of the request.

Inside of the server, you need to learn the Python programming language, the Google Datastore facility, how to generate Dynamic HTML easily using templates, and how to use the Google memory cache to make sure that your applications continue to be fast when being used by many users at the same time.

The browser technologies and HTTP topics are generic and apply to programming in any web application environment such as Ruby on Rails, PHP, Java Servlets, Django, Web2Py, or any of the literally hundreds of other web application frameworks. Learning these topics will be of use in any web programming environment.

Most of this book focuses on the unique aspects of programming in the Google App Engine framework. We cover Python, templates, the Datastore, and the memcache to give you a solid introduction to the App Engine environment and the Google Cloud.

What Is Google App Engine?

I recently attended a meeting at Google where they were giving away stickers for our laptops that said, "My other computer is a data center" (Figure 1-6). The implication was that we were learning to use Google App Engine, so we no longer needed any web servers or database servers to run the production instances of our applications. Our "other computer" was actually a bunch of computers and storage running somewhere deep inside of one of the many Google data centers around the world.

Figure 1-6. My other computer is a data center

Google's App Engine opens Google's production infrastructure to any person in the world at no charge. Much like Google gives us all free email with an amazing amount of long-term storage, we now have the ability to run the software that we write in Google's data centers (i.e., in the Google "cloud").

What Is a "Cloud"?

The term "cloud" is often used when we know how to use something at a high level but we are conveniently shielded from the detail about how it actually works. We know that we have ways to work with and use things in the cloud, but we don't bother looking at what is going on inside. Sometimes we refer to this concept as "abstraction"; we deal with something complex and detailed in a very simple and abstract way and are unaware of the many intricate details that may be involved. For most of us, the automobile is an abstraction. We use a key, steering wheel, gearshift, gas pedal, and brake to drive around and we seldom worry about the thousands of highly specialized parts that are combined to produce the car. Of course, when your car breaks down or performs badly, those details begin to matter a lot. And when we do not have the skills to address the details, we hire someone (a mechanic), paying the professional to dig into those details and give us back a nicely working "abstraction"—and of course a hefty bill listing all the details within the abstraction that needed some work.

The Internet is another abstraction/cloud. The Internet is often represented as a cloud (Figure 1-7) because although we know that all the computers are connected together, most people are generally unaware of the internal details of the links and routers that make up the Internet at any given moment. So the image of a cloud is a great way of representing all that hidden detail inside. We simply treat the Internet as an "abstraction" and use it—ignoring all the complex internal details.

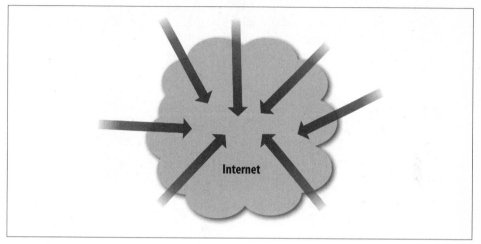

Figure 1-7. The Internet abstracted as a cloud

Why Did Google Build App Engine and Give It Away for Free?

The stated purpose of the creation of Google App Engine is to make the Web better. By empowering millions of new software developers to produce new applications for the Web, Google is hoping to encourage the growth of the Web. Another advantage of Google letting us see and use their scalable infrastructure is that we will help them find ways to improve their infrastructure and make use of it in novel ways. By opening App Engine up to the public, thousands of new bright developers are poring over every aspect of Google App Engine, testing, checking, poking, prodding, finding problems, and suggesting fixes and improvements. This process greatly builds the community of knowledge around the Google software environment, while keeping Google's costs low.

And although it is likely that companies like Yahoo!, Amazon, and Microsoft will counter with highly abstracted application clouds of their own, Google will have had the market to themselves for some time, building a lead and gaining momentum with developer loyalty. Once developers get used to something that works well, they usually are not in a hurry to change. When or if the other companies enter the application cloud market, they will certainly be playing catch-up.

What Is the Google Infrastructure Cloud?

In order to support its worldwide applications such as Google Search and Google Mail (Gmail), Google owns and maintains a number of large data centers around the world, each with thousands of computers and extremely fast networks connecting the data centers. There is plenty of speculation and amateur research that tries to track the number and locations of the Google data centers—but it is pretty safe to say that there are more than 20 large Google data centers scattered around the world. Figure 1-8 is an artist's depiction of what this might look like (please note that these locations are only approximate and not precise).

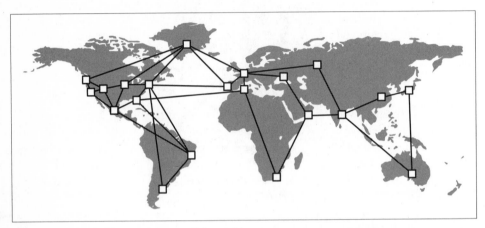

Figure 1-8. Google data centers around the world

Google carefully engineers every aspect of these centers, based on the number of users of their products, the penetration of Internet connectivity in various regions, the patterns of use over time, and many other factors. As usage grows and shifts, Google production engineers add or adjust network and computing resources to meet the changing demand.

Because Google buys so many computers and buys computers continuously, Google has carefully studied the cost, performance, reliability, energy use, and many other factors, to make sure that their investments in data centers are done wisely. As a result, the Google production infrastructure is so complex and so dynamic that even the internal programming teams at Google have no chance of keeping track of all the details and changes in the configurations in all the data centers. It would be a maintenance nightmare if the developers of Google Mail had code that depended on running on a particular server or even running in a particular data center. Any server can go away or be rebooted at any moment. It might even be possible for a large part of a data center to be shut down for maintenance or because of some significant power outage or other local issue.

So Google has developed a software framework—an *abstraction layer*—that hides all of the detail about where data is located or which software is running on which server in which data center. Software like Google Mail simply says, "I need the mail for *csev@umich.edu*" and the framework finds it and delivers it to the application. Because the Google Mail application does this pretty quickly for users anywhere in the world, you can bet that this abstraction/framework is very clever and very fast.

Once the framework that hides location and server detail from the programmer is in place, Google has great flexibility in terms of dynamic reallocation of resources to meet changing needs and demands. As one part of the world goes to sleep and another starts to wake up, data, software, and computation can be moved around the world, following the sun—and in those countries where people are sleeping, data centers can be dynamically reallocated to tasks such as spidering the Web, building indexes, performing backups, doing maintenance, or handling overflow load from servers in regions where the users are awake.

The software developers are completely unaware of the production configuration of the data centers, as it is changing on a moment-to-moment basis.

If you are thinking, "Wow—that must be pretty complex," you are right. One very important "competitive advantage" that distinguishes these mega-web companies is how well they can deploy cost-efficient scalable resources and provide quick, consistent, and reliable responses to users anywhere in the world. Every time we click their applications and search boxes, they make revenue, as we look at their ads all day long.

Enter the Application Engine

 This section is conjecture—it is not based on any internal knowledge of Google's approach or development.

For many years, Google had two main applications—Search and Mail. There were always a lot of secondary Google applications like Video or Sites, and Google internally encouraged a lot of experimentation. Small teams would form and try to build something that the world might find interesting. Google is legendary in labeling new services "Beta" to emphasize that they are under construction and will be improved upon for a long time. Because Google is committed to exploring innovative ideas, it probably tried to make the Google infrastructure increasingly easier to use for these new employees. It is also important to make sure that when a new application is introduced into the production environment, it is not allowed to consume resources in a way that would harm other production applications. So the cloud makes it easier for new employees to develop applications and protects the applications from each other by monitoring application activity and shutting down or throttling applications that "misbehave."

Once this approach was well understood for Google employees, it would have been a very logical step to see whether the environment could be further documented and ruggedized for use by the general public. Although it is almost certain that the actual Google applications written by Google employees can make use of resources that App Engine applications cannot access, it also is quite likely that the internal and external developer environments bear a striking similarity.

Your Application Must Be a Good Citizen in the Google Cloud

Because you are running your application on the Google infrastructure, along with the rest of the App Engine applications and the rest of the Google Applications, you need to follow a few rules. If your application misbehaves, it might be punished. The good news is that because the App Engine environment is completely "sandboxed," [*] App Engine blocks you from doing nearly all the things that Google does not want you to do. The Python environment that you run in App Engine has disabled the operations considered "unsafe" or "insecure." For example, you cannot write to the disk on the servers (you can write to the Datastore—just not to the disk on your local server). You cannot open a direct network connection from your App Engine application, either, as you are likely behind some of Google's firewalls; if you could make arbitrary network connections, you might be able to cause a bit of mischief with Google's other applications. You can retrieve the contents of a URL—you just cannot make your own network connections. These limitations are just commonsense rules to make sure that everyone lives happily together inside the Google cloud.

Google automatically monitors all the running applications (including yours) to make sure that no application uses so many resources that it might have a negative impact on other applications running in the cloud. Google measures the time it takes for your application to respond to each web request. When Google notices that your program is responding slowly or taking too many resources to respond to the request, the request is aborted. If your application abuses resources regularly, you might find yourself throttled or shut down all together. Google is not so concerned when your application is using lots of resources because it is very popular but is more concerned with ensuring that each time someone clicks on your application you use a reasonable amount of resources to handle each "click" or web request. It generally wants your application to be well-written and to make good use of the Google resources.

If your application begins to use a lot of resources because of increasing popularity, Google will happily start charging you for the resources.

[*] The term *sandbox* is used to indicate that multiple applications are kept in their own little sandbox—a place where it is safe to play without hurting others.

How the Cloud Runs Your Application

The best explanation of how the Google cloud works internally is that everything is "virtual." If you look at wired land-line telephones, the prefix of a phone number generally indicates something about the physical geographic location of the phone. On the other hand, many cellular phones have the same prefix, regardless of their physical location. When you make a call to a cellular number from a wired phone, the call is routed across wires into the cellular network and then somehow the cellular network "tracks down" your cellular phone and routes the call to the appropriate cellular tower that is physically near your phone.

In a noncloud environment, the Internet works like the wired phone network. Web servers have a fixed and known location. They are assigned an Internet Protocol (IP) address based on that known location, such as 74.208.28.177. Your IP address is like a phone number—the entire Internet knows where that IP address is located and can route packets across the links that make up the Internet to get the data to that physical server. You also assign the server a domain name, like *www.dr-chuck.com*, which lets Internet software use the Domain Name System (DNS) resolution to look up the numeric IP address (74.208.28.177) associated with the domain name as a convenience.

The Google cloud is more like a cellular network. Programs and data "roam around" the world and the web requests (like cellular calls) somehow find their way to your software, regardless of where in the world your software happens to be running. If you have an App Engine application running at a domain name of *cloudcollab.appspot.com*, Google can give this domain name a different IP address depending on what region of the world you are coming from. In the eastern United States, you might get one numeric IP address, and in South Africa, you might get another numeric IP address. Once Google gets your request into the Google network, it figures out which data center(s) can run your application or perhaps which data centers are already running your application. It probably picks a data center that is some combination of reasonably close and not currently overloaded or perhaps the data center where the data for your application is stored. If all of a sudden your application experiences a spike of traffic in the United Kingdom, Google will likely copy your program and some of your data to one of its data centers there and start your application in that data center and pass the incoming requests from the United Kingdom to your program running in the United Kingdom.

If your application is very popular, it might be running in a number of different data centers at the same time. Or if your application gets 10 requests per hour, it probably is not running anywhere most of the time. When Google sees a request for your application, it starts up a single copy somewhere and gives the request to your application. Once your application finishes the request, it is shut back down to conserve resources.

The most important point of this is that your application has absolutely no idea if or when it is running, where geographically it is running, and how many copies of it are running around the world. Google takes care of all those details for you completely and (thankfully) hides them from you. Somehow the requests from your users make it to your application and back to the end user—Google takes all the responsibility for making this happen quickly and efficiently.

Running an application in the cloud is kind of like flying business class across the Pacific Ocean between Australia and the United States. You are vaguely aware that you are going really fast inside of a highly complex device that you barely understand. The pilots, crew, maintenance people, chefs, logistics staff, traffic controllers, and gate agents all are making sure that your trip happens efficiently and comfortably—and that it is uneventful. All you know is that you sit in a recliner, watch a movie, eat a nice filet mignon, have a glass of red wine, lay the seat flat, sleep for a few hours, and wake up refreshed on a different continent.

Why You Really Want to Run in the Cloud

You might initially think that you don't want to run in the Google cloud because you want to make your own decisions and control your own destiny. You might want to run your own servers in your own facility and make all the decisions about your application. Perhaps you just like walking into a server room and seeing the hardware that is running the application. Although this sense of control might sound appealing at first, it is really just a lot of trouble and energy that does not advance the cause of your application. Here are a few of the things that you have to worry about when you run on your own servers: what operating system should I run? What version of the operating system is the most reliable? When do I apply vendor patches (especially those pesky security patches)? How do I protect my system from intruders? Do I need a firewall to protect my servers? How do I monitor my servers to detect when an intrusion happens and then how do I get notified? How far do I have to drive to the server room to reformat and reinstall the software at 4:00 a.m. so that it is back up by 10:00 a.m.? What database do I run? What version? What patches? Should I upgrade the memory of my database server, or should I add an additional disk to the RAID controller? Can I use a single database server, or do I need to cluster several database servers? How does the clustered database server get backed up? How long does it take to restore my database when there is a hardware problem with the database server's disk drives? How many application web servers do I need? I know that my application's peak usage is from 7:00 p.m. to 9:00 p.m. each day. Do I buy enough hardware to handle that peak load, or do I buy a little less hardware and just let the servers slow down a bit during the 7:00 p.m. to 9:00 p.m. period? If my application is so popular that it is used both in the United States and Europe, do I need to find a data center in Europe and put some hardware in Europe so that all the European users see a quick response time? When should I upgrade my hardware? Should I add more hardware and keep the old hardware or simply pitch the old hardware and install all new hardware? How much energy does my hardware take? Is there a way to reduce the energy footprint of my hardware?

And on and on. These problems do not go away just because you run on the Google infrastructure. But they are Google's problems, not your problems. You have outsourced these and hundreds of other subtle issues by running a production facility at Google. Google has some of the brightest production engineers in the world, who are very good at solving these problems and doing so very efficiently.

Although Google will charge you when your application begins to use significant resources, there is virtually no way that you could build the same scalable, worldwide, reliable, redundant, and efficient production environment anywhere near as cheaply as you can purchase those services from Google.

It is important to note that although Google App Engine is very exciting, because it is freely available to anyone to use and explore, there are many other available options for hosting applications on the Web. You should carefully investigate the appropriate production solution for your particular application.

The Simplest App Engine Application

You should consult the appendixes in this book for instructions on how to install Google Application Engine and run your first trivial application in Python. Once you have the App Engine environment installed, your first application consists of two files.

The first file is named *app.yaml*, and its purpose is to describe your application to App Engine:

```
application: ae-00-trivial
version: 1
runtime: python
api_version: 1
handlers:
- url: /.*
  script: index.py
```

I will cover the details of this file later; at a high level, it names the application and uses an asterisk as a wildcard, matching any string of characters so as to route *all* the incoming document requests (i.e., URLs) to the program named *index.py*.

The *index.py* file consists of three lines of Python:

```
print 'Content-Type: text/plain'
print ''
print 'Hello there Chuck'
```

The first line of the response is a header line, which describes the type of data being returned in the response. The second line is a blank line to separate the headers from the document, and the third line is the actual document itself. In effect, regardless of which document your browser requests, the program has a very simple and single-minded response, as shown in Figure 1-9.

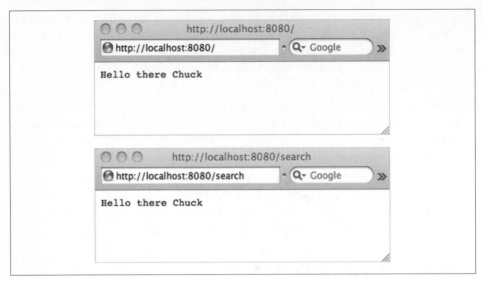

Figure 1-9. A simple App Engine application

Although this application is trivial, it can be deployed in the Google App Engine production cloud.

Summary

Welcome aboard Google App Engine. Your application will run in Google's best-of-breed data centers around the world. Google engineers take all the responsibility for the production environment for your application. All you need to worry about is whether your application works well, makes efficient use of resources, and makes your users happy.

If your application goes viral and usage takes off, Google's engineers swing into action, making sure that you have all the resources that you need and making use of the resources in Google data centers around the world.

If your application does not take off and is just a fun little place for you to putter around and experiment with your own creative ideas and share them with a few friends, Google lets you use their production infrastructure for free.

Once you have created and deployed your App Engine application, perhaps you too will need to add a sticker to your laptop that says, "My other computer is a data center." Or perhaps it would be more appropriate to have a sticker that says, "My other computer(s) is/are somewhere in one or more world-class data centers scattered around the world." (You might need to buy a bigger laptop for that one, though.)

Exercises

1. Explain how your responsibility as a developer changes when your application is hosted in Google's cloud environment versus when you build and support your own dedicated hosting facility.

2. Briefly describe the HTTP request/response cycle. What does it mean when your browser retrieves 40 documents to display your page? What are those 40 documents?

3. What is the purpose of the "handlers" entry in the *app.yaml* file?

## CHAPTER 2

HTML and CSS

Gonzalo Silverio

This chapter is an introduction to HTML and CSS. If you look around, there are hundreds of books with thousands of pages written on HTML or CSS. We could teach you everything there is to know about HTML and CSS, if we used very tiny print in this chapter. Instead, we will work through some example HTML and CSS and explain how they work. You will learn a useful amount of HTML and CSS, but there will still be much more to learn after you have read this chapter.

HTML (which, as mentioned earlier, stands for HyperText Markup Language) is the language that describes the meaning of web pages and CSS (Cascading Style Sheets) is a language that we use to tell the browser how to lay out web pages and control their formatting in the browser (Figure 2-1).

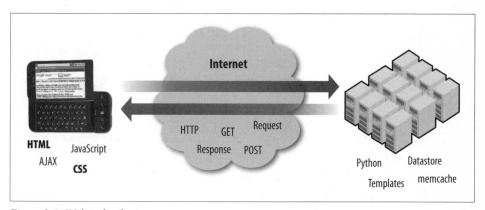

Figure 2-1. Web technologies

A Brief History of HTML and CSS

We are currently in the golden age of HTML and CSS, after many difficult and trying years. Be very thankful that you are not trying to learn HTML and CSS back in 2005, and be very thankful that you are not trying to learn HTML in 1999. From the moment that HTML was created until very recently, there was a continuous and often futile struggle to make pages look good across multiple browsers. The oversimplified history of HTML and CSS breaks down roughly as follows:

1990–1994	HTML was simple and pages looked pretty ugly. But it did not matter because we all liked grey backgrounds and purple links. We were just so pleased when our network connection was working that the look and feel of pages did not matter.
1995–1999	People and companies started getting serious about the Web, so they wanted their web pages to look nice. Because the browsers were competing with one another, each browser started adding in clever features to make it possible to make web pages pretty by writing some really obtuse HTML. Sadly each browser came up with its own approach to "pretty" web pages, and often pages that looked pretty in one browser looked horrible in another browser, and the HTML was really hard to write and to read and to maintain.
2000–2005	CSS was well defined, but each browser supported CSS differently and CSS support changed (and usually improved) each time a new version of a browser was released. It took years for people to stop using old browsers, so most serious websites needed to be compatible with several versions of multiple browsers, so we could not universally assume CSS. The resulting HTML was still far too obtuse.
2005–2008	All current browsers have good support for CSS and the oldest browsers in use had moderately good support. Internet Explorer 5 was the last popular browser that had flawed support for CSS. Internet Explorer 5 for Windows achieved about 70% of the CSS1 specification. At the end of 2006, Internet Explorer 5 represented about 4% of the browsers in use, and by the end of 2008, Internet Explorer 5 represented less than 0.1% of the browsers in active use.

So in 2009 and beyond, it is safe to assume that all the browsers we will encounter have good support for modern HTML and modern CSS. This is wonderful news because our HTML can be very simple and clean—all needed formatting can be done in CSS, and our pages will render nicely on every browser in common use. Whew! It took only 18 years to get it right.

In the rest of this chapter, we will show you how to write nice clean web pages. If you have some experience in HTML from the past, you may be surprised at how much we can do with very simple use of HTML and CSS.

HyperText Markup Language (HTML)

HTML allows us to "mark up" a text file to indicate that certain areas of the document are headers, paragraphs, lists, or other document elements. HTML treats the less-than (<) and greater-than (>) characters as special characters to separate the markup from the text. For example, in the following HTML fragment, we have a level-1 header and a paragraph:

```
<h1>Google App Engine: About</h1>
<p>
Welcome to the site dedicated to
learning the Google Application Engine.
We hope you find www.appenginelearn.com useful.
</p>
```

An HTML *tag* consists of a pair of angle brackets with a tag name inside them. The bracketed tags mark up the text that is between the start tag and the end tag. The `<h1>` tag indicates that the following text is a level-1 header. The `</h1>` indicates the end of the level-1 header. Similarly, `<p>` and the `</p>` indicate the beginning and end of a paragraph, respectively.

The browser reads this document, looks at the text, interprets the markup, formats the page, and displays the page as shown in Figure 2-2.

Figure 2-2. A simple HTML page

The markup is not shown, but the browser shows the level-1 header in a larger and bold font and leaves a blank line between the level-1 header and the paragraph. The paragraph is justified to fit in the space available given the width of the browser window. For example, if you widened the browser window, the text in the paragraph would be rejustified to fill the new space, as shown in Figure 2-3.

Extra whitespace in the text of an HTML document or the end of lines or even blank lines are ignored, as the browser justifies the text to fit into the space available in the browser window.

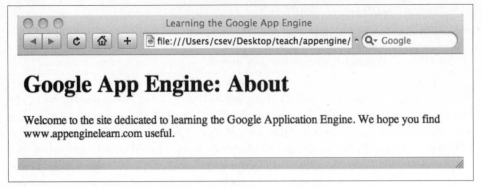

Figure 2-3. Rejustifying text as the browser is resized

You are probably wondering how we ever see a less-than or greater-than in an HTML page. We use the string < to display a less-than character and > to display a greater-than character. There are a number of special characters that can be displayed using an ampersand sequence:

```
<h1>HTML: Special Characters</h1>
<p>
Special characters are indicated by
the &amp; character. We can use this
to display &lt; and &gt;.
</p>
```

This HTML fragment would display as shown in Figure 2-4.

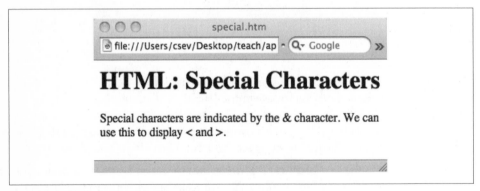

Figure 2-4. Displaying special characters

A Well-Formed HTML Document

Given that browsers need to display HTML pages that were authored over the past 20 years with many different styles of HTML, browsers are very tolerant of flawed and incomplete HTML. Browsers will read all kinds of HTML and display *something*. There is no guarantee that if you produce flawed HTML it will look the same or even similar on all browsers. When browsers encounter flawed or imperfect HTML, at some point the HTML is bad enough to cause the browser to go into what is called *quirks mode*. Quirks mode yields different results in different browsers. So if you produce nonstandard HTML, you cannot complain loudly in your blog that the browser is making your pages look bad.

If you want the browser to follow the "contract" for making pretty web pages across many web browsers, you have to follow the rules for the "contract." A well-formed HTML document has a line at the beginning that indicates that this web page is following the contract; the browser is then also expected to follow the contract. If you follow the contract, you can reasonably expect that your page will look the same across different browsers.

The following is a simple well-formed HTML document:

```
<!DOCTYPE html PUBLIC "-//W3C//DTD XHTML 1.0 Strict//EN"
 "http://www.w3.org/TR/xhtml1/DTD/xhtml1-strict.dtd">
<html xmlns="http://www.w3.org/1999/xhtml">
 <head>
  <title>Learning Google App Engine</title>
 </head>
 <body>
  <h1>Google App Engine: About</h1>
  <p>
  Welcome to the site dedicated to
  learning the Google Application Engine.
  We hope you find www.appenginelearn.com useful.
  </p>
 </body>
</html>
```

The first line of the document (the one that includes the word DOCTYPE) establishes that this page will follow the strictest and most modern standards for HTML. The rest of the document follows a few rules:

- The entire document is enclosed in one <html> ... </html> tag.
- There is a section of the document between <head> and </head> that describes the document. In this example, we give the document a title. The title is not displayed as part of the actual body of the document, but is often displayed elsewhere in the browser.
- The HTML content to be displayed in the browser is between the <body> ... </body> tag pair.

There are other rules as well, including all tags must be properly closed, properly nested, and lowercase.

The example document follows all of the rules. Thankfully, there is a service that we can use to check whether an HTML meets the contract that the DOCTYPE line agrees to—this type of service is called *validation*.

Validating Your HTML

There is a nice service that looks at your HTML and determines whether it violates any of the rules of strictly conforming HTML and makes sure that you meet the contract that you specify in your DOCTYPE. The validator is provided by the World Wide Web Consortium (W3C) at *http://validator.w3.org*.

You can go to this page and enter a URL for your website, upload a file with HTML, or paste the HTML into the site. The validator reads your HTML and tells you whether your HTML passes its tests, is properly formed, and complies with the contract specified in the DOCTYPE.

As shown in Figure 2-5, our HTML passed the validation test. If we had made a mistake in our HTML, we would have seen an error message, as shown in Figure 2-6.

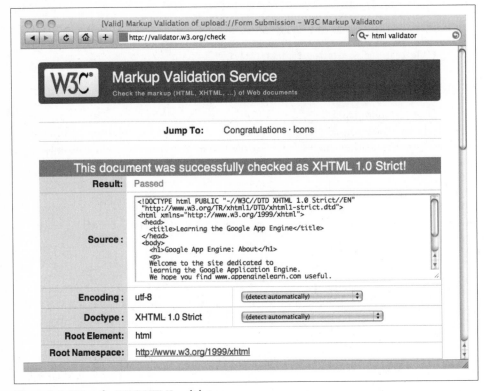

Figure 2-5. Using the W3C HTML validator

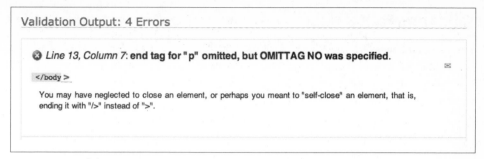

Figure 2-6. Invalid HTML

In the code used for the mistake example in Figure 2-6, we omitted the closing paragraph tag, </p>, in the input, which caused an error to be flagged. Although this error message is a pretty straightforward, sometimes the validator error messages can be quite cryptic and take a bit of skill to read. The best approach is to get a simple page properly validated and then build all your pages using the valid page as your template.

HyperText Links (Anchor Tags)

Let's continue looking at a few more HTML features that we will use in the pages that are in the rest of the book. We will look at how the HTML makes references from within one document to another document. We will also look at how we make lists in HTML.

In the following HTML fragment, we are showing only the contents of the <body> ... </body> section of the document:

```
<h1><a href="index.htm">AppEngineLearn</a></h1>
<ul>
 <li><a href="sites.htm">Sites</a></li>
 <li><a href="topics.htm">Topics</a></li>
</ul>
<h1>Google App Engine: About</h1>
<p>
Welcome to the site dedicated to
learning the Google Application Engine.
We hope you find www.appenginelearn.com useful.
</p>
```

In the level-1 header, we have the text AppEngineLearn. We surround this text with an "anchor tag" to indicate that this text is a hypertext reference. When the AppEngine Learn text is clicked on, the browser will navigate to the document named *index.htm*. The page renders as shown in Figure 2-7.

Figure 2-7. A basic HTML page

Although the level-1 header is larger and still in bold text, it is also underlined and blue or purple because the text is "clickable." If we look at the HTML and the anchor tag, we see a new syntax:

```
<a href="index.htm">AppEngineLearn</a>
```

There is a start `<a>` tag and an end `</a>` tag, which delimit the clickable text. However, in the start tag, there is some extra information, labeled `href`. These keyword/value pairs on tags are called *attributes*. Generally, any opening HTML tag can have one or more optional attributes.

In this case, the `href` attribute specifies the new document that is to be retrieved when the anchor text (`AppEngineLearn`) is clicked on. For this link, when we click on the text, our browser retrieves and displays the file *index.htm*.

We can see two other anchor tags in the example text as well:

```
<a href="sites.htm">Sites</a>
<a href="topics.htm">Topics</a>
```

These links allow us to navigate between several files that make up this web "site."

When we click on the text `Sites`, we are switched to the HTML document stored in the file *sites.htm*, and when we click on the text `Topics`, we are switched to the HTML document stored in the file *topics.htm*.

If you look at the rendered page in Figure 2-7, you see that the strings "Sites" and "Topics" are also underlined and purple or blue to draw our attention to the fact that these are clickable hypertext links.[*]

Multiple Files

In order for these links to work, you will need to place the HTML files in the same directory, as follows:

```
csev$ ls -l
-rw-r--r-- 1 csev staff 618 Dec 18 22:56 index.htm
-rw-r--r-- 1 csev staff 883 Dec 18 22:57 sites.htm
-rw-r--r-- 1 csev staff 679 Dec 18 22:57 topics.htm
csev$
```

Each of the files replicates the `<head>` ... `</head>` content and the first part of the `<body>` content to put a consistent navigation on each page. Following is the content of the *sites.htm* file:

```
<!DOCTYPE html PUBLIC "-//W3C//DTD XHTML 1.0 Strict//EN"
 "http://www.w3.org/TR/xhtml1/DTD/xhtml1-strict.dtd">
<html xmlns="http://www.w3.org/1999/xhtml">
 <head>
  <title>Learning Google App Engine</title>
 </head>
 <body>
   <h1><a href="index.htm">AppEngineLearn</a></h1>
   <ul>
    <li><a href="sites.htm">Sites</a></li>
    <li><a href="topics.htm">Topics</a></li>
   </ul>
   <h1>App Engine: Sites</h1>
   <p>
   Here are some sites we hope you find useful:
   </p>
   <ul>
    <li><a href="http://www.pythonlearn.com">
              Python Learn</a></li>
    <li><a href="http://www.appenginelearn.com">
              App Engine Learn</a></li>
    <li><a href="http://www.google.com/App Engine/">
              Google App Engine Site</a></li>
   </ul>
 </body>
</html>
```

Most of the page is identical to the *index.htm* file; only the last part of the body changes in the *sites.htm* file.

---

[*] Back in 1992, the choice was made to color links purple and blue to make the links to stand out from the text and encourage the first few thousand users of the World Wide Web to experiment and actually click on words.

When the pages are rendered, we can click on the links to move between the pages. Because the top half of the <body> content is always the same the navigation appears to be "permanent." In actuality, the whole page is being redrawn, but because the top part is identical, it appears to be present on all pages, so the navigation appears to be a "menu" that allows us to move from page to page.

Lists in HTML

In addition to these hypertext links, our HTML includes a list of items:

```
<ul>
 <li><a href="http://www.pythonlearn.com">
          Python Learn</a></li>
 <li><a href="http://www.appenginelearn.com">
          App Engine Learn</a></li>
 <li><a href="http://www.google.com/App Engine/">
          Google App Engine Site</a></li>
</ul>
```

We indicate the overall start and end of the list of items using the <ul> ... </ul> tags. Each of the entries in the list is indicated by a <li> ... </li> tags.

This particular list is an unordered list (ul), so when it is rendered, it is shown with a bullet to the left of each of the list items (li), as shown in Figure 2-8.

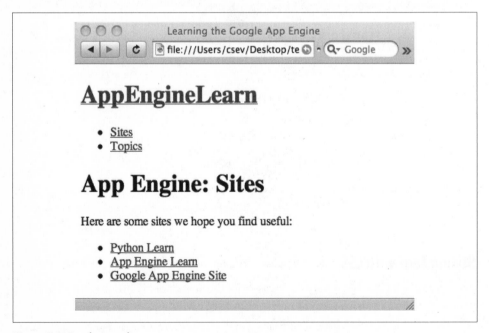

Figure 2-8. Rendering a list

Both the interpage navigation links and the list of sites are examples of unordered lists. You can see that the elements of the lists are indented and bullets have been added to each list element.

Specifying Styles Using CSS

When the browser reads and renders HTML, it has a set of built-in formatting rules for visually presenting various tags. For example, text within an anchor tag, <a>, is underlined and colored blue or purple (depending on whether the link has already been visited). The overall document is rendered in a Times Roman font.

Most of these default style choices date back to the early 1990s—and frankly, they're downright ugly. Before CSS, we would be tempted to add <font> and other tags throughout the HTML to override the default styles of the browsers. This clutter makes the HTML increasingly complex, hard to read, hard to maintain, and far less parsable for screen readers.

CSS gives us a lot of control over the look and feel of the document with little or no changes to the HTML, as shown in Figure 2-9.

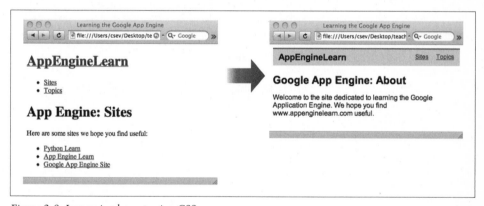

Figure 2-9. Improving layout using CSS

Next, we'll look at ways to change the styling of our document with no changes to the HTML. In the rest of the chapter, we'll transform the presentation of our HTML from nasty to classy, all without making any changes to our HTML.

Styling Tags with CSS

The syntax of a CSS rule is very different from the syntax of HTML markup. This is an example of a CSS rule:

```
body {
  font-family: arial, sans-serif;
}
```

Each CSS rules starts with a *selector*. The selector determines which part of the document this particular rule affects. The selector for this rule is "body," which means that this formatting rule is applied to everything between the **<body>** and **</body>** tags in the document (which is effectively the entire viewable document).

After the selector, there is an opening brace, {, followed by a number of formatting instructions, followed by a closing brace, }.

In this example, we have one formatting instruction. We are directing the browser to use the font family, `arial`, for the entire document, and—if the browser does not support the Arial font—to use any `sans serif` font. We have several options for including CSS in the HTML document. We can include the CSS in the main document using the **<style>** tag, as follows:

```
<!DOCTYPE html PUBLIC "-//W3C//DTD XHTML 1.0 Strict//EN"
 "http://www.w3.org/TR/xhtml1/DTD/xhtml1-strict.dtd">
<html xmlns="http://www.w3.org/1999/xhtml">
 <head>
  <title>Learning Google App Engine</title>
  <style type="text/css">
   body {
     font-family: arial, sans-serif;
   }
  </style>
 </head>
 <body>
   <h1><a href="index.htm">AppEngineLearn</a></h1>
   <ul>
    <li><a href="sites.htm">Sites</a></li>
    <li><a href="topics.htm">Topics</a></li>
   </ul>
   <h1>Google App Engine: About</h1>
   <p>
   Welcome to the site dedicated to
   learning the Google Application Engine.
   We hope you find www.appenginelearn.com useful.
   </p>
 </body>
</html>
```

The browser sees the **<style>** tag and reads the CSS rules and applies them to the document. With this change, our rendered document now looks as shown in Figure 2-10.

As you can see, the font in the entire document has switched from Times Roman to a more screen-friendly sans-serif font. As you will soon see, we have a lot of fine-grained control over look and feel of our document as well as document layout using CSS. Because CSS instructions can get quite lengthy, it is usually not a good idea to include them in the HTML document. Instead, put the CSS instructions in a separate file and include that file in the main document as follows:

```
<!DOCTYPE html PUBLIC "-//W3C//DTD XHTML 1.0 Strict//EN"
 "http://www.w3.org/TR/xhtml1/DTD/xhtml1-strict.dtd">
```

```
<html xmlns="http://www.w3.org/1999/xhtml">
 <head>
  <title>Learning Google App Engine</title>
  <link type="text/css" rel="stylesheet" href="glike.css"/>
 </head>
 <body>
 ...
```

Figure 2-10. Changing the default font

The CSS rules are stored in the file specified:

```
csev $ ls -l
total 32
-rw-r--r-- 1 csev staff   44 Dec 19 06:06 glike.css
-rw-r--r-- 1 csev staff  679 Dec 19 06:07 index.htm
-rw-r--r-- 1 csev staff  883 Dec 19 05:59 sites.htm
-rw-r--r-- 1 csev staff  679 Dec 19 05:59 topics.htm
csev $
```

If you look at the contents of the *glike.css* file, you'll see that it is a list of CSS rules:

```
body {
  font-family: arial, sans-serif;
}

a {
  color: blue;
}
h1 a {
  text-decoration: none;
  color: black;
}
```

We have added a second CSS rule to change the formatting of the anchor tags (i.e., hypertext links). We want the links throughout the document to be blue. When we see an anchor tag `<a>` *inside* of an `<h1>` tag, we do not want it to be underlined, so we set the `text-decoration` to none to eliminate the underlining and set the font color to black.

With these new changes, our page looks as shown in Figure 2-11.

Figure 2-11. Styling links

The normal links in the list are blue and underlined (default behavior) and the link inside the `<h1>` tag is black and not underlined.

With a surprisingly small amount of CSS, our page is looking much less ugly. In a way, it is unfortunate that the default styling that was chosen in the early 1990s was so garish. Luckily in 2008 and beyond, this can be quickly rectified by a bit of CSS. Because basic CSS is so simple, there should be no temptation to revert to formatting using `<font>` tags or other obsolete markup.

Exerting More Control over Markup

Now that you know how to change the styling of a tag or a tag within another tag, we need to move on to affecting the look of blocks of text. The `<div>` tag is how we mark blocks of our web page so that we can separately style each area of our document. We will divide the body of our document into two main areas. The top area is the navigation or "header," and it is the same across different documents. The bottom area is the "content," which changes completely from document to document:

```
<body>
  <div id="header">
    <h1><a href="index.htm">AppEngineLearn</a></h1>
    <ul>
     <li><a href="sites.htm">Sites</a></li>
     <li><a href="topics.htm" >Topics</a></li>
    </ul>
  </div>
  <div id="content">
    <h2>Google App Engine: About</h2>
    <p>
    Welcome to the site dedicated to
    learning the Google Application Engine.
    We hope you find www.appenginelearn.com useful.
    </p>
  </div>
</body>
```

When we add the `<div>` tag to our document, we add an `id` attribute so that we can uniquely identify a particular block in the HTML. We have now broken our document into a "header" area and a "content" area and can apply different styling to each area. Although the `id` attribute can be used on any tag, it is most commonly used on a `<div>` tag, splitting the document into major "chunks." You can use an `id` value (`content` or `header` in this example) only once in a particular document.

We can create CSS rules that apply to these newly defined blocks of our document. When we prefix the selector string with a hash character (#), it means that instead of applying to a tag in the document, the selector applies to the tag that has the matching `id` attribute:

```
body {
   font-family: arial, sans-serif;
}

#header {
 background-color: #dde;
  border-top: 3px solid #36c;
}

a {
   color: blue;
}

#header h1 a {
   text-decoration: none;
   color: black;
}
```

We set the background color of the entire `header` block to be light blue. We give the header block a slightly darker blue three-pixel border at the top of the `header` block.

We also change the selector for the anchor tag within the h1 tag to apply only when the tags are encountered inside the header block. This further narrows the application of this particular CSS rule.

The color string #dde indicates the color level of red, green, and blue—each of the three letters ranges from 0–9 and a–f, with 0 being the lowest and f being the highest. The color #000 is black and the color #fff is white. So the color #dde is pretty light, with a little more blue than red and green, so it looks light blue. The color #36c is a darker and deeper blue. There are many websites that can help you select these colors. Using the numeric versions of the colors gives the page designer precise control over their colors. With these changes, the page now looks as shown in Figure 2-12.

Figure 2-12. Styling blocks

The background color gives us a visual indication of the scope of our header block in our web page. You can see that we are now well under way to getting to the final look and feel of our page.

Validating CSS

Just like the HTML validator, there also is a CSS validator. You use it in a similar manner to the HTML validator. You can point the validator at a URL, upload a file, or paste in the text of your CSS. The validator is available at *http://jigsaw.w3.org/css-validator/*.

The validator reads your CSS, checks for errors, and produces a report that either indicates that your CSS is valid or lists its mistakes and shortcomings (Figure 2-13).

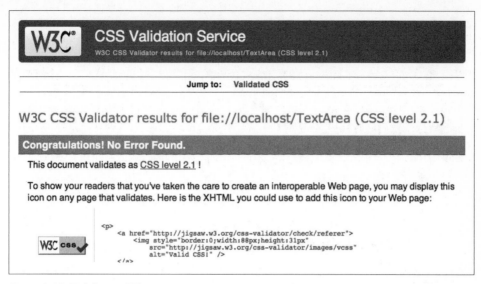

Figure 2-13. Validating CSS

The CSS validator is actually very useful when your CSS seems to be not working properly. The browser will generally be silent if you have an error in your CSS—that is, the browser will simply ignore the bits of CSS that are not the proper syntax. In these cases, using the CSS validator might save you hours of staring at your HTML and CSS and wondering whether you are crazy.

Tools to Help You Work with CSS

Another important tool for working with increasingly complex CSS is the Web Developer plug-in for the Firefox browser that is freely available from Chris Pedrick. Web developers have pretty much standardized on Firefox as their browser because of its support for web development. You can find and install the Web Developer plug-in at *http://addons.mozilla.org*.

When the Web Developer plug-in is installed, you will have an additional toolbar when you start Firefox. There are many useful options in this toolbar. The first one we will use is under Outline→Outline Block Elements.[†] When you enable the outlining of block elements, you can see the structure of your web page, including which elements are contained within other elements. If you have made a mistake in the structure or nesting of your HTML, you may be able to quickly identify and fix the problem just by looking over the block elements, as shown in Figure 2-14.

[†] An *inline tag* affects the formatting of HTML text without affecting the justification. A *block tag* (such as a <p> tag) causes justification of the current block to be stopped and a new block of text started.

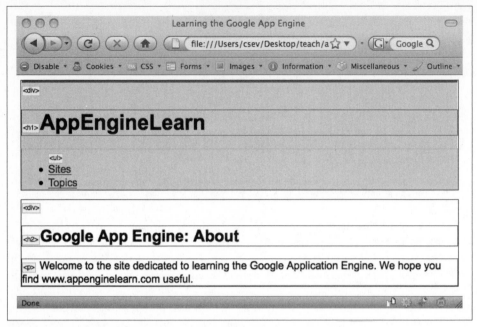

Figure 2-14. Outlining block elements with the Web Developer plug-in

With the Outline Block Elements feature enabled, we can see our header `<div>` as well as the `<h1>` and `<ul>` blocks within the header `<div>`.

As your web pages get even more complex and you gain skills using similar Firefox plug-ins, you will wonder how web designers survived without these important tools.

Building the Navigation Menu

Now let's build up our navigation menu by changing the layout of the blocks in our page using CSS. Until now, the blocks have appeared one after another from top to bottom in the order that they appear in the document. We are going to take a bit more direct control of our blocks and get the look and feel that we like. The first thing we will do is make the list elements (`<li>`) render using inline layout instead of block layout. Then we take the `<h1>` content and push it over to the left side of the header `<div>` and the list of navigation links in the `<ul>` and push that to the right side of the header `<div>`.

Here are the CSS rules to move these elements around within the "header" `<div>`:

```
#header {
  background-color: #dde;
  border-top: 3px solid #36c;
  height: 100%;
  overflow:hidden;
}
```

```
#header h1 {
  font-size: 20px;
  float: left;
  vertical-align: middle;
}

#header li {
  font-size: 14px;
  display: inline;
}

#header ul {
  list-style: none;
  float:right;
  vertical-align: middle;
}
```

For the header `<div>` itself, we set the height to 100% and the overflow to hidden. In order to lay the `<h1>` element on the left and the `<ul>` on the right, we "float" them left and right. Floated element children are taken out of the flow of the document, which means that `#header` is technically empty and will not lay out enough vertical space to wrap the two children unless specifically told to do so; hence the `height: 100%;` and the `overflow:hidden` rules.[‡] We set the font size on the `<h1>` link and float it to the left of the header `<div>` and align it vertically with the vertical center of the header `<div>`. We tell the individual list elements to render inline (rather than render as a block) so that they come out horizontally (next to one another) rather than vertically (stacked on top of one another).

Finally, we float the `<ul>` to the right of the header `<div>` and align it vertically with the vertical middle of the header `<div>`. We also specify that there should be no bullets on our list by setting the `list-style` to `none`.

When this is completed, the page will render with the navigation all tucked nicely into a bar at the top of the page, as shown in Figure 2-15.

If we view the page in Firefox with block outlining turned on, it is not as pretty, but you can see how the `<h1>` block migrated to the left of the header `<div>` and the `<ul>` block migrated to the right of the header `<div>`, as shown with Outline Block Elements turned on, in Figure 2-16.

We are almost done! Figure 2-17 shows our current page and our desired ultimate page.

They almost look identical, but there are some subtle differences—and when you look closely, our final result actually looks much better.

[‡] This is just one example of a useful and nonobvious advanced CSS technique. This chapter should be thought of as just the start of your education about CSS techniques.

Figure 2-15. Moving navigation to the top of the page

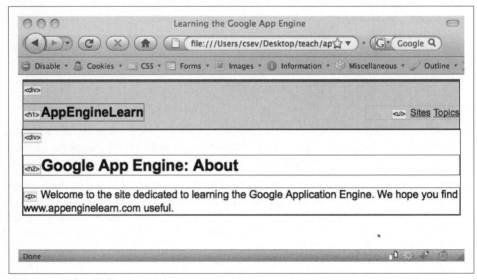

Figure 2-16. Floated block-level elements

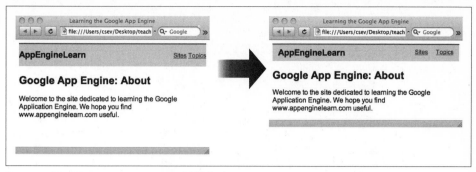

Figure 2-17. Adjusting spacing around block elements

The CSS Box Model

Our remaining task is to nudge our blocks around a bit so that we have a pleasing amount of space around the blocks. Having a bit of space will make our page easier to read and use and generally look more professional.

When each block is laid out, it takes up a certain amount of space based on the font size, text wrapping, number of characters, and so on. You can even force the height and width of a block's content to particular values using CSS. Once the size of the content has been established, we can add space around the content, using some combination of these three CSS values (see Figure 2-18):

- *Padding* adds a specified amount of space around the block's content and inside of the border. The padding space takes its background color from the content itself.

- Outside of the padding, there is an optional *border*. The border is usually a line around the content, which can have a style, color, and thickness. Often the border is a different color than the background color to visually offset the block from the rest of the page.

- Outside of the border, there is the *margin*. The margin is additional space outside of the border of the block element. The margin is used to ensure that there is some space between the parent element and the block.

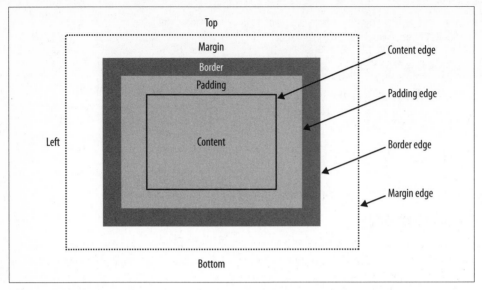

Figure 2-18. CSS box model

Each of these can be independently set on the right, left, top, and bottom of each block element, giving a great deal of flexibility. The units of these values can be in pixels or "em-units." An em-unit is equivalent to the height of the capital M of the default or inherited font size. Often all three of these values (padding, border, and margin) are used when we place a colored border around a block element. If there is no border and no background color in the block element, there is not much difference between margin and padding.

We make several changes to the CSS to nudge our blocks around, add some borders, and add some padding so that the layout looks more natural:

```
#header {
  background-color: #dde;
  border-top: 3px solid #36c;
  height: 100%;
  overflow:hidden;
  padding: 7px;
  margin-top: 5px;
}

#header h1 {
  font-size: 20px;
  float: left;
  vertical-align: middle;
  margin: 0;
  padding: 0 0 0 .3em;
}

#header li {
```

```
    font-size: 14px;
    display: inline;
    padding: .5em;
}

#header ul {
  list-style: none;
  text-align: right;
  float:right;
  vertical-align: middle;
  margin: 0;
  padding: 0;
}
```

With these changes, our page is finally laid out nicely, as shown in Figure 2-19.

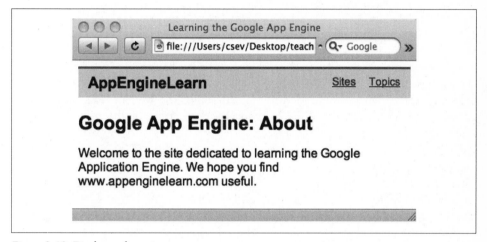

Figure 2-19. Final page layout

The page also looks very natural as the browser window is resized.

Adding Navigation Hints for Users

So far we have worked exclusively on the main page (*index.htm*). Let's add one more feature to the menu. When we are in a page other than *index.htm* (i.e., *sites.htm* or *topics.htm*), let's change the look of that link to give users a subtle clue as to which page they are on. We would like to change the link to the current page from blue to black and remove the underline.

To do this, we add a `class` attribute to the link on the currently selected page. The class attribute is very similar to the `id` attribute, except that the `class` attribute can be used over and over on any number of tags in the document. The general notion is that we use the `id` attribute to identify major blocks of our page and we use the `class` to format elements that may be repeated many times in the page. In this case, we are using a `class` because we might want to later add another navigation area in the `#content` area and then we can simply reuse the `class` attribute.

Make the following change to the navigation in the *topics.htm* file:

```
<div id="header">
 <h1><a href="index.htm">AppEngineLearn</a></h1>
 <ul>
  <li><a href="sites.htm">Sites</a></li>
  <li><a href="topics.htm" class="selected">Topics</a></li>
 </ul>
</div>
```

This gives us a handle so that we can style tags with `class="selected"` differently. To style this tag, we add the following to our CSS:

```
#header li a.selected {
  color: black;
  text-decoration: none;
}
```

The selector on this CSS rule says, "Within the `div` that has an `id` of header, when you are inside of an `<li>` tag *and* you find an anchor tag with a class of `selected`, make the color black and remove the underline from the link." So we can reach in and very precisely change the `selected` link, leaving the formatting of the rest of the page unchanged.

We make a similar change to the *sites.htm* page, indicating that the "Sites" link is the currently selected link so that we are consistent across pages.

The resulting pages render as shown in Figure 2-20.

The navigation link for the current page properly shows up in black with no underline.

Summary

This chapter has covered a lot of ground, starting from basic HTML markup to the CSS box model and the layout of navigation menus using floating `<div>` tags. To truly understand the details of all that we just covered, you'd probably need several complete books.

The focus in this chapter was merely to show one end-to-end example including both simple and complex topics in order to expose you to the kinds of things you can do with HTML and CSS.

Figure 2-20. Pages with navigation indicators

Exercises

1. Give a brief history of the major phases of the Internet.

2. How do you represent special characters such as "less than" or "greater than" in HTML?

3. In the late 1990s, HTML became increasingly complex, as designers used HTML features like tables to control the look and feel and layout of a page. What is the current best practice approach for specifying the look and feel and layout of a page in 2008?

4. What does it mean when someone says that the HTML should be marked up based on the "semantics" of the page?

5. Give an example of (a) a self-closed HTML tag and (b) an attribute on an HTML tag.

6. What is the purpose of the `alt` attribute on the `img` tag?

7. In the following CSS rule, why is there more than one font specified?

```
body {
  font-family: "Trebuchet MS", Helvetica, Arial, sans-serif;
  font-size: x-large;
}
```

8. What is the difference between the `class=` and `id=` attributes on a tag?

9. In the CSS box model, is the margin inside or outside the border?

10. What CSS property (`font-family`, `color`, and so on) is used to change a list from being displayed vertically to being displayed horizontally?

11. Describe two things that you should keep in mind when designing a web page for accessibility.

12. How does the float CSS attribute affect the layout of a web page?

13. What is the purpose of the `<head>` area of the HTML document?

## CHAPTER 3

Python

Although HTML and CSS tell the browser how to display a page, the real power of your application will come when the HTML is dynamically generated by your Google App Engine application. Building HTML using a program is how a website shows dynamic information, such as a list of items pulled from a catalog database. Then the website allows you to pick an item and place it in your shopping cart and then a few screens later, it takes your credit card number and sells you the items. All of this requires programming. We write our instructions on how to handle incoming requests in a programming language called Python.

You will need to write a program that receives the incoming requests from the browsers and handles the request by reading and/or writing some data and then sending the next page of output back to the browser. In the next chapter, we will talk about the Hyper-Text Transport Protocol (HTTP) and the request/response cycle in more detail. In this chapter, you get a quick introduction to the Python programming language as used in Google App Engine.

What Is Programming?

When a request comes from a browser into your web application, you must respond with a response. Let's imagine for a moment that somehow all the requests were routed to you personally and you had to produce a response by hand for each request. It would be very similar to how telephone operators made manual phone connections in the early 1900s.

If you had to respond by hand to every request from a browser, your application would be very slow and likely not very popular or successful. And your life would become very boring because you would be doing something very simple over and over again.

If you learn to write a program to produce the response automatically, you can delegate all of the manual work of receiving requests and making responses to the program that you write and the microprocessors that are running your program in the Google cloud.

Being able to delegate the task of receiving a request from a browser and producing the response sounds mighty convenient. And it is—it will allow you to take a weekend off while the microprocessors are doing the work. But there is one catch: you must explain to the microprocessor the exact series of steps to be taken each time a request is received. If you can explain the steps in sufficient detail, the microprocessor can do the work for you millions of times per second.

You must express the exact steps you want to perform in a programming language called Python because that is the language that Google App Engine understands. In this chapter, you learn the basic syntax and grammar of Python before you learn the basic steps of our web application. So although some of this chapter may seem simple and trivial, unless you are an experienced programmer, please take the time to read the chapter and get a sense of the Python language so that the rest of the book makes better sense.

About Python

Guido van Rossum created Python in 1990. The primary impetus for Python was to make a language that was powerful and capable and at the same time very easy to use and learn. Guido named Python after the British comedy program *Monty Python's Flying Circus*. Perhaps this name was chosen to communicate the groundbreaking notion that programming should be fun and playful.[*]

The syntax for Python is very simple; the language is designed to be intuitive, yet powerful. Other languages of the time, like C, used very dense and cryptic syntax with many special characters that each had its own special meaning.

For example, here is a (somewhat contrived) loop to print each character of a string in C with lots of special characters and syntax that have great meaning to skilled C programmers:

```
for(ch=mystring; *ch; ch++ ) {
   printf("%c",*ch);
}
```

And here is the loop in Python:

```
for ch in mystring:
    print ch
```

In the 1990s, C was far more popular than Python because writing in C was very similar to writing raw low-level assembly code. So C programs were very small and very fast and very cryptic. In the early 1990s, the typical computer was a 25Mhz Intel 486 with

---

[*] Other languages of the same time period had very unfun names like COBOL (Comprehensive Business-Oriented Language) or FORTRAN (FORmula TRANslation). The C language was so named because its predecessor was named "B."

640 KB of memory. Small and fast programs were very important and a cryptic programming language such as C was a necessary price to pay.

Over the years, computers have become much faster and now sport a lot more memory. Another trend is that people who do not have formal training in computer science are finding that knowing a little bit about programming is very helpful. People doing work in fields such as chemistry, biology, or the social sciences increasingly find a need to write simple programs to manipulate data as part of their basic work.

Over time, many of these fields have adopted Python as the programming language for their projects—it is simple enough to learn without necessitating a degree in computer science, and it has many powerful features that make it very well suited for data manipulation.

Increasingly, computer science and informatics teachers are discovering that Python is an excellent first language to teach. Because the language is simple, agile, clean, and powerful, students are able to master the language far more quickly. This means that students can write richer and more interesting programs in their first programming course. Students can quickly see how writing software can actually solve problems that might be useful to them. Students who want to go further in computer science can still learn systems languages such as Java, C, and C++ for their professional career. In many ways, learning Python first deepens their ultimate understanding of the richness of programming when they learn more systems-oriented languages.

Google internally prefers that software be written in one of three languages: Java, C++, or Python. Given that Google had extensive experience with Python, it was quite a natural step for it to choose Python as the first language supported by Google App Engine. Given that the goal of App Engine is to greatly broaden participation in web application development, it makes a lot of sense to use a language that is very popular both inside and outside of computer science, with a particular focus on being very easy to learn.

Installing Python

This chapter assumes that you have Python installed on your computer. If your computer does not come with Python preinstalled, visit *http://www.python.org* to download and install a copy for your system.

Some of the examples in this chapter are Python programs that are to be edited in a file and executed by running Python on your computer, which looks like this:[†]

```
python myfile.py
```

And other examples in this chapter use Python in interactive mode, in which you simply start Python and enter commands as follows:

[†] See *www.pythonlearn.com* for details on how to install and run Python on your computer system.

```
python

Python 2.5.2 (r252:60911, Feb 22 2008, 07:57:53)
Type "help", "copyright", "credits" or "license" for more information.
>>> print "Hello"
Hello
>>>
```

Python uses three greater-than signs to indicate that it is waiting for input. The prompt changes to three dots (...) when you are entering a block of code. When you are running Python interactively, each statement executes as you type it in.

The Essence of Programming

When we write a program, we are describing a series of steps using a formal programming language with a very specific syntax. In a sense, a program is like a recipe for cooking a particular dish, or perhaps the instructions for putting a child's new toy together that comes "some assembly required."

In a program, assembly instructions, or a recipe, there are four basic patterns of steps:

Sequential steps

Normally, steps happen in order. Once one step is completed, we move on to the next step; sometimes the steps are even numbered. An example of this might be: (1) add 300 grams of flour, (2) add 100 ml of milk, (3) add one egg.

Conditional steps

Sometimes we skip a step. Depending on some condition, we decide to do a step or not do a step. An example of a conditional step in our recipe might be: (4) if you are cooking at more than 2000 meters above sea level, add a second egg. Often these conditional steps are expressed using the word "if."

Repeated steps

Sometimes we do a step over and over until some condition is satisfied. An example of a repeated step might be: (5) blend the mixture with a fork until nearly all the lumps are gone. Words like "while," "repeat," or "until" are often used to describe repeated steps.

Stored and reused steps

Sometimes we end up with a set of steps that we will want to do over and over again the same way each time. Instead of repeatedly describing the steps each time they are needed, we describe them once and store them for later use. Then, when we need the steps, we call them in and use them. Sometimes we define the stored steps ourselves, and other times we use stored steps created by someone else. An example of a stored step in a recipe might be: (6) open the flavor packet and pour the contents into the bowl. Somewhere out there, the recipe for making whatever is in the flavor packet is known, but that is not our problem. The flavor packet has been provided to us and we simply use it at the appropriate moment in our preparation.

So our recipe ends up looking like this:

```
add 300 grams of flour
add 100 ml of milk
add an egg
if altitude > 2000:
  add an egg
while there are too many lumps:
  beat mixture with a fork
open and add provided flavor packet
```

One thing to note is that we naturally use indentation to indicate the conditional and repeated steps. For example, in the previous example, it is important to know whether we beat the mixture all the time or only when we are above 2,000 meters. Looking at the indentation, it is pretty clear that we always beat the mixture, regardless of altitude. Also, because `open and add provided flavor packet` is not indented, it is clear that we do this only once, not many times.

The indentation can tell us which statements are part of a conditional or repeated block. The recipe would end up with a very different outcome if it were written as follows:

```
add 300 grams of flour
add 100 ml of milk
add an egg
if altitude > 2000:
  add an egg
  while there are too many lumps:
    beat mixture with a fork
  open and add provided flavor packet
```

If the altitude is less than or equal to 2,000 meters, we won't end up with tasty biscuits; instead, we will end up with some badly mixed wallpaper paste.

When the computer tells us that there is a syntax error, it is because it cannot understand our instructions. Even with all the claims of machine intelligence and the advances of computers, they are still pretty simple-minded creatures that like clear and explicit instructions in a very formal language.

Input, Processing, and Output

Another basic pattern in programming is input, processing, and output. The basic idea is that a typical program gets some input, does some processing, and produces some output.

A simple three-line program in Python that directly demonstrates input, processing, and output is a program to convert elevator floor numbers. When we use an elevator in the United States, the lobby floor is floor number 1. When we use an elevator in the rest of the world, the lobby floor is floor number 0.

Here is our program to handle this complex conversion task:

```
usf = input('Enter the US Floor Number: ')
wf = usf - 1
print 'Non-US Floor Number is',wf
```

The first line of the program calls the Python function named `input` to display a prompt string and read a number putting the number in the variable `usf`. A variable is a temporary storage area where we keep data for use later in the program.

The second line of the program takes the input data, subtracts 1, and stores the new value in a variable called `wf`. The third line produces some output using the Python `print` statement.

When we run the program, it functions as follows:

```
python elev.py
Enter the US Floor Number: 2
Non-US Floor Number is 1
```

We edit the program in a file called *elev.py* and run the program by calling Python and giving Python the filename. The program prompts us for the U.S. floor number, and we enter 2. The program does its conversion and then prints out the equivalent floor number for the rest of the world.

This program demonstrates both sequential steps and stored/reused steps. Our program starts at the first step and proceeds through the third step. The call to `input()` and the use of `print` are examples of using predefined code that is built-in to Python (like the flavor packet from the recipe example).

Conditional Steps: A Number-Guessing Web Application

Our next Python example will be a number-guessing game. The user is repeatedly asked for a number and then told whether her guess is too low, correct, or too high. Figure 3-1 shows what this web application will look like.

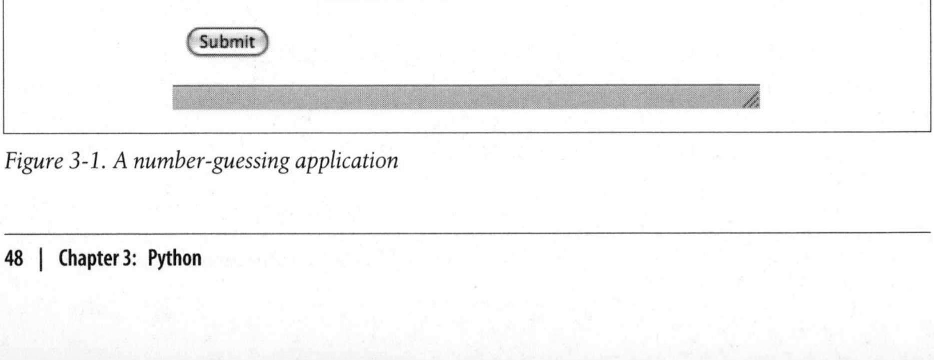

Figure 3-1. A number-guessing application

The user will be able to guess the number repeatedly and get feedback on every guess. Hopefully, with enough feedback and enough guesses, she will eventually figure out the secret number.

Here is the source code for the application:

```
print 'Your guess is', guess

answer = 42

if guess < answer :
  print 'Your guess is too low'

if guess == answer :
  print 'Congratulations!'

if guess > answer :
  print 'Your guess is too high'
```

For the moment, we will ignore how to make the HTML in the browser display the form and how the data from the browser finds its way into the variable guess. Just assume for now that the number from the web form ends up in the variable named guess.

The first thing the program does is print out the value for guess. This helps assure us that the guess variable really contains the number that we expect. Then we store the secret value in a variable named answer.[‡] Then we have three conditional statements. The first if statement checks whether the guess is too low, the second checks whether the guess is correct, and the third checks whether the guess is too high. In each case, a single line of output is printed if the condition is true. The conditional statements are carefully constructed so that only one of the three if statements is true, so only one line of output comes out, regardless of the value of guess.

The expressions guess < answer, guess == answer, and guess > answer are logical expressions that look at the value of guess and answer and decide whether the logical expression is true or false. If the logical expression in an if statement evaluates to true, the indented statements are executed. If the logical expression evaluates to false, the indented statement(s) are skipped. We call these *conditional* statements because whether they execute is controlled by the result of the logical expression in the if statement.

Often there is a situation in which we want one set of statements to execute if the logical expression is true and another set of statements to execute if the logical expression is false. We use the else keyword to indicate that there is one of two paths and that the logical expression is simply choosing between one of the two alternatives.

Here is another version of our program that uses the else capability:

[‡] To help understand why 42 is the answer, type the string "the answer to life the universe and everything" into Google's search box—all lowercase and no quotes.

```
print 'Your guess is', guess

answer = 42

if guess == answer :
  print 'Good guess'
else:
  print 'Bad guess'
```

Now this program functions a bit differently than our original program, but it does nicely demonstrate the use of the else. If the logical expression (guess == answer) evaluates to true, we print Good guess. If the logical expression evaluates to false, we run the else: code and print Bad guess.

Figure 3-2 shows a map view of the if-then-else that shows how the program executes. It is choosing between the true path and the false path based on the logical expression.

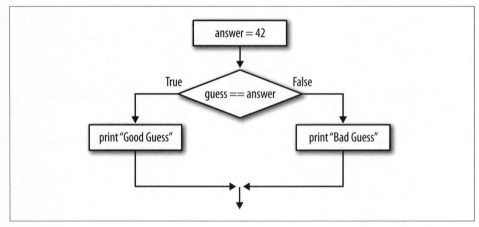

Figure 3-2. If-then-else

We might want to help the user who has a bad guess by giving a little more detail, as follows:

```
print 'Your guess is', guess

answer = 42

if guess == answer :
  print 'Congratulations!'
else:
  if guess < answer :
   print 'Your guess is too low'
  else:
   print 'Your guess is too high'
```

This example shows the concept of *nesting*—a very important concept because it allows us to nest a statement within another statement. Nesting is what allows us to create very complex programs using the four simple concepts of sequential, conditional, repeated, and stored and reused steps.

As programmers, we communicate which groups of statements belong to which block of code by changing the indentation. We indent the entire second `if` statement (`guess < answer`) to indicate that it is part of the `else` clause in the first `if` (`guess == answer`). Figure 3-3 is a visual representation of this.

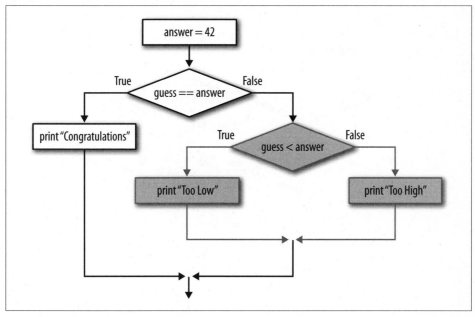

Figure 3-3. Nesting if-then-else statements

By carefully controlling indents, we can communicate how we want the program to handle our conditional statements.

It turns out that this pattern of nesting `if`s within `if`s is so common that we have a special way of representing this logic flow by using the `elif` (i.e., `else if`) statement instead of nested `if` statements. That is, here's yet another way we could write this program:

```
print 'Your guess is', guess

answer = 42

if guess == answer :
  print 'Congratulations!'
elif guess < answer :
  print 'Your guess is too low'
else:
  print 'Your guess is too high'
```

You can add as many `elif` clauses as you like. Python checks the first clause (`guess == answer`) and if this is true, Python runs the indented code. If (`guess == answer`) is false, it checks the next `elif` (`guess < answer`) and if the logical expression on the `elif` evaluates to true, it runs the indented code block. If none of the `if` or `elif` logical expressions evaluates to true, it falls through, and the code in the `else` block is executed. You can add as many `elif` statements as you like, and the `else` statement is optional. A diagram of this example code is shown in Figure 3-4.

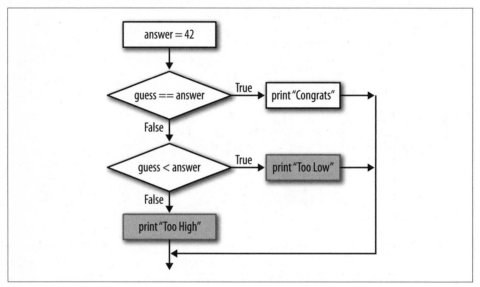

Figure 3-4. Multibranch if statements

You can see that Python sequentially looks for logical expressions that are true, and when it finds one, it executes the indented code and then is all done with the block. If none of the logical expressions is true, it falls down into the else statement. You can think of both the `elif` and `else` clauses as part of the `if` statement.

Variables and Expressions

Another important aspect of this program is its use of variables. *Variables* are the programmer's way of giving names to areas of the computer's memory. When we have some data that we want to keep and then use later in the program, we put the data in a variable. We call them "variables" because their contents can vary. We can set a variable to hold one value, and then later in the program, we can set it to another value. Once we set a variable to a value, it holds (remembers) that value until we change it or the program ends.

The primary way that we set variables is through an assignment statement:

```
answer = 42
```

The equals sign (=) is used in most programming languages to indicate variable assignment. You will notice that in the previous if statements, we used double equals (==) in the logical expression when we were checking for equality. In English, we would read the previous statement as "Assign the value 42 into the variable named answer."

If we go back to our elevator floor conversion program, we can take a closer look at the assignments statements and variables:

```
usf = input('Enter the US Floor Number: ')
wf = usf - 1
print 'Non-US Floor Number is',wf
```

This program has two assignment statements and two variables. The first statement asks the user for a number; this number is returned to us as the result of calling the input function. Because we want to use that value later, we assign the value to be stored in the variable usf.

In the second statement, we have an assignment statement that has an expression on the righthand side. The expression (usf -1) is requesting that Python do a computation. In English, we are saying, "Retrieve the current contents of the variable usf and subtract one from that value." The assignment statement tells us what to do with the results of the expression after the expression has been computed (i.e., place this new value into the variable wf).

Then the final statement is a print statement that prints out a string, followed by the current contents of the variable wf.

Actually, we can put expressions anywhere that is expecting a value. We could shorten the previous program as follows:

```
usf = input('Enter the US Floor Number: ')
print 'Non-US Floor Number is', (usf-1)
```

We are using an expression on the print statement and printing out the result of the expression instead of storing it in a variable and then printing out the variable. The parentheses around (usf -1) are not necessary, but they help emphasize that it is an expression that is evaluated before the printing is done.

Naming Variables

As programmers, we can pick any variable names we like, as long as the names follow a few simple rules. In Python, variables must start with a letter or underscore (_) and may consist of any combination of letters, underscores, and numbers:

```
Legal Variable Names: x, usf, _food, food16, FOOD
Illegal Variable Names: 42secret, :usf, value-7
```

Upper- and lowercase is significant in Python variables. For example, usf and Usf are different and distinct variables.

Often programmers who are just starting out have trouble choosing variable names as they write their code because there is so much choice. Beginning programmers also have trouble looking at example code because it is hard to pick out which parts of the syntax are necessary because they are part of the language and which parts of the syntax are just things that were chosen by the programmer. In the following code:

```
usf = input('Enter the US Floor Number: ')
wf = usf - 1
print 'Non-US Floor Number is',wf
```

the `input` and `print` are part of Python. You can look them up in the Python manual. The variable names `usf` and `wf` were chosen by the person who wrote this sample program.

It is a good idea to select variable names that are mnemonic[§] so that we can more easily remember what we put into the variable. In this case, we name two variables as follows: `usf` stores the United States floor number and `wf` stores the worldwide floor number. In a three-line program, we really don't need any memory aids, but as you look at code samples throughout the book, you'll notice that the variable names are generally chosen to make sense.

For example, if we were feeling diabolical and wanted to challenge the reader of our program, we could write the same program as follows:

```
dsjdkjds = input('Enter the US Floor Number: ')
xsjdkjds = dsjdkjds - 1
print 'Non-US Floor Number is', xsjdkjds
```

As the programmer, you can choose any variable name you like. In this example, we chose variable names that are complete gibberish and differ by only a single letter. The program still functions the same because Python cares only that you use variable names that match exactly from the variable assignment to the place where you use the variable. However, anyone else who looks at this code will have trouble understanding what things mean in the program. So we choose mnemonic names to convey to the human reader what we intended to store in a particular variable.

Constants

We already have been using constants. Constants are values that we put into the program. Here we highlight the constants used in our sample program:

```
usf = input('Enter the US Floor Number: ')
wf = usf - 1
print 'Non-US Floor Number is', wf
```

We have two string constants and a single integer constant (1). We call these values *constants* to contrast them with variables. A variable can hold many different values as the program runs; a constant is a single value that never changes.

[§] Mnemonic means "memory assisting."

Handling Text Data Using Strings

So far all of our expressions (calculations) have been done with numbers. You can do the kinds of operations that you might expect with numbers: add, subtract, multiply, divide, and so on.

It turns out that although doing numeric calculations is an important task within a computer, increasingly programming is concerned with textual data such as names, addresses, or URLs.

Python has very good built-in support for processing textual data. We have already seen string constants with quotes. You can actually use either single quotes or double quotes for Python string constants. We prefer single quotes in Python code because we use double quotes in HTML code.

You can assign a string into a variable—pretty much like a number. We could rewrite our number guessing program as follows, putting strings into variables:

```python
print 'Your guess is', guess

answer = 42

if guess == answer :
  msg = 'Congratulations!'
elif guess < answer :
  msg = 'Your guess is too low'
else:
  msg = 'Your guess is too high'

print msg
```

Instead of doing the `print` in each of the conditional statements, we simply store a string in the variable named `msg`, and at the end we print out the contents of the variable `msg`. The result is the same. We have just used a string variable to store the message instead of printing it directly.

One thing that makes strings powerful in Python is that we can look at each character in the string individually or pull out a portion of the string (a *substring*). Think of a string as a list of characters in order. The first character in the string is the [0] character.

In this example, we are running Python interactively; we can type Python statements and have them immediately execute:

```python
python
>>> txt = 'guess=25'
>>> print txt[0]
g
>>> print txt[1]
u
>>>
```

The three greater than characters (>>>) are just Python asking us for the next line of Python to execute. You can see that the first character (i.e., [0]) is the letter g and the

[1] character is the letter u. If you think back to the elevator example, strings and the square bracket lookup operation are similar to elevators outside the United States. Both the first floor/character are labeled with zero.[||]

You can also pull out a portion of the string by adding a colon and ending character to the brackets as follows:

```
>>> print txt[2:4]
es
>>> print txt[2:5]
ess
>>>
```

The rule for the number after the colon is that we go *up to but not including* character four. So the syntax [2:4] really includes only characters two and three.

One nice bit of Python syntax allows you to omit the first or second number; it is assumed to be the beginning or end of the string, respectively:

```
>>> txt = 'guess=25'
>>> print txt[:5]
guess
>>> print txt[6:]
25
>>>
```

Remember that the second number [:5] is up to but not including the character at position 5.

You can also add strings together using the plus sign. It may seem a little strange at first, but it will seem natural pretty quickly. Adding strings is simply concatenating them:

```
>>> think = 'happy' + 'thoughts'
>>> print think
happythoughts
>>>
```

If you wanted to add a space between the words, just add the space:

```
>>> think = 'happy' + ' ' + 'thoughts'
>>> print think
happy thoughts
>>>
```

Using the String Library

Python includes an extensive library of functions to manipulate strings. We can use the string library to perform many tasks without resorting to writing lots of simple loops

---

[||] Although starting at zero might feel very counterintuitive at first, it turns out to have a lot of advantages, both in elevator labeling and character lookup in strings.

to look through strings. The Python string library has many features that I do not describe here. For now we will look at just the `find()` feature.

You use `find()` to search for the occurrence of one string within another. The `find()` method either returns the position of the search string or `-1` to indicate that the search string was not found.

Here is a simple example of using `find()` in a string:

```
>>> txt = 'guess=25'
>>> print txt.find('=')
5
>>> print txt.find('pizza')
-1
>>>
```

We did `find()` an equals sign character (=) at position 5 in our string and the string `'pizza'` was not found at all in our string. The `find()` method returns an integer number indicating the first position of the search string or `-1` to indicate "not found."

There are several different string library methods available: `lowercase()`, `rfind()`, `split()`, `strip()`, `rstrip()`, `replace()`, and many more. For more documentation on Python capabilities, go to *http://docs.python.org/library/stdtypes.html*.

Types and Conversion

We have seen situations where we store integer numbers in a variable and at other times we store strings in a variable. It turns out that Python is very aware of the kind of data that we are placing in our variables. The technical term for the kind of data in a variable or constant is called its *type*. We say that a variable is an *integer type* or that a variable has a *string type*.

We can even ask Python what type a particular variable is using the built-in `type()` function:

```
>>> txt = 'guess=25'
>>> print type(txt)
<type 'str'>
>>> pos = txt.find('=')
>>> print pos
5
>>> print type(pos)
<type 'int'>
>>>
```

The variable `txt` is of type `str`. When we call the `find()` method and search for an equals sign, we get an integer number that we store in the variable `pos`. Then when we ask Python the type of `pos`, it tells us that `pos` is an integer.

We can add two integers and we can add two strings. But can we add a string and an integer? What happens?

```
>>> txt = 'abc' + 'def'
>>> print txt
abcdef
>>> num = 36 + 6
>>> print num
42
>>> huh = 'abc' + 6
Traceback (most recent call last):
  File "<stdin>", line 1, in <module>
TypeError: cannot concatenate 'str' and 'int' objects
>>>
```

Python complains that we are trying to do something that is not allowed, as indicated by the `Traceback` message. So our program is being stopped in its tracks and the `Traceback` is a helpful message indicating where our program was executing when it stopped.

The message provides the category of error that it encountered (i.e., a `TypeError`) and gives some detail about it.

You can find a list of the kinds of errors (exceptions) and their descriptions at *http:// docs.python.org/library/exceptions.html*.

When we try to add a string and a number, Python complains. The simple fix is to convert the number to a string using the built-in `str()` function and then concatenating the strings together:

```
>>> huh = 'abc' + str(6)
>>> print huh
abc6
>>>
```

The `str()` function takes an expression as its input parameter and converts the parameter to a string and returns the string to us. Once the integer 6 is converted into a one-character string with a 6 character in it, we can successfully concatenate the `abc` and the `6` together.

If we can convert from an integer to a string, we should be able to convert from a string to an integer. You probably already guessed that this is accomplished using the `int()` function. It takes a string as input and returns an integer. Of course, the characters in the string must be a properly formatted number, or we will get a traceback:

```
>>> print int('12')
12
>>> print int('x49')
Traceback (most recent call last):
  File "<stdin>", line 1, in <module>
ValueError: invalid literal for int() with base 10: 'x49'
>>>
```

Let's say that we are presented with a string that looks as follows:

```
'guess=25'
```

We want to pull out whatever number comes after `guess=` and then convert that number to an integer. Here is a sequence of Python string operators that accomplish that task:

```
>>> txt = 'guess=25'
>>> pos = txt.find('=')
>>> sub = txt[pos+1:]
>>> print sub
25
>>> print type(sub)
<type 'str'>
>>> ival = int(sub)
>>> print ival
25
>>> print type(ival)
<type 'int'>
>>>
```

First, we find where the equals sign is located in the string. Then we pull out a substring that starts one character past the equals sign through the end of the string [`pos+1:`]. We now have a string with the number's characters—we see that it is of type `str`. Then we use `int()` to convert `sub` to an integer and store it in `ival`. Just to make sure, we check the type of `ival` and verify that it is an integer.

Variables with Many Values at the Same Time: Lists

So far we have seen integer variables and string variables—in each variable, we can store a single value. When we put a new value into a variable, we overwrite the old value. Python supports several kinds of (types of) variables that can store multiple values at the same time.

Let's say we wanted to keep track of our friends—that is, we wanted to keep a list of our friends. In Python, we can use a `list` variable as follows:

```
>>> pals = list()
>>> pals.append('Glenn')
>>> pals.append('Sally')
>>> pals.append('Joe')
>>> print pals
['Glenn', 'Sally', 'Joe']
>>> print type(pals)
<type 'list'>
>>> print len(pals)
3
>>>
```

Initially we make a new variable and create an empty `list()`. Then we append three strings to the list using the `append()` method. When we print out the list, we see the three pals we added to our list. If we ask Python to tell us the type of the `pals` variable, it says that `pals` is a `'list'`. We can even use the built-in function `len()` to find out how many strings we have in our list named `pals`.

Lists have and maintain an order and we can pull out any of the items in the list. We use the square bracket syntax to pull an element out of a list, much like how we pull a particular character out of a string using square brackets. And we continue to use the non-American elevator numbering rules—the first element is [0] and the second element is [1] and so on.

```
>>> print pals[0]
Glenn
>>> print pals[2]
Joe
>>>
```

We can also change an element in a list by using the square bracket syntax and as assignment statement:

```
>>> print pals
['Glenn', 'Sally', 'Joe']
>>> pals[2] = 'Joseph'
>>> print pals
['Glenn', 'Sally', 'Joseph']
>>>
```

We can see that the third element in our pals list was changed from 'Joe' to 'Joseph'.

There are many other list operations that are provided by Python. For example, if we want to sort the list, we call the sort() method on the list:

```
>>> pals.sort()
>>> print pals
['Glenn', 'Joseph', 'Sally']
>>>
```

There are many different methods available for list beyond append() and sort(): remove(), insert(), index(), reverse(), and more. Lists in Python are very powerful and very helpful tools that we can use to solve problems.

Repeated Code: Loops

Once we have a list that contains some number of things, we need a way to do something to each of those elements in the list. This is one of the more common places where we end up with the repeated code pattern. We call this pattern *looping* because we write a block of code and then loop through it over and over again.

Python has a for loop that is ideal for looping through a list of items. To loop through the list of items in the previous example, we can write the following for loop:

```
>>> pals = list()
>>> pals.append('Glenn')
>>> pals.append('Sally')
>>> pals.append('Joseph')
>>> print pals
['Glenn', 'Sally', 'Joseph']
>>> for x in pals:
```

```
...  print x
...
Glenn
Sally
Joseph
>>>
```

You can see that the **for** loop went through the list of pals, and for each pal in the list, it executed a **print** statement.

Take a look at just the **for** loop code:

```
for x in pals:
  print x
```

The **for** and **in** are part of the Python language, much like **print** or **if**. Also notice that the **for** line ends with a colon (:), indicating the start of a block of code and the loop body is indented below the **for**. In this example, the loop body is only one line. But loop bodies can be any number of lines and can include more complex code.

Another important part of the **for** statement is the **iteration variable**. Because the body of the loop (**print x**) is going to be executed one time for each string in our list, inside the loop body we need to know which of the **pals** we are processing. The iteration variable in this example is **x**. The loop will run three times (the size of our list), and each time the loop runs, **x** will refer to the particular value for the element of the list that we are processing.

In a sense, the **for** loop executes as follows:

```
>>> x = pals[0]
>>> print x
Glenn
>>> x = pals[1]
>>> print x
Sally
>>> x = pals[2]
>>> print x
Joseph
>>>
```

The **for** statement knows how many strings are in the **pals** list and steps through them one at a time, with the variable **x** being assigned the successive values in the **pals** list.

This is why Python uses the keyword **in** as part of the syntax of the **for** loop:

```
for x in pals:
  print x
```

The way to think of this **for** look in English is "for each of the elements in pals, set **x** to that element and then execute the loop body." We shorten that to **for x in pals:** to save some typing. We can also put more code in the loop body:

```
>>> for pal in pals:
...  print 'A Pal'
...  print pal
```

```
...
A Pal
Glenn
A Pal
Sally
A Pal
Joseph
```

In this example, we change the iteration variable from x to something more mnemonic. We call the iteration variable pal. We also put a second print statement in the body of the for loop to show multiple statements in the indented block.

We can also loop through each of the characters in a string using a for statement. A string can be thought of as a list of characters:

```
>>> txt = 'guess=25'
>>> for x in txt:
...   print x
...
g
u
e
s
s
=
2
5
>>>
```

Again, we use x as our iteration variable. The for loop goes through the characters in the string in order and assigns each successive character in the string to x and then executes the loop body.

We can look for a particular character in the string by adding an if to the body of the loop:

```
>>> txt = 'guess=25'
>>> for x in txt:
...   print x
...   if x == '=' :
...     print 'Found an Equal Sign!'
...
g
u
e
s
s
=
Found an Equal Sign!
2
5
>>>
```

The loop runs and we always print out the character. If the character is =, we print out an additional joyous message indicating that we found an equals sign.

Python's Backpack: Dictionaries

Python lists are very useful: (a) they keep things in order, (b) they can be sorted, and (c) we can look up the second element. We can solve many important aspects of our data management problems with lists.

However, some problems need more flexibility than Python's list feature gives us. Sometimes we want a "backpack" or "purse" or "handbag" that we can put a bunch of things into and get those things back out. We will organize our backpack by labeling everything that we put into it. We label items as we put them in and then use the labels to pull the items back out.

So far in our pals example, each pal has a first name. What if we wanted some more detail about each pal such as a first name, last name, email address, phone number, and so on. We can use a Python dictionary to store this information nicely. So we create an empty dictionary using `dict()` and fill it up with labeled items:

```
>>> pal = dict()
>>> pal['first'] = 'Glenn'
>>> pal['last'] = 'Golden'
>>> pal['email'] = 'glenng@umich.edu'
>>> pal['phone'] = '517-303-8700'
>>> print pal
{'phone': '517-303-8700', 'last': 'Golden', 'email': 'glenng@umich.edu', 'first':
'Glenn'}
>>>
```

We use the assignment statement with the dictionary key in square brackets to fill up our new dictionary with labeled items. We label the items in our backpack with strings like `'first'`, `'last'`, `'email'`, and `'phone'`. When we print out our dictionary named `pal`, we see a series of entries with the label (or key), a colon, and then a value. It is important to note that the dictionary (like a backpack or purse) does not keep the items in a particular order. It just labels each item so that we can get it back.

If we want to get an item back, we use the bracket syntax to look up or retrieve the item from our dictionary:

```
>>> print pal['phone']
517-303-8700
>>>
```

Just like in a list, where we can look up at item at position 2 using square brackets, in a dictionary we can look up the item that has the label `'phone'` using square brackets. If we try to look up an item and it is not there, we get an error:

```
>>> print pal['age']
Traceback (most recent call last):
 File "<stdin>", line 1, in <module>
KeyError: 'age'
>>>
```

We get the dreaded traceback error and our program is stopped cold in its tracks. Luckily dictionary objects have a method called get(), which is more forgiving. When we use get(), we give it a value to use if the key is not found:

```
>>> print pal.get('age','Age not available')
Age not available
>>> print pal.get('phone', 'Phone not available')
517-303-8700
>>>
```

If the label/key is not found when get() is called, the second parameter to the get() method is returned instead of a traceback. If the label is present in the dictionary, the proper value is returned.

The Python dictionary is used in many places because we can put any combination of key/value pairs in the dictionary without knowing in advance what we will be putting into the dictionary. A dictionary is Python's way of passing around a bag of stuff with labels on each item.

Looping Through a Dictionary

We often need to loop through a dictionary to do something to each of the items stored in the dictionary. Again, we use the for statement, this time with a slightly different syntax. The iteration variable (z in this example) loops through the keys/labels in the dictionary:

```
>>> print pal
{'phone': '517-303-8700', 'last': 'Golden', 'email': 'glenng@umich.edu', 'first':
'Glenn'}
>>> for z in pal:
... print z
...
phone
last
email
first
>>>
```

If we want the keys and values, we use the key from the iteration variable to look up the value using the key as follows:

```
>>> for key in pal:
... print key, pal[key]
...
phone 517-303-8700
last Golden
email glenng@umich.edu
first Glenn
>>>
```

In the example loop, we change the name of iteration variable to key to make it more mnemonic. Now on each line, we see both the key and the value for each entry in the

Python dictionary. For each iteration through the loop, `key` takes the string that is the label for the entry and then we look up the value using the bracket syntax `pal[key]`.

Dictionaries have many capabilities beyond those shown here. Python has a built-in function called `dir()` that lists the capabilities of an object like our `pal` dictionary:

```
>>> dir(pal)
['clear', 'copy', 'fromkeys', 'get', 'has_key', 'items', 'iteritems', 'iterkeys',
'itervalues', 'keys', 'pop', 'popitem', 'setdefault', 'update', 'values']
```

You can check out the Python documentation to see details on what each of these methods is used for.

You can actually use the `dir()` function on any Python variable or constant to see what capabilities are available. This is an abbreviated list of what can be done to a String object:

```
>>> dir('Hello')
['capitalize', 'center', 'count', 'decode', 'encode', 'endswith', 'expandtabs',
'find', 'index', 'isalnum', 'isalpha', 'isdigit', 'islower', 'isspace', 'istitle',
'isupper', 'join', 'ljust', 'lower', 'lstrip', 'partition', 'replace', 'rfind',
'rindex', 'rjust', 'rpartition', 'rsplit', 'rstrip', 'split', 'splitlines',
'startswith', 'strip', 'swapcase', 'title', 'translate', 'upper', 'zfill']
>>> print 'Hello'.upper()
HELLO
>>>
```

You can find the detail on the methods available for Python lists, dictionaries, or strings in many Python books and online sources.

Stored and Reused Code: Python Functions

Now we take a look at the last of our core patterns (sequential, conditional, repeated, and store/reuse). We actually have been using the reuse part of the pattern all along. We have been using parts of Python that are provided as part of Python itself:

```
>>> txt = 'guess=25'
>>> print len(txt)
8
>>>
```

What is `len()` and where did it come from? This is an example of some code that was written and provided for us by Python. The code was written and stored in Python and ready for us to reuse it at any time.

In Python, these items are called *functions*. The word "function" is taken from the mathematical notion of a function, which takes an input and returns an output. The `len()` function takes a string as its input and returns an integer as its output.

We can write our own functions and use them to help make our programs more readable. When we create a function as a programmer, generally our main purpose is to capture a bit of useful code so we can use it several places instead of writing it over and over in each of those places.

Here is a trivial example of a function that shows simple store and reuse:

```
>>> def welcome():
...    print 'Hello'
...
>>> welcome()
Hello
>>> welcome()
Hello
>>>
```

The def keyword starts a function *definition*. As we define our function, we name our function welcome. Function names follow the same rules as variable names. After the function name, we have some optional parameters to be passed into the function. In this example, we have no parameters, so we have empty parentheses (). The def statement ends with a colon (:) to indicate that we are starting a block of code. The def keyword is best thought of as "*define function*," as it signals the start of a block of code that defines a function. The def keyword also tells Python not to execute the following block but instead to store it for later reuse.

The body of our function is a single print statement. Notice that after the function definition is done, there is no output. We just see Python asking for the next command with the >>> prompt. This is because Python did not execute the print statement; the print statement was simply stored under the name welcome for later use:

```
>>> def welcome():
...    print 'Hello'
...
>>>
```

Now we actually call the function using the name that we gave it in the def statement:

```
>>> welcome()
Hello
>>> welcome()
Hello
>>>
```

By putting the parentheses after an identifier, we are telling Python, "Go find that function named welcome and execute it." Python goes and finds the stored code for welcome and runs it, and we see the print statement come out. And then we ask to run it again and the print statement comes out again.

We defined the function once and reused it twice. We kept this example trivial to focus on the storing and reusing and to emphasize that when Python encounters the function definition (def), it does not execute the code because Python only stores it for later.

Functions become much more powerful and useful when we give parameters to them as follows:

```
>>> def welcome(name):
...   print 'Hello',name
...
>>> welcome('Glenn')
Hello Glenn
>>> welcome('Sally')
Hello Sally
>>>
```

When we use a parameter in our function, it allows us to do something slightly different each time we call the function by passing in different parameters on each call to the function. In the function definition, we add parameters within the parentheses. In this example, our `welcome()` function accepts a single parameter, which we call `name` within the function. Within the function, our `print` statement prints out both the welcome message and the name parameter.

The `name` parameter is called a *formal parameter*. Formal parameters are very similar to the iteration variable in a `for` statement. The `name` variable simply represents whatever is the first parameter when the function is called. The `name` variable lasts only during the block of function code. Formal parameters can take on different values on each call.

So when we call the `welcome()` function twice with a different parameter each time, the `print` statement shows us the value for `name` on each call.

So far all the functions that we have shown as examples just execute code. A function can also return a value back to the code that is calling the function. This is how the `len()` function works:

```
>>> txt = 'guess=25'
>>> print len(txt)
8
>>>
```

The `len()` function takes the variable `txt` as its input, does some magical work, and then returns an integer, which we immediately print out, because we called the `len()` function on a `print` statement.

We can do something similar. Let's say we want our program to be able to welcome in several languages. We can write a function that determines the proper greeting based on the language code, as follows:

```
>>> def greet(lang):
...   if lang == 'es':
...     return 'Hola'
...   elif lang == 'fr':
...     return 'Bonjour'
...   else:
...     return 'Hello'
...
>>> print greet('en'),'Glenn'
Hello Glenn
>>> print greet('es'),'Sally'
Hola Sally
```

```
>>> print greet('fr'),'Michael'
Bonjour Michael
>>>
```

So our **greet()** function takes as its formal parameter a string indicating our preferred language. Within **greet()**, we use a simple multibranch **if** for each of the languages that we support. When the language matches Spanish (**'es'**), we execute the **return** statement giving the string **'Hola'** as the parameter to the **return** statement.

The **return** statement causes the function execution to stop and return to the code that called the function. In addition, the parameter on the return is the *return value* of the function, and it is used where the function was called. So when our function is called as follows:

```
>>> print greet('fr'),'Michael'
Bonjour Michael
>>>
```

the **greet()** function is called with **'fr'** as the parameter. The **greet()** function runs and eventually gets to **return 'Bonjour'**, which transfers control back to the **print** statement with the string **'Bonjour'** coming back to become the first parameter to the **print** statement.

If you find the idea of making a function call as part of a **print** statement a bit confusing, the following is equivalent and a bit more explicit as to what is going on:

```
>>> xgr = greet('fr')
>>> print xgr,'Michael'
Bonjour Michael
>>>
```

In this version, we call the **greet()** function with **'fr'** as the parameter. The **greet()** function executes and returns **'Bonjour'**, which we store in the variable **xgr**. In the next statement, we print out the contents of the **xgr** variable and the string **'Michael'**. This produces the same output as when we called the **greet()** function right in the **print** statement in the previous example.

Turning Traceback to Our Advantage Using Try and Except

So far, we have characterized traceback errors as a bad thing by implying that it means that we have done something wrong. Indeed, a traceback does mean that we have sufficiently confused Python to the point where Python does not know what to do next, so it gives up.

Remember the use of the **int()** function, which converts strings to integers? It gets pretty upset when the string does not contain numbers:

```
>>> print int('42')
42
>>> print int('fortytwo')
Traceback (most recent call last):
 File '<stdin>', line 1, in <module>
```

```
ValueError: invalid literal for int() with base 10: 'fortytwo'
>>>
```

Python saw that we gave it letters instead of numbers and gave up. Sometimes programmers actually are prepared to deal with this kind of error; all we really need to know is that it happened, and we can write some code to deal with the error situation.

We use the `try` and `except` statements in Python to tell Python that we know what we want to do if Python encounters an error. As the programmer, we are taking responsibility for dealing with the error.

Here is a simple example of `try`/`except` in action:

```
>>> try:
...   print int('fortytwo')
... except:
...   print 'Oops!'
...
Oops!
>>>
```

As we know that `int()` might blow up, we take out a bit of insurance on it. Instead of just calling `int()`, we call `int()` in a `try` block. If the code in the `try` block works without error, the `except` block is skipped. However, if anything goes wrong in the `try` block, the `try` block is terminated and the `except` block is executed. In the previous example, the `int()` fails, but Python knows that it is in a `try` block, so instead of giving us a traceback, Python runs the `except` block—so we see the `'Oops!'` message.

A more sensible example would be to make a function that safely converts a string to an integer and returns –1 if the conversion fails. Because our program is expecting positive numbers as input, we can use a negative number as an error indicator:

```
>>> def safeint(sval):
...   try:
...     return int(sval)
...   except:
...     return -1
...
>>> print safeint('fortytwo')
-1
>>> print safeint('42')
42
>>>
```

Our function takes a string parameter as its parameter. It will try to convert it to an integer and if we are successful, we return the new value. If the `int()` conversion fails, Python will not give a traceback, but will instead continue with the `except` code and return -1.

As a result, we can call the function with any string, and if there is an error in the conversion, we simply get –1 instead of a traceback, and the program blows up.

Object-Oriented Python

The object-oriented approach is a very important technique for building complex applications effectively. Python has excellent support for object-oriented programming.

Even in this chapter, you are already using objects. Python strings, lists, and dictionaries are all examples of Python objects. The `dir()` function lists the available methods in a class or object.

The key to object-oriented programming is the notion of an **object**, which contains both capabilities, such as the `find()` method on a string, as well as data. In particular, we can have many **instances** of objects. Our program can have hundreds or thousands of strings at any given moment and each of the strings has some data (attributes) as well as capabilities (methods).

We can also define our own classes, which can be used to create objects. A **class** is a template that defines the nature and makeup of objects. When you want to make a new object, use the **class** to construct it.

The following is the definition and use of a very simple **class**:

```
class Simple():
 num = 0
 def addone(self):
  self.num = self.num + 1
  return self.num

x = Simple()
x.addone()
x.addone()
print x.addone()
```

When we put this code into a file and execute the program, the value printed is 3 because the number inside the object has been incremented three times.

This class is named `Simple` and has one data attribute (`num`) and one method `addone()`. We create a new object (instance of the class) by constructing the object using `Simple()` and storing that new object in the variable x. We can call the `addone()` method on our object. Each call to `addone()` adds 1 to the `num` value inside of the x object.

Within the `addone()` method, the `self` parameter refers to the particular instance of the object. For example, if we added the following code:

```
Y = Simple()
y.addone()
print 'Y=',y.addone()
print 'X=',x.addone()
```

it would print out 1 for y and 4 for x. We now have two instances of `Simple` objects. Each of the objects has its own copy of the `num` variable. In the `addone()` method, `self.num` is how each object refers to its own copy of the `num` variable.

We cover object-oriented aspects of Python in more detail as they come up—in Chapter 5, as well as in the remainder of the book.

Comments in Python

Although most of the time when we write Python, we are communicating with Python itself, often we want to include information in our source code for humans to read. These comments usually help explain what is going on in our program to some other human, who might be reading the program and trying to figure it out. Surprisingly often, the human you are communicating with is you in the future, as you try to look back at your code and try to (again) figure out what you intended.

Python ignores anything on a line after it encounters a # character. Here is our first program, with a few comments:

```
# This program helps travelers use elevators
usf = input('Enter the US Floor Number: ')
wf = usf-1 # The conversion is quite simple
print 'Non-US Floor Number is',wf
```

Python comments can either be at the end of a line of Python code or stand on a line by themselves.

The Tao of Programming

We are nearly at the end of this quick introduction to Python. If this is your first experience programming, it might take a while to get the hang of programming. You may feel a bit discombobulated for a while. Feeling a bit confused until you get a sense of the big picture is perfectly normal. The most important thing you can do is to relax and keep trying.

As a beginning programmer, you will likely go through three phases:

- In the first phase, you hate the computer and you hate Python. It seems that no matter what you do, Python always tells you "Syntax error" or "Traceback." You read the book, and try to get things right and gingerly hand a bit of code to Python. Python seems to dislike you personally and nearly always rejects your submission as "not worthy." You start to feel like an insignificant worm that Python hates and rejects your "almost perfect" submissions no matter how hard you try. Sadly, many people get to this point in their first programming class, give up, and vow to choose a career that is as far from technology as possible.

- In the second phase, you realize that when Python is telling you "Syntax error" or "Traceback," it means that Python has become confused and does not know what to do next. Python is kind of like a puppy. A puppy will listen to whatever you say and seem interested in everything you are saying but a puppy only understands a few words like "food," "fetch," "sit," or "walk." In the second phase, you begin to feel superior. You realize that when Python gives you an error, Python shows that it needs to keep coming to you for help and guidance and purpose. Python is nothing without you. You are the wise and powerful programmer. Sometimes you write a loop to make Python sum up all the numbers between one and a million just to show it who is boss.

- In the third phase, you realize that Python is actually a great help to you and that Python represents the collective intelligence of hundreds of programmers who have given you some powerful and brilliant tools and capabilities. When you face a problem, you are not alone—you are facing the problem with the programmers who built Python at your side. All you need to do is use the right bits of Python and combine them to solve your particular problem. Sometimes when you are in a hurry, your instructions have a little mistake. When you make a mistake, Python courteously gives you an error message that includes clues as to what Python thinks you have done wrong. After a while, you will be able to quickly look at the error messages and have the clues jump out at you so that you can fix the tiny mistake you have made. You and Python are partners who help each other along the way.

It takes a while to make it to the third phase of programming, in which it becomes fun and Python feels like a powerful tool that enables you to encode your instructions so that the computer can handle tasks for you—whether that task is running a web server or processing a large amount of data that you want to analyze.

Summary

This chapter aimed to compress the high-level details of an entire programming class into a few pages. Even if you are a little confused at this point, keep moving forward! Often students find that larger and more complex examples make more sense than the trivial examples in this chapter. Larger examples have two advantages: (1) they generally are really trying to accomplish something that makes sense, and (2) you can see more steps and how we use all the patterns together to accomplish the task.

This chapter can also be a useful reference as you look through the more complex examples later in the book. Later chapters also will have areas that describe more advanced aspects of Python.

Exercises

1. How does the Python language compare to lower-level languages such as C in terms of the kinds of applications that are appropriate for each language?

2. What are the four basic patterns of programming? What are the four kinds of "steps"?

3. What does it mean when we "nest" a block of code within another block of code? Give an example of a nested block of code.

4. What is the function of the `else:` statement when an `if:` and several `elif:` statements have been used?

5. In the following code, which line will never be executed?

```
if x < 2 :
  print 'Below 2'
elif x >= 2 :
  print 'Two or more'
else :
  print 'Something else'
```

6. In the following code, which line will never be executed?

```
if x < 2 :
  print 'Below 2'
elif x < 20 :
  print 'Below 20'
elif x < 10 :
  print 'Below 10'
else :
  print 'Something else'
```

7. What is the purpose of an iteration variable in a `for` loop in Python?

8. What is a mnemonic variable? Why do we use mnemonic variable names?

9. After you have some experience writing Python code, describe what it means to have an "indentation error."

10. Type the following code into Python and see what happens:

```
x = 5
if x < 10 : print 'Small'
else: print 'Big'
```

When might this "contracted" form of a statement be useful?

11. What is a constructor? What are we constructing? Give an example of a constructor.

12. What is the difference between a class and an object in object-oriented programming?

13. What is the main difference between a function and a method?

14. What function in the Python string library is used to strip whitespace characters from the right side of a string?

15. Give an example of the following Python types: string, integer, list, and dictionary.

16. What is the purpose of the Python `type()` function? What is the purpose of the Python `dir()` function?

17. Run the following Python code in the Python interpreter:

```
>>> x = input('Type something ')
Type something [1,2,3]
>>> print x
[1, 2, 3]
```

```
>>> print type(x)
>>> <type 'list'>
```

What does this tell you about the Python `input()` function? How might you use
this capability in a program?

18. What will the following Python code print out?

```
a = 'Hello world'
print a[8]
```

19. When you store data in a Python list, how is the data stored and how do you look
up a particular item?

20. When you store data in a Python dictionary, how do you retrieve an item? What
dictionary method do you use to retrieve an item, providing a default value if the
item does not exist in the dictionary?

21. What element of the Python language is used to recover from errors and provide
alternate processing instructions when an error is encountered?

22. What will the following code print out?

```
zz = { 'Sam': ['Joe', 'Fred'], 'Fred': ['Sally', 'Joe'] }
print zz['Fred'][0]
```

Describe what this data structure might represent.

## CHAPTER 4

Sending Data to Your Application

So far we have looked a bit at HTML and CSS in the browser as well as at the Python programming language that we will use within the server.

In this chapter, we start to put it all together by looking at the HyperText Transport Protocol (HTTP) and how the browser interacts with the server. This interaction between the browser and server across the Internet is called the request/response cycle because the cycle of the browser making a request to the server and getting a response from the server happens over and over as we browse the Internet. The request/response cycle is the middle portion of Figure 4-1.

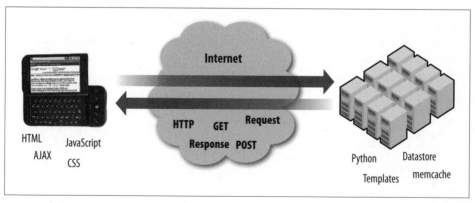

Figure 4-1. The request/response cycle

Making an HTTP Request

When you type a Uniform Resource Locator (URL) into the address box of your web browser and press Enter, you are asking your browser to retrieve a particular document somewhere on the Web. The URL *http://www.dr-chuck.com/page1.htm* can be broken down into three parts (as shown in Figure 4-2):

- The first part of the URL indicates which network protocol is to be used when your browser contacts the host and requests the document. Usually the protocol is either *http://* or *https://*, indicating HTTP or secure HTTP, respectively. Sometimes you will see a URL that starts with *ftp://*, indicating that the File Transfer Protocol (FTP) must be used to retrieve the document.
- The second part of the URL is a host that is connected to the Internet. In this example, the hostname is *www.dr-chuck.com*.
- The third part of the URL is the document that we are to retrieve from that host. In this example, the document is */page1.htm*.

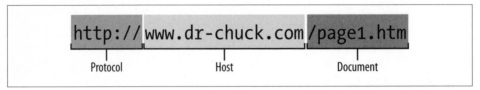

Figure 4-2. The parts of a URL

Using the information in the URL, the browser can retrieve the requested document following the rules of the HTTP protocol. The browser first makes a connection on the default port 80 to the host *www.dr-chuck.com*. Once the connection is established, the browser requests the document by sending the following command:

```
GET http://www.dr-chuck.com/page1.htm HTTP/1.1
```

The GET indicates that this is a simple request to GET a document. This command indicates which type of HTTP request (or HTTP method) we are making. Other HTTP methods include POST, PUT, and DELETE.

The server running at *www.dr-chuck.com* receives this request, finds the document *page1.htm*, and returns the following HTML as the HTTP response:

```
<h1>The First Page</h1>
<p>
If you like, you can switch to the
<a href="http://www.dr-chuck.com/page2.htm">
Second Page</a>.
</p>
```

And then it closes the connection. This completes our first HTTP request/response cycle.

The browser then reads and parses the returned HTML in the HTTP response and renders a page that looks like Figure 4-3.

Figure 4-3. A simple web page

If you were to click on the Second Page link, the browser would see the `href` value of *http://www.dr-chuck.com/page2.htm* and repeat the steps of an HTTP `GET` request by making another connection to *www.dr-chuck.com* on port 80 and sending the following command:

```
GET http://www.dr-chuck.com/page2.htm HTTP/1.1
```

And the server would respond with the following HTML document:

```
<h1>The Second Page</h1>
<p>
If you like, you can switch back to the
<a href="page1.htm">
First Page</a>.
</p>
```

Figure 4-4 shows this interaction showing the `GET` request being sent from the browser to the web server and the web server returning the HTML document as the response.

Note that in the second page, our hypertext reference (`href`) is simply `page1.htm`. If the protocol and host are omitted from the hypertext reference, it assumes the same protocol and host as the current document was retrieved from. This lets pages be moved more easily from host to host. If the `href` includes the full protocol and hostname, it is called an *absolute reference*, and if these are omitted, it is called a *relative reference* because the `href` is assumed to be relative to the current document.

We can happily go back and forth between the first and second pages—with each click, the browser makes a connection to the host on port 80, sends an HTTP `GET` request for the document, and then displays the HTML, which is returned in the HTTP response.

Hacking the HTTP Protocol

The HTTP protocol is simple enough that we can actually emulate the protocol by hand. We can make the same connection as the browser and send the same command to the server and see the server return our HTML document over the connection.

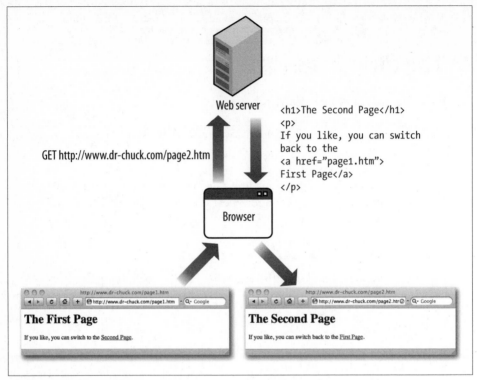

Figure 4-4. The request/response cycle

To make this connection directly, we use the `telnet` command built into most operating systems. Start a Windows command-line interface or Mac OS X Terminal program and run the following `telnet` command to connect to HTTP port 80 on *www.dr-chuck.com*:

```
$ telnet www.dr-chuck.com 80
Trying 74.208.28.177...
Connected to www.dr-chuck.com.
Escape character is '^]'.
GET http://www.dr-chuck.com/page1.htm
<h1>The First Page</h1>
<p>
If you like, you can switch to the
<a href="http://www.dr-chuck.com/page2.htm">
Second Page</a>.
</p>
Connection closed by foreign host.
$
```

Once the connection is established, we type the `GET` command with the requested document and press Enter. The web server will respond with the HTML of the requested document.

The HTTP protocol has many more options and features, but you have now successfully hacked the most basic aspect of the HTTP protocol.

The HTTP Protocol Standards

One of the reasons that the Web is so successful is that all of the details of the network protocols are very carefully documented in open and public specifications. These standards are quite mature and in wide use across many different software and hardware environments. The Internet Engineering Task Force (IETF; *http://www.ietf.org*) is the standards organization responsible for the creation and maintenance of these Internet standards.

The IETF standards are called Requests for Comments or RFCs. The basic idea when developing an RFC is that engineers produce a straw man standard and request that the rest of the IETF review the documents and provide any comments on how the standard should be fixed and/or improved. At some point, when the comments are properly addressed, the specification matures and goes into use.

The HTTP protocol is covered by a number of different RFCs. The main RFC that provides the groundwork for the HTTP protocol is RFC-1945, which was written by Tim Berners-Lee, Roy T. Fielding, and Henrik Frystyk Nielsen in May of 1996. You can view the text of this RFC at *http://tools.ietf.org/rfc/rfc1945.txt*.

Look on page 22 of the specification for a description of the GET request that we just sent to our server to request a document. As you look through the table of contents of RFC-1945, you can begin to see the complexity and richness of the HTTP protocol. If you take a few minutes and read closely, you will also see that the details of HTTP are described very precisely, which makes it easier to write interoperable software from multiple sources.

Watching HTTP in Action

As you move forward, you will need to debug the interactions between your browser and the server, as well as many other interactions. An essential tool to help you understand and debug many aspects of web programming in the browser is the Firebug plug-in for Firefox, written by Joe Hewitt.

Firebug is a great complement to the Web Developer plug-in for Firefox, which you should have already installed (see Chapter 2). To install the Firebug add-on, go to *https://addons.mozilla.org* and search for Firebug. Follow the instructions and install the plug-in. Once the installation is complete, you should have a small bug icon in the lower-right corner of the Firefox window.

To start Firebug, click on the bug icon in the lower-right corner of Firefox. The screen will split in two, with your original web page in the top half and the Firebug console in the lower half. You can adjust the size of each half by dragging the border bar up or down. When you first visit a site, you may need to enable Firebug for the site, as shown in Figure 4-5.

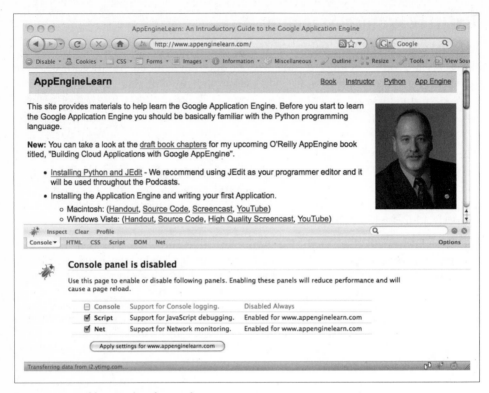

Figure 4-5. Enabling Firebug for a website

Once you have enabled Firebug for the site, switch to the Net tab in the Firebug interface and click the Refresh button to reload your web page.

As the page reloads, you will see a new line in the Firebug window each time the browser makes a new HTTP request, as shown in Figure 4-6. Initially, it requests the document from *http://www.appenginelearn.com* but in that document there are references to Java-Script, CSS, and image files. When the browser sees a reference to one of these embedded files, it issues additional GET requests to retrieve those files. The browser made 11 separate GET requests to assemble the documents needed to render this page. You can see the amount of time it took for each request and the amount of time it took to produce the entire page.

Next, you learn how the browser sends data to the server for processing using the HTTP POST request.

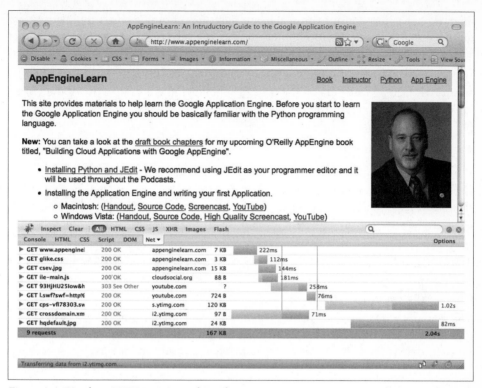

Figure 4-6. Watching HTTP activity with Firebug

HTML: Building a Form

The number-guessing application is back. We will first build the HTML for the form to prompt for user input and then write the App Engine code to handle the input and play the game, as shown in Figure 4-7.

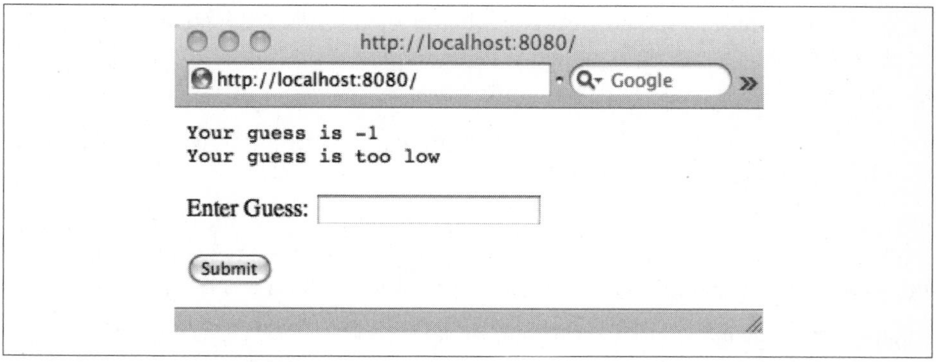

Figure 4-7. A simple HTML form

To review the rules for our game, the computer has chosen a secret number; we are given a number of chances to submit a guess to the server. The server tells us whether our guess is high, low, or correct. Hopefully, over time, we'll arrive at the right number.

In order to make an interactive web page that prompts for input and sends it to the server, we need a `<form>` tag on the page. The following is a sample use of the `<form>` tag to create the input portion of the example page:

```
<form method="post" action="/">
<p>Enter Guess: <input type="text" name="guess"/></p>
<p><input type="submit"/><p>
</form>
```

In the `<form>` tag, we have several attributes. The `method` attribute tells your browser that we will be sending the data to the server using an HTTP `POST` and the `action` attribute tells your browser where to send the form data when the Submit button is clicked.

The form itself is made up of HTML interspersed with `<input>` tags. There are a number of different types of `<input>` tags: `text`, `submit`, `button`, `checkbox`, `file`, `hidden`, `image`, `password`, and `reset`. For now we will focus on `text` and `submit`.

The text input area provides an area on the web page for the user to type in data. We give the text area a `name` so that when there are multiple text areas on a form, we can keep the data from each input area separate when it is sent to the server.

You can have multiple forms on a single page and have hypertext links on the page in addition to form submit buttons. Depending on where the user clicks on the page, the next HTTP request may be a `GET` or `POST` request. If the user clicks on the Submit button within a form, the browser makes a `POST` request and sends the form data along with the `POST` request.

Sending Form Data to the Server Using POST

If you recall, when we talked about the HTTP `GET` request, we said that the web browser makes a connection to the host on port 80 and then sends a single line with the `GET` request, including the document that is being requested:

```
GET http://www.dr-chuck.com/page2.htm HTTP/1.1
```

When we make a `POST` request, we send additional data to the server along the same connection, as shown in Figure 4-8.

The first line is the `POST` request that includes the URL to which the post is being sent. Then a number of informative messages to the server about the type of browser that is being used, how the `POST` data is encoded, how much `POST` data is present, and so on.

Then, after all the informative messages, we see the actual `POST` data. It is a very simple *keyword=value* format, in which the field name (as specified in the HTML) is the

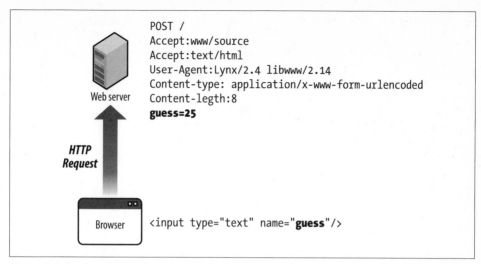

```
                        POST /
                        Accept:www/source
                        Accept:text/html
                        User-Agent:Lynx/2.4 libwww/2.14
                        Content-type: application/x-www-form-urlencoded
        Web server      Content-legth:8
                        guess=25
```

Figure 4-8. Sending data to the server using POST

keyword and the text which was typed into the form is the value. So in this example, the POST data is:

```
guess=25
```

The POST data goes into the server, just like an HTTP GET response, and the server does some processing and then returns some HTML to the browser as an HTTP response that the browser displays as the new page. So both a POST and GET HTTP request give us a new page for display in the browser.[*]

Handling Form Data in the App Engine Server

So far pretty much everything we have done up to this point in the book has been what we call *flat HTML*. We place an HTML document in a file and we can look at that file from our laptop or put the file up on a web server and view the HTML from the Web. When you are working with flat HTML, a server is optional.

To handle a POST request and generate dynamic HTML based on the POST data, we must run software on a server. So to complete our guessing game, we will need to write an App Engine program in Python.

Our browser will (1) make the POST request to our web server, and the web server will (2) run our Python program, which will produce (3) the HTTP response with the new HTML for display on the browser, as shown in Figure 4-9.

---

[*] Later, you will learn about Asynchronous JavaScript and XML (AJAX) and its ability to update parts of pages, but for now, we will keep it simple and replace the entire page.

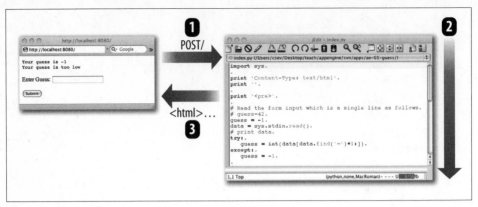

Figure 4-9. Responding to a POST request

So now we need to make a simple App Engine program. For instructions on how to set up and start App Engine on your system, see the appendixes.

This application will consist of two files. The first file is *app.yaml*, which names the application and decides how to route the incoming URLs, as follows:

```
application: ae-01-guess
version: 1
runtime: python
api_version: 1

handlers:
- url: /.*
  script: index.py
```

In the handlers section, we keep things really simple and route all the incoming document URLs (/.*) to a program file called *index.py*. The *app.yaml* file is in a format called Yet Another Markup Language (YAML). YAML uses a simple syntax to represent keywords and values and structured data using colons (:) and indenting.

We do the main work in the *index.py* file. Through the magic of the App Engine framework, the code in *index.py* is started when a request comes into the server and runs from top to bottom for each request. The POST data is available to us as standard input, which we access using a built-in feature of Python called *sys.stdin*.

The basic outline of the program is to check any POST data and parse the POST data to find the numeric value of the guess. Then we check to see whether the guess is correct, high, or low, and print out an appropriate message, and then print out the HTML for the <form>, so the user can submit a new guess if they like:

```
import sys

print 'Content-Type: text/html'
print ''
```

```
print '<pre>'

# Read the form input which is a single line
# guess=25
guess = -1
data = sys.stdin.read()
# print data
try:
    guess = int(data[data.find('=')+1:])
except:
    guess = -1
print 'Your guess is', guess
answer = 42
if guess < answer :
    print 'Your guess is too low'
if guess == answer:
    print 'Congratulations!'
if guess > answer :
    print 'Your guess is too high'
print '</pre>'

print '''<form method="post" action="/">
Enter Guess: <input type="text" name="guess"><br>
<input type="submit">
</form>'''
```

Stepping through the code, here's a description of what is happening at each step:

- In the first line, we do an import sys to make the "sys" library available to us so that we can read the standard input. The "sys" library is a collection of functions that come with Python.

- We print out a header line indicating the content type and a blank line to signal the start of the actual HTML. You will notice when you view source later that you do not see any the header line(s). This is because the header lines are part of the HTTP response but not part of the HTML document.

- Then we use sys.stdin.read() to pull in the raw POST data from the incoming request. If this is a GET request, we will not get any data on stdin.

- Then we use Python string functions to split the guess=25 string into parts and pull out the number after the equals sign and convert it from a string to an integer (see Chapter 3 for details on the string parsing in this line of code). Because we may have no data or improperly formatted data, we put the string parsing and conversion in a try/except block. If anything goes wrong, we set the guess variable to –1.

- Next we use a series of if statements to check whether the incoming guess is correct, high, or low, and then print out an appropriate message.

- At the end of the program, we print out the text of the HTML form using Python multiline string syntax. In Python, if you start a string with triple quotes (''' '''), the string continues until it finds a matching set of triple quotes—even if the string continues for multiple lines.

This program runs for every request regardless of whether it is a GET request or a POST request.

To run this application, create a folder named *ae-01-guess* and put the *app.yaml* and *index.py* files into the folder as shown previously. Assuming that you have installed App Engine following the instructions in the appropriate appendix, you should be able to start App Engine in the command or terminal window by typing the following command in the folder above the *ae-01-guess* folder:

```
apps csev$ dev_appserver.py ae-01-guess/
INFO 2008-12-27 14:30:27,023 appcfg.py] Server: appengine.google.com
INFO 2008-12-27 14:30:27,386 dev_appserver_main.py] Running application ae-01-guess
on port 8080: http://localhost:8080
```

Once the application is running, we can navigate to *http://localhost:8080/* by typing the URL into our browser. When we enter the URL, the browser makes an HTTP GET request to retrieve the document. As there is no POST data, the code in the `try` block will fail and `guess` will be `-1`, so the first screen will look as shown in Figure 4-10.

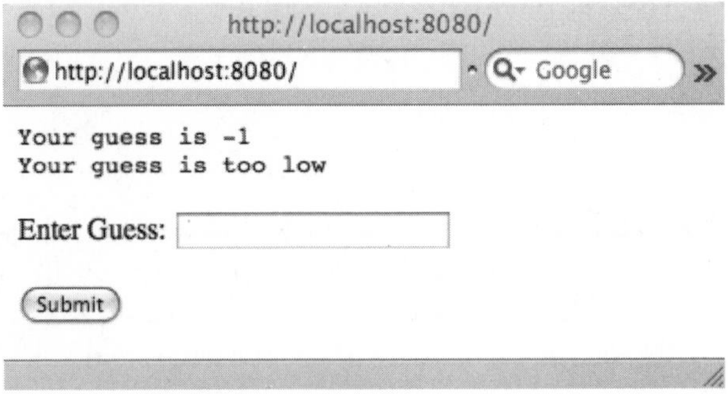

Figure 4-10. The first screen of the guessing game

If you view the source of this page, you will see the following HTML, which was generated by our Python program:

```
<pre>
Your guess is -1
Your guess is too low
</pre>
<form method="post" action="/">
<p>Enter Guess: <input type="text" name="guess"/></p>
<p><input type="submit"></p>
</form>
```

This HTML is simply the accumulated output of all the `print` statements in our *index.py* program. As the *index.py* program runs, its standard output forms the HTML response that is sent to the browser.

If we enter a guess such as 100 and click Submit, our browser sends an HTTP POST to our application. This time the standard input contains the string `guess=100`, so the code in the try block succeeds in parsing the input guess and we GET the output shown in Figure 4-11.

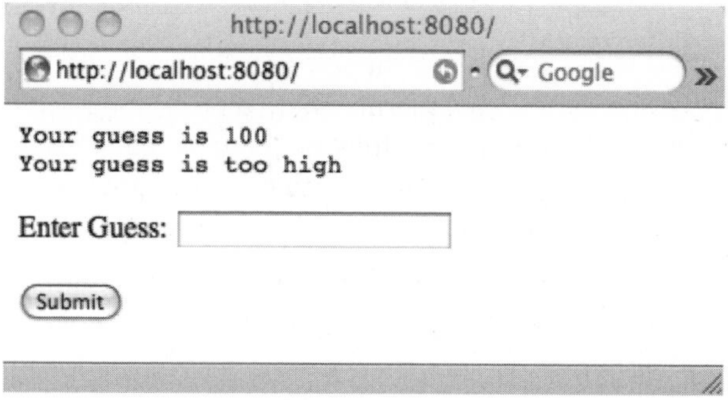

Figure 4-11. After an incorrect guess

As we continue to make guesses, the browser sends POST requests to our server program and we GET responses—until hopefully we arrive at the correct answer.

Make sure to test your application to confirm that it properly handles numbers that are too high, too low, and just right. Also test to see whether the program does something meaningful when you leave the text input blank and click Submit or enter nonnumeric data in the field and click Submit. It is always a good idea to think through how to test your applications quickly and thoroughly. One general approach is to come up with a series of inputs that make sure that your test sequence touches every line of your program at least once.

Sending Form Data to the Server Using GET

We usually send form data to the server using a POST, but it is also possible to send form data to the server using GET. Just change the method to GET as shown:

```
<form method="get" action="/check">
<p>Enter Guess: <input type="text" name="guess"/></p>
<p><input type="submit"/><p>
</form>
```

When you send form data using GET, the parameters are appended to the document that is being requested, as follows:

```
GET /check?guess=25
```

If you use the GET method to pass in form data, instead of the data appearing on sys.stdin(), it appears as part of an environment variable named QUERY_STRING. We would have to change the previous example program to detect when we were processing a GET request and parse the incoming guess value from the query string instead of from standard input.

When we use the App Engine webapp framework, it automatically knows how parameters are passed differently using GET and POST and handles both cases on our behalf.

App Engine Log

Web applications get their input from browsers and send their output back to browsers, so it is sometimes a little hard to figure out what is happening inside of the program. This is especially true when someone else is using your application and complaining that it is breaking.

This type of situation is where the application log is really helpful. The log is a place that you can monitor your application's behavior, even when other users are using the application in their browsers.

Depending on how you are running your App Engine, the log is either in a command window/terminal or available from the Google Launcher. In either case, the log is a series of messages that are updated in real time as HTTP requests are received and the program produces the results. Here is a sample log for the application we just ran:

```
apps csev$ dev_appserver.py ae-01-guess/
INFO 2008-12-27 14:30:27,023 appcfg.py] Server: appengine.google.com
INFO 2008-12-27 14:30:27,386 dev_appserver_main.py] Running application ae-01-guess
on port 8080: http://localhost:8080
INFO 2008-12-27 14:30:37,454 dev_appserver.py] "GET/HTTP/1.1" 200 -
INFO 2008-12-27 14:30:44,464 dev_appserver.py] "POST/HTTP/1.1" 200 -
INFO 2008-12-27 14:31:10,850 dev_appserver.py] "POST/HTTP/1.1" 200 -
INFO 2008-12-27 14:31:13,820 dev_appserver.py] "POST/HTTP/1.1" 200 -
```

You can see as the App Engine server starts up and is ready to receive requests on port 8080 (instead of the default HTTP port of 80). You can see a single GET request for the "/" document when we initially load the page and then three POST requests as we are making guesses to try to find the secret number.

The "200" is an HTTP status code that is being returned to the browser and that indicates the success or failure of each request. Some common HTTP status codes are: 200 = Success, 301 = Document has been moved (redirect), 404 = File not found, and 503 = Server Unavailable/Overloaded.

Our first application keeps things really simple—for example, we did not differentiate between which code we ran for a GET request and which code we ran for a POST request. We skimmed by this little problem by using a **try**/**except** block and knew that a GET request would have no data and the **except** block would cope with that situation.

But our user interface might have looked a little better if we had checked to see whether this was a GET request and not do the guess parsing or guess checking at all. We would only look at and parse the POST data if we actually get a POST request.

It turns out that we have access to the HTTP method and many other details regarding our incoming HTTP request through CGI environment variables (explained in the following section).

Looking at All the Data Available on an HTTP Request

There is a lot of data available to our program in addition to the POST data. The App Engine environment makes this data available to our application for each incoming request so that we can do things differently based on this information.

The environment variables fall into three categories:

- Variables describing the server environment (SERVER_SOFTWARE or SERVER_NAME)
- Variables describing the request data (REQUEST_METHOD, HTTP_USER_AGENT, or CONTENT_TYPE)
- Variables describing the browser environment variables (HTTP_USER_AGENT, HTTP_ACCEPT, and so on)

You can find documentation about these parameters at *http://hoohoo.ncsa.uiuc.edu/cgi/in.html*. This is a very old website that describes the Common Gateway Interface (CGI), which was the way that the very first web servers passed input data from an HTTP request into application code running on the server.

We will write an application that reads and dumps out all the information available to our application. We call this the "dumper" program because it just looks at its input and dumps it out.

The dumper program consists of a very simple *app.yaml* file and a single *index.py* Python file that contains the complete code of our App Engine program.

The *app.yaml* file names our application and routes all incoming requests to the *index.py* script as before:

```
application: ae-02-dumper
version: 1
runtime: python
api_version: 1

handlers:
- url: /.*
  script: index.py
```

The logic for our dumper program is completely contained in the *index.py* file:

```
import os
import sys

print 'Content-Type: text/html'
print ''
print '<form method="post" action="/" >'
```

```
print 'Zap Data: <input type="text" name="zap"><br/>'
print 'Zot Data: <input type="text" name="zot"><br/>'
print '<input type="submit">'
print '</form>'

print '<pre>'
print 'Environment keys:'
print ''
for param in os.environ.keys():
    print param, ':', os.environ[param]
print ''

print 'Data'
count = 0
for line in sys.stdin:
  count = count + 1
  print line
  if count > 100:
    break

print '</pre>'
```

Let's walk through each of the parts of the dumper program's *index.py*.

The first print sends the HTTP response headers, followed by a blank line to indicate the start of the HTML document:

```
print 'Content-Type: text/html'
print ''
```

When you select View Source on an HTML page, you are not shown the response headers because they are not part of the HTML document. However, with the Firebug plug-in, you can see the HTTP response headers under the Net tab, as shown in Figure 4-12.

The next set of print statements produces the HTML for a form that we use to send some more complex POST data to our program. This form now has two input text areas named zap and zot, so we can see what happens with multiple input areas:

```
print '<form method="post" action="/" >'
print 'Zap Data: <input type="text" name="zap"><br/>'
print 'Zot Data: <input type="text" name="zot"><br/>'
print '<input type="submit">'
print '</form>'
```

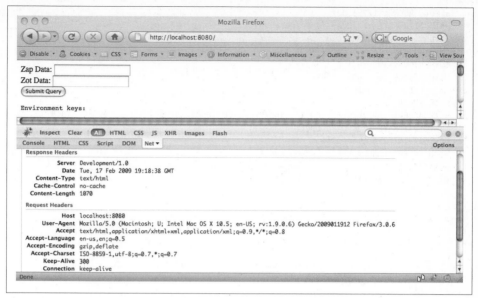

Figure 4-12. HTTP headers on a response

The form is quite basic, with two text fields and a Submit button. The next lines of the program read in a set of variables passed to our program as a Python dictionary. These are the *environment* or CGI variables. They are a combination of the server configuration as well as information about the particular request itself.

We iterate through the keys in the dictionary and then print the keys and values, separated by a colon character, using a Python for loop:

```
print '<pre>'
print 'Environment keys:'
print ''
for param in os.environ.keys():
    print param, ':', os.environ[param]
print ''
```

The output from this section is as follows:

```
HTTP_REFERER : http://www.appenginelearn.com/
SERVER_SOFTWARE : Development/1.0
SCRIPT_NAME :
REQUEST_METHOD : GET
HTTP_KEEP_ALIVE : 300
SERVER_PROTOCOL : HTTP/1.0
QUERY_STRING :
CONTENT_LENGTH :
HTTP_ACCEPT_CHARSET : ISO-8859-1,utf-8;q=0.7,*;q=0.7
HTTP_USER_AGENT : Mozilla/5.0 (Macintosh; U; Intel Mac OS X 10.5; en-US; rv:1.9.0.5)
Gecko/2008120121 Firefox/3.0.5
HTTP_CONNECTION : keep-alive
SERVER_NAME : localhost
```

```
REMOTE_ADDR : 127.0.0.1
PATH_TRANSLATED : /Users/csev/Desktop/teach/appengine/apps/ae-02-dumper/index.py
SERVER_PORT : 8080
AUTH_DOMAIN : gmail.com
CURRENT_VERSION_ID : 1.1
HTTP_HOST : localhost:8080
TZ : UTC
USER_EMAIL :
HTTP_ACCEPT : text/html,application/xhtml+xml,application/xml;q=0.9,*/*;q=0.8
APPLICATION_ID : ae-02-dumper
GATEWAY_INTERFACE : CGI/1.1
HTTP_ACCEPT_LANGUAGE : en-us,en;q=0.5
CONTENT_TYPE : application/x-www-form-urlencoded
HTTP_ACCEPT_ENCODING : gzip,deflate
PATH_INFO : /
```

Data

Because this is an HTTP GET request, there is no data to print.

You can consult the CGI documentation for the details on each of the previously mentioned variables: *http://hoohoo.ncsa.uiuc.edu/cgi/in.html*.

When we are programming at the CGI level, we are using the old mystical ways of the early web server programs. We won't use this pattern for much longer, but it is good to start by understanding the low-level details and then delegate the handling of those details to a web framework.

The last part of the *index.py* program dumps out up to the first 100 lines of POST data, if the data exists:

```
print 'Data'
count = 0
for line in sys.stdin:
  count = count + 1
  print line
  if count > 100:
    break
```

According to CGI rules, the POST data is presented to the application via its standard input. In Python, we can read through the predefined file handle *sys.stdin* to access our POST data using a Python for loop.

If you look at the bottom of the initial output of the program, you will see that there is no POST data because when you navigate to *http://localhost:8080*, the browser issues an HTTP GET request for the initial document (/).

To test POST data dumping code, we must enter some data into the Zap and Zot input fields and click the Submit button, as shown in Figure 4-13.

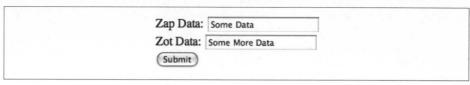

Figure 4-13. Entering form data

When we click Submit, our browser sends a `POST` request, which we can immediately see in the `REQUEST_METHOD` variable change from `GET` to `POST`:

```
Environment keys:

HTTP_REFERER : http://www.appenginelearn.com/
SERVER_SOFTWARE : Development/1.0
SCRIPT_NAME :
REQUEST_METHOD : POST
HTTP_KEEP_ALIVE : 300
SERVER_PROTOCOL : HTTP/1.0
QUERY_STRING :
   ...
```

And if we scroll down to the bottom of the output, we can see the actual `POST` data:

```
GATEWAY_INTERFACE : CGI/1.1
HTTP_ACCEPT_LANGUAGE : en-us,en;q=0.5
CONTENT_TYPE : application/x-www-form-urlencoded
HTTP_ACCEPT_ENCODING : gzip,deflate
PATH_INFO : /

Data
zap=Some+Data&zot=Some+More+Data
```

To make parsing easier, the `POST` data is encoded by escaping spaces and special characters. Each parameter starts with an ampersand (&) to distinguish its new parameters from the data of the previous parameter. To make sense of this input, we would have to parse the input data using string parsing and then unescape the data to get back to the actual data that was typed into the form.

There are two ways to encode `POST` data. The easy way to encode the `POST` data is called "application/x-www-form-urlencoded"; this approach concatenates all the data into a single line of input as shown earlier. The more complex way to encode `POST` data is called multipart/form-data and is described in the next section.

Advanced: Multipart POST Data with File Upload

Let's dig a little deeper into the complexity of the HTTP protocol before we sit back and delegate all the hard work to the App Engine framework in the next chapters.

This is our last "low-level" example—and after you play a bit with this code, you will probably be quite content to learn and use the framework that nicely hides all the detail of the protocol from us.

Take the sample code (*ae-02-dumper*) and make the following changes to the form code:

```
print '<form method="post" action="/" enctype="multipart/form-data">'
print 'Zap Data: <input type="text" name="zap"><br/>'
print 'Zot Data: <input type="text" name="zot"><br/>'
print 'File Data: <input type="file" name="filedat"><br/>'
print '<input type="submit">'
```

We have switched to a multipart encoding of the data and added an input field of type `filedat` so that we can attach a file to this request. If you are uploading file data from a form, you are required to encode the form data as multipart. You can look at the documentation for multipart encoding in RFC-2046, section 5.1.3: *http://tools.ietf.org/html/rfc2046#section-5.1.3*. (It was written by Ned Freed and Nathaniel S. Borenstein in 1996.)

If you skim this document, you'll notice that it appears complex, but if you read it closely, you'll see that the rules for looking at multipart data are very clear and precise. It is quite possible to write programs to handle the incoming data reliably. The key is that this code should be written only once and made available to programmers like us to use so that we can ignore all the details.

To see our program produce the multipart data, run the program again, type in some data, select a file, and then click Submit (Figure 4-14).

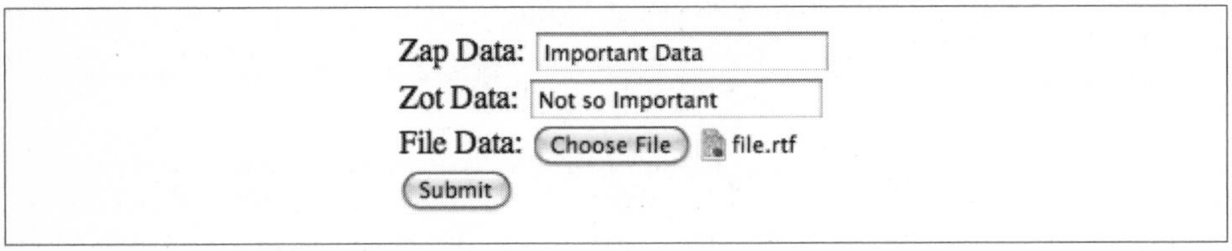

Figure 4-14. Uploading a file using a form

When you click Submit, the program will produce the following output (abbreviated here):

```
GATEWAY_INTERFACE : CGI/1.1
HTTP_ACCEPT_LANGUAGE : en-us,en;q=0.5
CONTENT_TYPE : multipart/form-data; boundary=--------------------------
5152045303884710066681910962
HTTP_ACCEPT_ENCODING : gzip,deflate
PATH_INFO : /

Data
--------------------------5152045303884710066681910962

Content-Disposition: form-data; name="zap"

Important Data

--------------------------5152045303884710066681910962
```

```
Content-Disposition: form-data; name="zot"

Not so Important

---------------------------515204530388471006681910962

Content-Disposition: form-data; name="filedat"; filename="file.rtf"

Content-Type: application/rtf

{\rtf1\ansi\ansicpg1252\cocoartf949\cocoasubrtf350

{\fonttbl\f0\fswiss\fcharset0 Helvetica;}

{\colortbl;\red255\green255\blue255;}

\margl1440\margr1440\vieww9000\viewh8400\viewkind0

\pard\tx720\tx1440\tx2160\tx2880\tx3600\tx4320\tx5040\tx5760\tx6480\tx7200\tx7920\t
x8640\ql\qnatural\pardirnatural

\f0\fs24 \cf0 Here is an rtf file. Yay!}

---------------------------515204530388471006681910962--
```

You can see that the input data that is sent to our application now consists of a number of lines. Each of the fields in the form has a separate section in the input stream coming from the browser. The browser chooses a section boundary string and tells us the boundary string as one of the environment variables.

When the file data is listed—the browser simply sends in all the data in the file—the file that was chosen was in Rich Text Format (RTF), and it was very small. The uploaded file could be anything such as an image—and it could be very large—the browser simply sends all the data in the file through the connection, and then, when all the file data has been sent, the browser sends the boundary string.

This why when you send a file with a form, it can take quite a while if your upstream network connection is slow. It's because the browser is patiently sending all the file data up to the server on the HTTP connection. The browser often gives a progress bar as the file is uploaded to give you some sense of how much data has been sent so far.

We won't bother writing Python code to parse this multipart data format—it has already been done for us in the App Engine framework. Just remember that you *could* write that code if you wanted to, by spending some quality time with RFC-2046. But for now, we will focus on writing our application instead of writing a bunch of HTTP parsing code.

Summary

In this chapter, we took a look at how the HyperText Transport Protocol (HTTP) operates in some detail. We have examined how the browser makes requests to the server and how the server processes those requests and returns an HTTP response.

We looked at how form data is passed into the server, as well as a whole series of server environment variables that are made available to our application by App Engine.

App Engine gives us a very primitive Common Gateway Interface (GCI)—compliant interface with environment variables, standard input, and standard output, which we can make use of if we choose to write our applications at a low level. We can examine all the data that App Engine makes available to our scripts.

Ultimately, programming at this low level is only of passing interest because we will delegate much of the detail of handling the request and response to the built-in web application framework in Google App Engine. However, as we switch to depending more on the framework in upcoming applications, it is good to have a general sense of what is really going on at a low level.

When we use the framework for the first time, our code may initially seem a little more complex, but the framework takes care of a myriad of small details of parameter passing, parsing, headers, and conversion. Given that details can get pretty intricate in HTTP pretty quickly, learning and programming in the App Engine framework is a small price to pay for the benefits that we gain in our productivity and the reliability of our applications. It is always good to use existing code instead of building and debugging your own code from scratch—particularly if that code is supported and also used by Google.

Exercises

1. What are the three parts of a Uniform Resource Locator?
2. What is the HyperText Transport Protocol command to retrieve a document?
3. How are special characters encoded in the Request-URI? Hint: Look on page 24 of the 1996 version of RFC-791 (source: *http://tools.ietf.org/html/rfc791*).
4. What command would you use to "hack" HTTP and connect directly to a web server to retrieve a document "by hand"?
5. Use the Firebug extension in Firefox to watch the network activity for a Google.com page and then time your favorite band's MySpace page (or any band's). How many documents and how many milliseconds (1/1000 of a second) are required for each page?
6. What is the purpose of the `action` attribute on a form tag in HTML?
7. Give an example of a checkbox input tag in HTML (this will require a bit of research online).

8. What Python object is used to pass in all of the data from a form to an App Engine application (string, dictionary, list, integer)? Why is this a good data structure to represent incoming form data?

9. What is the purpose of the `import sys` statement in an App Engine application?

10. In the URL *http://localhost:8080/*, what does the 8080 mean? Why is it there?

11. Why is a `try/except` needed in the simple application used in this chapter? What would happen if you did not use `try/except` ? Try it and see what happens.

12. When do you use HTTP `GET` and when do you use HTTP `POST`?

13. True or false: You must use HTTP `POST` to send form data to an application.

14. Why are logs important to a developer when a web application is in production?

15. When would you use multipart form data on a `POST` request?

## CHAPTER 5

The App Engine webapp Framework

Now that we have written a few low-level App Engine applications, it is time to begin to develop our application using the high-level Web Application (webapp) framework that is provided as part of Google App Engine.

This chapter reimplements the number guessing-application using the App Engine webapp framework instead of using low-level HTTP directly. The low-level capabilities that we used in the previous chapter are not gone—they are just hidden beneath a layer that has been added for our convenience.

The webapp library takes care of many of the mundane details of the HTTP interactions. The webapp framework handles all details, like parameter parsing, multipart parameter formats, and so on.

Although using the webapp framework may initially look a little more complex than the lower-level code, in the long run, your web applications will be far smaller and you won't end up reading RFC documents to make sure that your program is compliant with the subtle details of the HTTP protocol. Your programs won't break because you did not notice some small detail in the protocol until a user started using a different browser than the ones that you used for testing.

A Trivial App Engine Application

Recall the very first example of the web application; it consisted of two files. The first file is *app.yaml*:

```
application: ae-00-trivial
version: 1
runtime: python
api_version: 1

handlers:
- url: /.*
  script: index.py
```

The second file is *index.py* and consists of three lines of Python:

```
print 'Content-Type: text/plain'
print ''
print 'Hello there Chuck'
```

It is pretty hard to get much simpler than that. To accomplish the same task using the web application framework, it takes a few more lines of code to get things connected. Most of this code is "plumbing" to get things properly set up and connected. The plumbing may initially seem to be a bother, but we will explain it all and as your programs get richer and more complex, there will be less plumbing and more of your cool programs.

An Equivalent Trivial webapp Application

To write the same program using the webapp framework, we start with a very similar *app.yaml* file, as follows:

```
application: ae-03-trivial
version: 1
runtime: python
api_version: 1

handlers:
- url: /.*
  script: index.py
```

The same application using the webapp framework is shown in the *index.py* file:

```
import wsgiref.handlers
from google.appengine.ext import webapp

class MainHandler(webapp.RequestHandler):

  def get(self):
    self.response.out.write('Hello there Chuck\n')

def main():
  application = webapp.WSGIApplication([
      ('/.*', MainHandler)],
      debug=True)
  wsgiref.handlers.CGIHandler().run(application)

if __name__ == '__main__':
  main()
```

This initially looks like a lot of plumbing surrounding a single line of code. Let's look through the program in sections. The top two lines:

```
import wsgiref.handlers
from google.appengine.ext import webapp
```

indicate that we will be using some existing code from Google's libraries. The import statements ensure that the *webapp* and *wgisref* libraries are available to our application.

The next section of code defines a Python class called `MainHandler`:

```
class MainHandler(webapp.RequestHandler):
  def get(self):
    self.response.out.write('Hello there Chuck\n')
```

Our `MainHandler` class will "handle" the incoming requests. In our definition of `MainHandler`, we are extending the `webapp.RequestHandler` class so that we inherit all its capabilities.

If the incoming request is an HTTP `GET` request that is sent to `MainHandler`, the `get()` method within `MainHandler` will automatically be called. We define the `get()` method within the `MainHandler` class to write a single line of output to the HTTP response object and return.

The call to `self.response.out.write()` is a little more clumsy than using the `print` statement from prior examples, but it does allow the webapp framework to help you do things like automatically generate HTTP response headers such as Content-Type and make sure that all the headers are sent out before the HTML document.

The next section of the code is a function called `main()`, which sets up the plumbing so that incoming requests are routed to our `MainHandler` for handling:

```
def main():
  application = webapp.WSGIApplication([
    ('/.*', MainHandler)],
    debug=True)
  wsgiref.handlers.CGIHandler().run(application)
```

This bit of code is best translated as "Create a new web application, and route all the URLs that come to this application (`/.*`) to the `MainHandler` class; once the application has been created and configured with its routing, run the application."

The *app.yaml* file described earlier routes various incoming URLs *between* various Python programs (*index.py* and so on) and the routing within *index.py* determines further routing *within* the application. This "plumbing," which routes URL patterns to various handlers that make up our application, will make more sense as our applications get more complex and handle more than one URL pattern. We just mention it here as necessary magic framework plumbing without the need for you to fully understand it yet.

The only remaining code in our application calls the `main()` function when the program first starts up:

```
if __name__ == '__main__':
  main()
```

Remember that the code within `main()` is not executed when Python reads the function definition (*def*)—the `main()` function is executed when it is called in the previous lines.

The Handler Callback Pattern

The handler callback pattern is very common in object-oriented programming and was used in the previous example. The basic idea is that we hand over the main responsibility for handling something to a framework (i.e., a large amount of code that we did not write). We let the framework call one of our handler objects back at some important moment when it wants us to participate in the handling of the request.

This pattern is used in many situations, ranging from graphical user interfaces to message and event handling. We initially communicate to the framework those "happenings" or events that we are interested in and point the framework at a bit of our code to "handle" those events. That is why we use the convention of naming these bits of code with "Handler" in their names. These objects are designed to "handle" an incoming HTTP request, as shown in Figure 5-1.

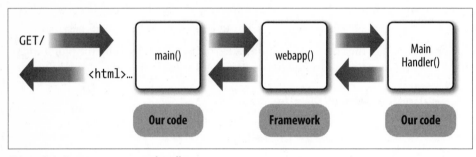

Figure 5-1. Routing requests to handlers

The incoming HTTP GET request arrives to our main() function. Instead of handling the request directly, we set up the *webapp* framework and tell it under what conditions (URLs that match /.*) and where (MainHandler) to call us back when it needs some "assistance" from us.

Then the framework starts up and looks at the HTTP GET request, figures out which kind of request it is, parses all of the data, and converts file input if necessary. Then it calls out MainHandler, using either the get() or post() method as appropriate.

Looking at the Handler Code

The MainHandler we defined earlier was capable of handling only incoming GET requests. We can easily add another method to the MainHandler class to indicate how we want to handle incoming POST requests as follows:

```
class MainHandler(webapp.RequestHandler):

  def get(self):
    self.response.out.write('Hello there Chuck\n')
```

```
def post(self):
    self.response.out.write('Hello POST Chuck\n')
```

In order to handle both incoming requests, we create two methods that we provide to the framework in our `MainHandler` class: a `get()` method and a `post()` method. The framework will look at the incoming request and call the proper method for us. If the request is a `GET` request, the framework will call the `get()` method, and if the request is a `POST` request, the framework will call our `post()` method, as shown in Figure 5-2.

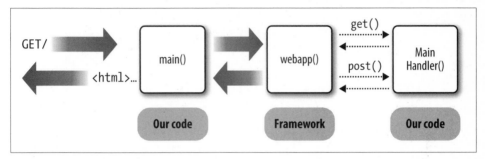

Figure 5-2. Handling both GET and POST requests

So far, this is a pretty trivial application—even with its support for `POST`.

What Is "self" and Why Is It There?

You may be wondering why the parameter `self` is added to the methods of our `MainHandler` class and why, inside of the `MainHandler` class, we use `self` to prefix things like `self.request` and `self.response`.

The use of `self` is part of Python's object-oriented approach. When we define the `MainHandler` class, we are defining a pattern (i.e., like a cookie cutter) to make lots of instances of `MainHandler` objects (i.e., cookies). To process your incoming HTTP requests, the framework calls the `MainHandler` objects to do the work.

In Figure 5-2, it is implied that `main()` calls the framework on every incoming request and then the framework calls `MainHandler` immediately and directly. And this is likely to be the way most requests are handled when your application is handling low traffic levels.

However, we can think of the framework a little more abstractly and imagine how the framework might behave differently if we were handling millions of requests per second. The previous figure can be redrawn to emphasize that the code in `main()` is telling the framework (registering) our intention with respect to routing of URLs to particular handlers. And then the framework receives the requests and passes them to the appropriate handler, as shown in Figure 5-3.

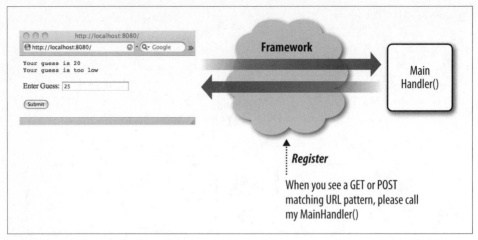

Figure 5-3. Working with a framework

Once the routing has been established with the framework, there is no further need to involve the `main()` code until the program is revised because the framework knows where to route incoming requests.

Now assume that your application experiences a high level of traffic, to the point that one `MainHandler` simply cannot handle the load. The framework can detect the situation, and because the `MainHandler` class is a template, the framework can construct as many `MainHandler`s as it likes. Each of these `MainHandler` instances is distinct and unique, and they operate independently of each other. During periods of heavy traffic, the framework can create many copies of `MainHandler` and route requests to the least-busy `MainHandler` as the load changes, as shown in Figure 5-4.

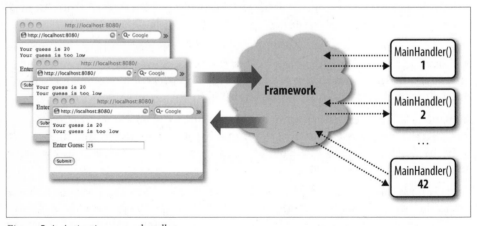

Figure 5-4. Activating many handlers

If the framework made many instances of the `MainHandler` class, each class might be doing something quite different at any moment. Each instance (1,2, ... 42) of the class could be handling a different HTTP request and producing a different HTTP response. A different user may be logged in and she may be trying to guess a different number.

We need a way for each instance of the `MainHandler` class to be able to have its own place to store data. This is the purpose of the `self` variable in Python. The `self` variable means "this instance" or "this copy." Using `self` allows `MainHandler` number 42 to be working on something different than `MainHandler` number 1. So when we write our output to `self.response.out.write()`, the `self` bit makes sure that we are working on the correct response.

When we write our program, we have no idea whether the framework will create one instance of our `MainHandler` class or if it will create many instances. We do not know whether those instances will run on one server in one data center or be spread around the world, handling requests locally.

This detail does not matter at all to us. We write our code using the object-oriented approach and give the framework the flexibility to reconfigure our application as it sees fit and as conditions change. This is called *abstraction* because there are a lot of details about how this works that we will never know—and frankly we don't really care. As long as the Google framework and Google engineers make sure that our application runs properly and quickly, it is just not our concern. It is one of the nice aspects of living snug and warm in the Google infrastructure cloud.

Number Guessing Using the webapp Framework

We can once again revisit our number-guessing game and implement the game as a webapp. Following is the source code for the completed program *index.py*:

```
import wsgiref.handlers
from google.appengine.ext import webapp

class MainHandler(webapp.RequestHandler):

  formstring = '''<form method="post" action="/">
<p>Enter Guess: <input type="text" name="guess"/></p>
<p><input type="submit"></p>
</form>'''

  def get(self):
    self.response.out.write('<p>Good luck!</p>\n')
    self.response.out.write(self.formstring)

  def post(self):
    stguess = self.request.get('guess')
    try:
      guess = int(stguess)
    except:
      guess = -1

    answer = 42
```

```
      if guess == answer:
        msg = 'Congratulations'
      elif guess < 0 :
        msg = 'Please provide a number guess'
      elif guess < answer:
        msg = 'Your guess is too low'
      else:
        msg = 'Your guess is too high'

      self.response.out.write('<p>Guess:'+stguess+'</p>\n')
      self.response.out.write('<p>'+msg+'</p>\n')
      self.response.out.write(self.formstring)

def main():
  application = webapp.WSGIApplication([
    ('/.*', MainHandler)],
    debug=True)
  wsgiref.handlers.CGIHandler().run(application)

if __name__ == '__main__':
  main()
```

If you compare this program to the previous program, you'll see that the "plumbing" code is identical. We set up the framework and route all incoming URLs to MainHandler. All our changes that make this application different from the previous application are contained in the MainHandler class:

```
class MainHandler(webapp.RequestHandler):

  formstring = '''<form method="post" action="/">
<p>Enter Guess: <input type="text" name="guess"/></p>
<p><input type="submit"></p>
</form>'''

  def get(self):
    self.response.out.write('<p>Good luck!</p>\n')
    self.response.out.write(self.formstring)
```

We define a multiline string variable called formstring that holds the HTML for the form for our guessing game. When we receive a GET request, we send back a "Good Luck" message and then print the formstring, resulting in Figure 5-5.

If you were to view the source of the page, you'd see this:

```
<p>Good luck!</p>
<form method="post" action="/">
<p>Enter Guess: <input type="text" name="guess"/></p>
<p><input type="submit"></p>
</form>
```

The HTML response is produced by repeated calls to self.response.out.write(). We pass a string into each of the calls. Note that within a string the \n is a special character that ends a line and starts a new line. If we want our HTML source to end up on separate lines, we must include this character where appropriate, as in:

```
self.response.out.write('<p>Good luck!</p>\n')
```

Because whitespace and newline characters are generally ignored in HTML, we could omit the newline character (\n), but it does help in debugging to be able to look at the returned HTML and have it be readable.

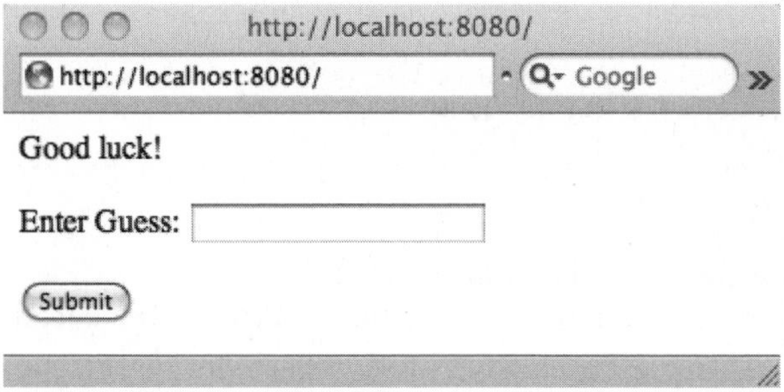

Figure 5-5. A number-guessing application

If we enter a guess, as shown in Figure 5-6, and click Submit, the browser will send our application an HTTP POST request with the form data as input.

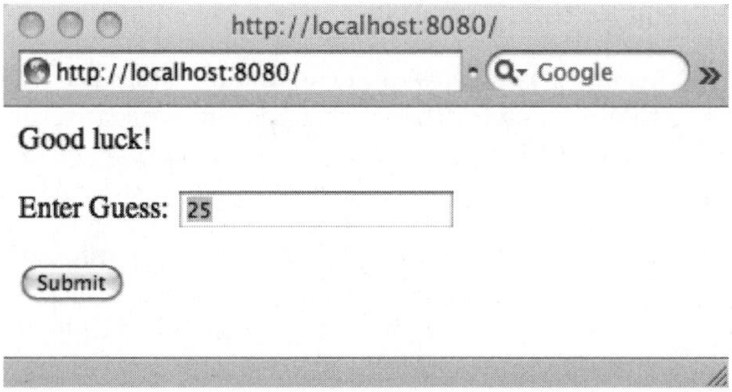

Figure 5-6. Entering a guess

The webapp framework will automatically notice the POST request and route it to the post() method in the MainHandler class:

```
def post(self):
    stguess = self.request.get('guess')
    try:
        guess = int(stguess)
    except:
        guess = -1

    answer = 42
    if guess == answer:
```

```
    msg = 'Congratulations'
elif guess < 0 :
    msg = 'Please provide a number guess'
elif guess < answer:
    msg = 'Your guess is too low'
else:
    msg = 'Your guess is too high'

self.response.out.write('<p>Guess:'+stguess+'</p>\n')
self.response.out.write('<p>'+msg+'</p>\n')
self.response.out.write(self.formstring)
```

The first thing that we do is use the `self.request.get()` from the framework to get the input value for the form field named `guess`.

This is an example of where the framework has saved us a good deal of effort. If you recall from the last chapter, the `POST` data in the HTTP request is encoded, and escaped, and in keyword/value format. And if the form data is encoded as multipart form data, the `POST` data is still more complex.

Thankfully, this is all hidden from us; the framework parses whichever format it sees and hands us the data for the `guess` field.

The `self.request.get()` returns a string value (hence the mnemonic name `stguess`), so we must convert our string guess to an integer using the `int()` function. We place the integer conversion safely in a `try/except` block and set `guess` to `-1` if we encounter any error in the conversion.

Once we have the integer `guess` and `answer`, we use a four-branch `if` that sets a message to be given to the user. We check for the correct answer, a negative number caused by an error, a low guess, and a high guess. Based on the `if`, we set the `msg` variable to contain an appropriate string.

At the end, we use `self.response.out.write()` to output a paragraph that shows the guess in string form using string concatenation (+), print out a paragraph with the message, and then print out the form to yield a page that looks like Figure 5-7.

Viewing the page source reveals the following:

```
<p>Guess:25</p>
<p>Your guess is too low</p>
<form method="post" action="/">
<p>Enter Guess: <input type="text" name="guess"/></p>
<p><input type="submit"></p>
</form>
```

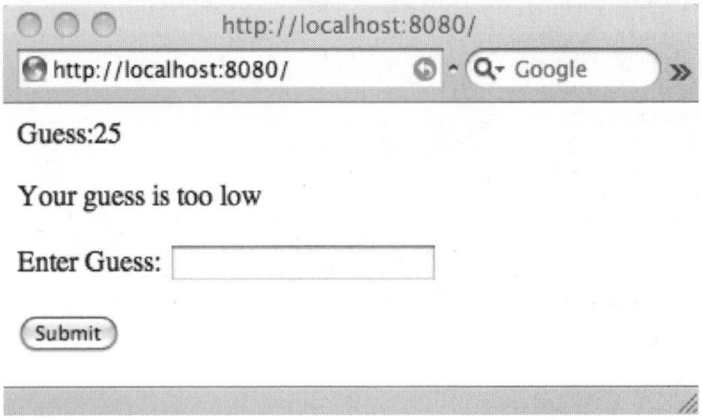

Figure 5-7. An incorrect guess

Web Server Logs

Because our software takes incoming HTTP requests and produces an HTTP response, often in some end user's browser halfway around the world, it is a little hard to figure out what happened when something goes wrong. Usually, if your program fails, users shake their heads and switch to another website in disgust. They don't call you and talk for a while about what they did that went wrong and what strange messages they saw. And you do not want them calling you at all hours of the night when they encounter an error. You would be far happier if, in the morning, you could see what went wrong by looking in the log.

A *log* is generally a file or window that contains messages from your program. You have been using logs all along. Figure 5-8 shows an example log when your application is running locally.

When the App Engine server is running, the log streams out to the window in which you started the AppServer. When you upload your application to the Google infrastructure, it still maintains a log that you can check in a browser.

You can look at the log of a production web application at any time and see what is happening, as shown in Figure 5-9. You can see successful activities, get a sense of patterns of interaction, and see errors in the log.

After a while, you will get used to the logs and their patterns and rhythms. Once you become familiar with your application, it is almost like watching the screens in the Matrix: after a while, it just starts to make sense to you.

In addition to the default logging that App Engine provides for you, you can add your own logging messages to your application, as shown here:

```
import logging
import wsgiref.handlers
from google.appengine.ext import webapp

class MainHandler(webapp.RequestHandler):

  formstring = '''<form method="post" action="/">
<p>Enter Guess: <input type="text" name="guess"/></p>
<p><input type="submit"></p>
</form>'''

  def get(self):
    self.response.out.write('<p>Good luck!</p>\n')
    self.response.out.write(self.formstring)

  def post(self):
    stguess = self.request.get('guess')
    logging.info('User guess='+stguess)
    try:
. . .
```

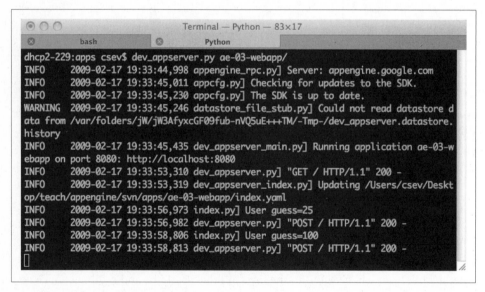

Figure 5-8. Web server log

When you add a `logging` statement to your code, it shows up in the log interspersed with the other messages. If you watch the log, you can see your "customers" make progress toward the winning answer.

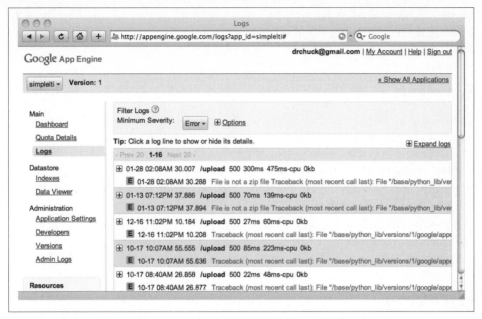

Figure 5-9. Viewing logs when your application is in production

If you look closely at the following log, it might seem that perhaps this game is too hard; the customer is showing signs of frustration as he plays the game:

```
INFO 2008-12-28 02:50:18,654 dev_appserver.py] "GET/HTTP/1.1" 200
INFO 2008-12-28 02:50:26,422 index.py] User guess=20
INFO 2008-12-28 02:50:26,430 dev_appserver.py] "POST/HTTP/1.1" 200
INFO 2008-12-28 02:50:31,853 index.py] User guess=100
INFO 2008-12-28 02:50:31,860 dev_appserver.py] "POST/HTTP/1.1" 200
INFO 2008-12-28 02:50:36,591 index.py] User guess=50
INFO 2008-12-28 02:50:36,599 dev_appserver.py] "POST/HTTP/1.1" 200
INFO 2008-12-28 02:50:43,786 index.py] User guess=30
INFO 2008-12-28 02:50:43,795 dev_appserver.py] "POST/HTTP/1.1" 200
INFO 2008-12-28 02:50:48,478 index.py] User guess=35
INFO 2008-12-28 02:50:48,490 dev_appserver.py] "POST/HTTP/1.1" 200
INFO 2008-12-28 02:52:52,412 index.py] User guess=Grrr.
```

The judicious use of logging messages allows you to track your program internally and is particularly helpful when things are not going well—you can put a message in the log when you encounter strange or error conditions.

As the user does not see the log, you can add plenty of detail to help you figure out the source of the problem—particularly given that you will be looking at the log hours after the actual error occurred in your application.

You can see why some of the error messages err on the side of verbosity and provide far more detail than you might need. You often need to reconstruct what happened; the log provides the only clues to what went wrong.[*]

Summary

The Google App Engine webapp framework moves us toward an object-oriented approach to handling our HTTP requests and responses. We initially set things up by creating a web application and giving it a routing table to call us back to handle the incoming requests. Then the framework parses and interprets the incoming HTTP requests and calls the correct methods in our handler code to process the input data and prepare the HTTP response.

We also looked at how application logs are used in a web application to help you monitor what is happening when your application is running and potentially experiencing errors, as you are not in contact with the ultimate end users of your application.

Exercises

1. What are the advantages of using the webapp framework in Google App Engine instead of writing a "straight-up" application, as described in the previous chapter?

2. In a webapp program, what do the following lines of code accomplish?

```
application = webapp.WSGIApplication(
    [('/.*', MainHandler)],
    debug=True)
```

3. Why are the handlers in a webapp objects instead of just a set of functions?

4. Why do handlers use `self.response.write()` instead of `print` to produce their output?

5. The variable "self" is simply a naming convention. What concept does the name "self" represent? What would be another good mnemonic variable name to use instead of "self"?

6. How might the Google cloud take advantage of the object-oriented nature of a webapp-based application?

7. What is the purpose of triple quotes (`'''`) in Python?

8. How is the "submit" HTML input type displayed in a browser?

[*] Reference: *http://code.google.com/appengine/articles/logging.html*.

## CHAPTER 6

Templates

Although it is possible to generate all of the HTML of your application from within strings in Python, this is generally a poor way to author HTML. In particular, it means that every time you want to change a bit of the generated HTML, you need to dig through the program, find the strings, and then change the HTML code:

```
formstring = '''<form method="post" action="/">
<p>Enter Guess: <input type="text" name="guess"/></p>
<p><input type="submit"></p>
</form>'''
```

At the same time, our web application needs to have some parts of the web pages be generated dynamically as part of the code of the web application—either based on the user's input or based on some information retrieved from the Datastore.

The compromise that solves both problems is a *template*. A template is a file that contains mostly HTML with specially marked areas of the template that are replaced by data passed into the template from the Python code when the template is rendered.

There are many different template languages and syntaxes. The default template syntax used by Google App Engine is borrowed from the Django project (*http://www.django project.com*).

Template Syntax

The template syntax in Google App Engine augments the HTML by using curly braces to identify where we are giving commands to the template system. The template for our number-guessing program when we are responding to a GET request is in the file *index.htm*:

```
<p>{{ hint }}</p>
<form method="post" action="/">
<p>Enter Guess: <input type="text" name="guess"/></p>
<p><input type="submit"></p>
</form>
```

Templates have special "hot areas" where text from Python can be substituted into the output produced by the template. The area in the template that will be replaced with data from Python is between double curly braces. In between the double curly braces, hint is a key that is used to determine which piece of data from the Python code to put into the template to replace {{ hint }}.

We use a different template after the user has made a guess—we want to show both his guess and then the hint in the template *guess.htm*:

```
<p>Your Guess: {{ stguess }}</p>
<p>{{ hint }}</p>
<form method="post" action="/">
<p>Enter Guess: <input type="text" name="guess"/></p>
<p><input type="submit"></p>
</form>
```

This template has two areas to be replaced with data provided from Python.

By convention, we put the templates into a directory named *templates*, as shown in Figure 6-1. This way we can easily keep HTML templates separate from the Python code.

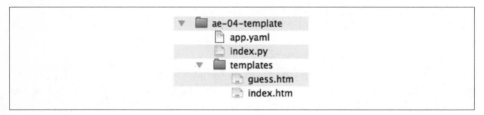

Figure 6-1. Directory structure

Naming the folder *templates* is not a rule—it is a convention. Following the convention is a good idea because it means that other developers will immediately know where to find the templates in your application.

Using the Templates from Python

To display the template in Python we add code to *index.py* to "render" the template and then print the output of the render process to the HTTP response. To render a template, App Engine reads through the template file, looks for the marked areas to substitute with the values from Python, and produces the merged output.

Following are the needed changes to make our number-guessing program use a template instead of writing out the HTML directly from Python:

```
import os
import logging
import wsgiref.handlers
from google.appengine.ext import webapp
```

```
from google.appengine.ext.webapp import template

class MainHandler(webapp.RequestHandler):

  def get(self):
    temp = os.path.join(
          os.path.dirname(__file__),
          'templates/index.htm')
    outstr = template.render(
          temp,
          {'hint': 'Good luck!'})
    self.response.out.write(outstr)
```

We add an `import` statement to make the template library available to our application.

Within the `get()` method, the first line looks up the full path to the template file by using the path to the currently executing file and adding *templates/index.htm* to the end of the current file's path.

The actual template processing is done in the `template.render()` line. This takes two parameters: the first is the location of the template file from the previous step (stored in the variable `temp`) and the second is a Python dictionary object, which contains the strings to be placed in the template where the {{ hint }} entries are found. The results of the substitution of the variables into the template are returned as a string in the variable `outstr`.

The text returned from the `template.render()` in `outstr` will look as follows:

```
<p>Good Luck!</p>
<form method="post" action="/">
<p>Enter Guess: <input type="text" name="guess"/></p>
<p><input type="submit"></p>
</form>
```

The data from the Python dictionary is now substituted into the template as it is rendered. Figure 6-2 shows a diagram of the rendering process.

The process is simple: the render engine looks for the "hot spots" in the template, and when it finds a spot where a substitution is required, the renderer looks in the provided Python dictionary to find the replacement text:

```
outstr = template.render(
      temp,
      {'hint': 'Good luck!'})
self.response.out.write(outstr)
```

The final step in our `get()` method is to write `outstr` to the HTTP Response.

The template language is actually quite sophisticated. We will look at more of the capabilities of the template language later in this chapter.

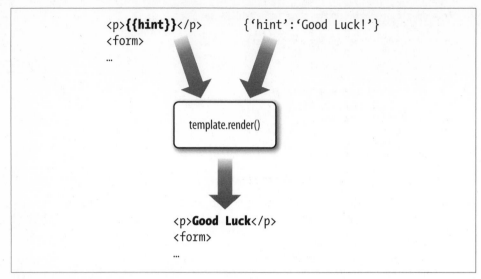

Figure 6-2. The rendering process

The Number-Guessing Game Using Templates

We can easily rewrite our number-guessing game to use templates instead of generating the HTML from strings in Python. We create the two template files (*index.htm* and *guess.htm*) as shown earlier, and place them in the *templates* folder.

We then make the following changes to our `MainHandler` code:

```
from google.appengine.ext.webapp import template

class MainHandler(webapp.RequestHandler):

  def get(self):
    temp = os.path.join(
          os.path.dirname(__file__),
          'templates/index.htm')
    outstr = template.render(
          temp,
          {'hint': 'Good luck!'})
    self.response.out.write(outstr)

  def post(self):
    stguess = self.request.get('guess')
    msg = ''
    guess = -1
    try:
      guess = int(stguess)
    except:
      guess = -1

    answer = 42
    if guess == answer:
```

```
    msg = 'Congratulations'
elif guess < 0 :
    msg = 'Please provide a number'
elif guess < answer:
    msg = 'Your guess is too low'
else:
    msg = 'Your guess is too high'

temp = os.path.join(
        os.path.dirname(__file__),
        'templates/guess.htm')
outstr = template.render(
        temp,
        {'hint': msg, 'stguess': stguess})
self.response.out.write(outstr)
```

We make sure to import the template library at the beginning of our program, and then in the `get()` method, we render the template *index.htm* passing in the string `Good Luck!` as the text that will be substituted for `{{ hint }}` in the template.

In the `post()` method, we render the *guess.htm* template and we pass in two strings. We pass in the hint value, which comes from the logic of the program in the `msg` variable, and the guess, provided by the user under the label of **stguess** so it can be placed in the template where the `{{ stguess }}` is found.

In each case, we call `self.response.out.write()` to send back the results of the render process to the browser.

When we first start the application, it looks like Figure 6-3.

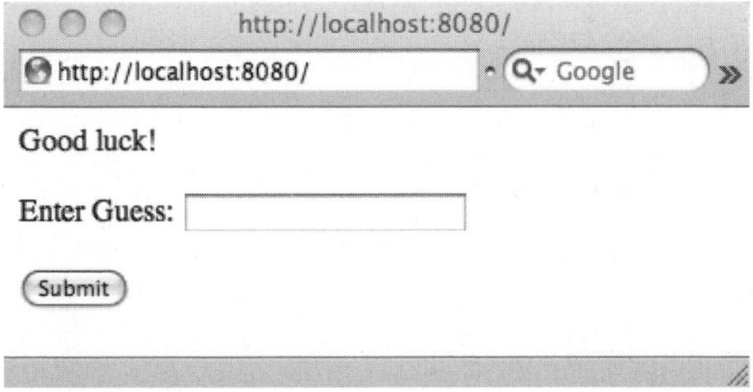

```
http://localhost:8080/
http://localhost:8080/          Q▾ Google    »

Good luck!

Enter Guess: [                    ]

( Submit )
```

Figure 6-3. The guessing game

Viewing the page source reveals the HTML that is produced by the rendering step:

```
<p>Good luck!</p>
<form method="post" action="/">
<p>Enter Guess: <input type="text" name="guess"/></p>
<p><input type="submit"></p>
</form>
```

We cannot detect which parts of the HTML came from the template and which parts of the HTML came from the Python code—our browser simply receives and displays the merged HTML.

Although templates may initially seem like more of a bother than a help, as your program grows in size and complexity, templates are an important way to keep your program organized.

Abstraction and Separation of Concerns: "Model View Controller"

The concept of templates is not unique to Google App Engine. As web applications can quickly get quite complex, it is very important to be organized and for each area of functionality to have its place. Following commonly understood patterns helps us keep track of the bits of the program. A well-known pattern helps you understand your own code and helps other programmers understand your code so that they can help you develop or review your application.

One of the most common programming patterns in web-based applications is called Model-View-Controller, or MVC for short. Many web frameworks, such as Ruby on Rails and Spring MVC, follow the MVC pattern.

The MVC pattern splits the code of a web application into three basic areas:

Controller
> The code that does the thinking and decision making.

View
> The HTML, CSS, and other elements that make up the look and feel of the application.

Model
> The persistent data that we keep in the datastore.

In a Google App Engine program, the various "handlers" in our *index.py* file are examples of Controller code and the HTML in the templates is an example of a View.

We will encounter the Model in Chapter 8, where we will revisit the MVC pattern and explore it in more detail.

Building a Multiscreen Application

We will now leave our number-guessing game behind and pick up where we left off in Chapter 2, in which we were building a multiscreen application with navigation between the screens. We will use and expand this application as the example for the remainder of the book.

If you recall, we had three web pages and clever navigation between the pages. We used CSS to style the pages and tuck the navigation up into a top bar across each page. We had even changed the styling of the currently selected page to give the user a visual clue as to which was the current page, as shown in Figure 6-4.

Figure 6-4. Navigation clues

In the HTML and CSS chapter, we edited and viewed these files as static HTML and CSS in a single directory. Now we will put these files into an App Engine application. We will set up the directories as shown in Figure 6-5.

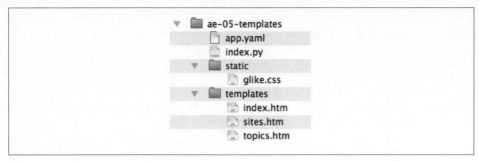

Figure 6-5. Directory layout for templates

We put the HTML files in the *templates* folder and place the CSS file (*glike.css*) into a new folder called *static*. The *static* folder contains files that do not change—they may be CSS, JavaScript, or image files.

We will need to make only slight changes to the files; initially, we just copy in the CSS and HTML files in their respective folders into a new App Engine application.

Static Files in App Engine

We indicate that the *static* folder holds "unchanging" files and gives them a URL by adding an entry to the *app.yaml* file:

```
application: ae-05-templates
version: 1
runtime: python
api_version: 1

handlers:
- url: /static
  static_dir: static

- url: /.*
  script: index.py
```

We add a new handler entry with the special indicator to map URLs that start with */static* to the special *static* folder. And we indicate that the material in the *static* folder is not dynamically generated.

The order of the URL entries in the handler section is important. In the *app.yaml* file just shown, App Engine first checks to see whether an incoming URL starts with */static*, and if there is a match, the content is served from the *static* folder. If there is no match, the "catchall" URL (*/.**) routes all other URLs to the *index.py* script. Because the handler entries are checked in the order that they appear in the file, it is important that the catchall URL be the last entry in the file.

The convention is to name the folder *static*. You technically could name the folder and path (*/static*) anything you like. The *static_dir* directive (like the script directive) is an *app.yaml* directive and cannot be changed. But the best approach is to follow the pattern and name the folder and path *static*.

The advantage of placing files in a *static* folder is that it does not use your program (*index.py*) for serving these files. As you may be paying for the processor usage of the Google servers, avoiding processor usage on serving *static* content is a good idea. The *static* content still counts against your data transferred—it just does not incur extra processor costs by running these files through *index.py*.

Even more importantly, when you indicate that files are *static_dir*, it allows Google to distribute these files to many different servers geographically and leave the files there. This means that retrieving these files from different continents may be using Google servers closest to the user of your application. Thus your application can scale to far more users efficiently.

Google also makes sure to set the response headers properly for these static files so that the browser is encouraged to cache these files, further reducing the load on your application and increasing its responsiveness.

Referencing Static Files

The only change we need to make is to properly reference the *glike.css* CSS file from the *index.htm*, *sites.htm*, and *topics.htm* files. Because the CSS file is now in the *static* folder with a */static* path, we make the following change to each of the HTML files:

```
<html xmlns="http://www.w3.org/1999/xhtml">
 <head>
   <title>App Engine - HTML</title>
   <link href="/static/glike.css" rel="stylesheet" type="text/css" />
 </head>
 <body>
   <div id="header">
```

When App Engine sees the URL that starts with */static*, it routes it to one of its many distributed copies of the CSS file and serves up the content.

Generalizing Template Lookup with Multiple Templates

In the number-guessing example, there were only two templates, so we hardcoded the name of the template when we wanted to do the rendering operation. Sometimes you are in a handler that knows the exact name of the template, so it can follow the hardcoded pattern.

Other times, you want to have a bunch of templates and serve them up with paths, such as:

```
http://localhost:8080/index.htm
http://localhost:8080/topics.htm
http://localhost:8080/sites.htm
```

We can create general-purpose code to look up a template based on the incoming path of the request (i.e., the document that is being requested).

We can take advantage of the fact that part of the incoming HTTP request is the path to the requested document. For example, if the browser is requesting the page *http:// localhost:8080/topics.htm*, the document being requested is */topics.htm*.

We can retrieve the document string from the incoming request using `self.request.path`. We can then check whether we have a template that matches the incoming document name and render that template. If we are given a path for which we do not have a template, we simply give them the *index.htm* template.

Here is the controller code to accomplish this using `self.request.path`:

```
class MainHandler(webapp.RequestHandler):

  def get(self):
    path = self.request.path

    temp = os.path.join(
          os.path.dirname(__file__),
          'templates' + path)

    if not os.path.isfile(temp):
        temp = os.path.join(
            os.path.dirname(__file__),
            'templates/index.htm')

    outstr = template.render(temp, { })
    self.response.out.write(outstr)
```

In the `get()` method of `MainHandler`, we first pull in the document that was requested by the browser from `self.request.path` and concatenate the current working directory of *index.py* with "templates" and the requested document using `os.path.join()`.

Then we check to see whether this file exists; if the file does not exist, we use the template *index.htm*.

Once we have chosen our template, we call `template.render()`. For now we have no substitutable values in the templates, so we send in an empty dictionary `{ }` as the second parameter to the render call.

Once the render is complete, we send the rendered output to the HTTP response using `self.response.out.write()`.

We are taking advantage of the fact that the `self.request.path` variable shows the path/ document that is being requested by the browser for each request. In the log output in Figure 6-6, you can see each path being requested using a `GET` request.

You can see the browser requesting a path like */sites.htm*, which renders from the template and then, when the browser sees the reference to the */static/glike.css*, it does another `GET` request to retrieve the CSS, which is stored in the *static* folder.

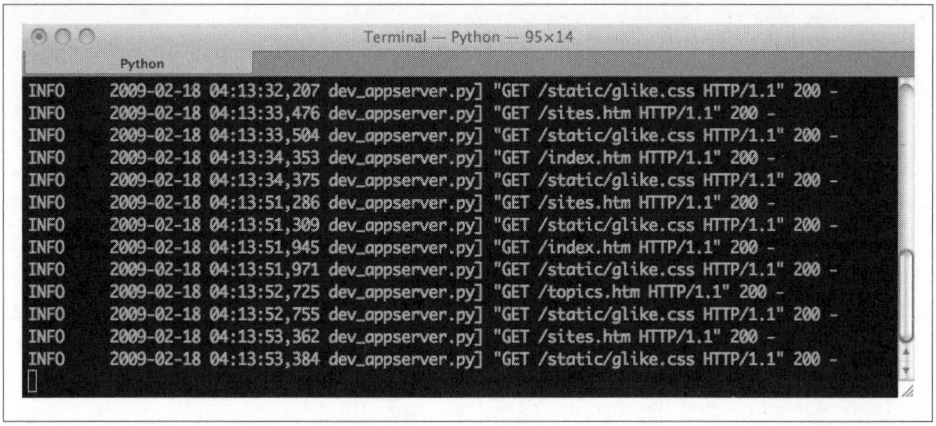

Figure 6-6. Requesting documents in the log

The `self.request.path` starts with a slash (/), so when it is appended to *templates*, the file path that we hand to the render engine as its first parameter is:

```
templates/sites.htm
```

which is exactly where we have stored our templates.

Extending Base Templates

We have only begun to scratch the surface of the capabilities of the template language. Once we have successfully separated our views (HTML and CSS) from the controller (Python), we can start looking at ways to manage our views more effectively.

If you look at the example HTML files used as templates in this application, you will find that the files are nearly identical, with a few small differences between each file. Most of the content is identical and copied between files:

```html
<html xmlns="http://www.w3.org/1999/xhtml">
 <head>
   <title>App Engine - HTML</title>
   <link href="/static/glike.css" rel="stylesheet" type="text/css" />
 </head>
 <body>
   <div id="header">
     <h1><a href="index.htm">App Engine</a></h1>
     <ul>
       <li><a href="sites.htm">Sites</a></li>
       <li><a href="topics.htm">Topics</a></li>
     </ul>
   </div>
   <div id="bodycontent">
     <h2>App Engine: About</h2>
     <p>
     Welcome to the site dedicated to
     learning the Google App Engine.
```

```
            We hope you find www.appenginelearn.com useful.
          </p>
        </div>
      </body>
    </html>
```

The only things that change between the files are (1) which link is selected (i.e., class="selected") and (2) the information in the bodycontent div. All the material in the <head> area and nearly all material in the header div are identical between files.

We create a significant maintenance problem for ourselves by repeating this common text in many (perhaps hundreds) files in our application. When we want to make a change to this common text, we have to carefully edit all the files and make the change, which is tedious and error-prone. It also means that we have to test each screen separately to make sure that it is updated and working properly.

To solve this problem, we create a special template that contains the common material for each page. Then the page files include only the material that is different. Here is a sample page file that is making use of the base template, the new *index.htm* template file:

```
{% extends "_base.htm" %}
{% block bodycontent %}
      <h2>App Engine: About</h2>
      <p>
      Welcome to the site dedicated to
      learning Google App Engine.
      We hope you find www.appenginelearn.com useful.
      </p>
{% endblock %}
```

The template language uses curly braces and percent signs to indicate our commands to the render engine. The first line says this page starts with the text contained in the file *_base.htm*. We are starting with *_base.htm* and then *extending* it.

The second line says, "When you find an area marked as the bodycontent block in the *_base.htm* file, replace that block with the text in between the block and endblock template commands."

The *_base.htm* file is placed in the *templates* directory, along with all the rest of the template files, as shown in Figure 6-7.

The contents of the *_base.htm* file are the common text that we want to put into each page, plus an indication of where the body content is to be placed:

```
    <head>
      <title>App Engine - HTML</title>
      <link href="/static/glike.css" rel="stylesheet" type="text/css" />
    </head>
    <body>
      <div id="header">
        <h1><a href="index.htm">App Engine</a></h1>
        <ul>
          <li><a href="sites.htm">Sites</a></li>
          <li><a href="topics.htm">Topics</a></li>
```

```
      </ul>
    </div>
    <div id="bodycontent">
        {% block bodycontent %}
            Replace this
        {% endblock %}
    </div>
  </body>
</html>
```

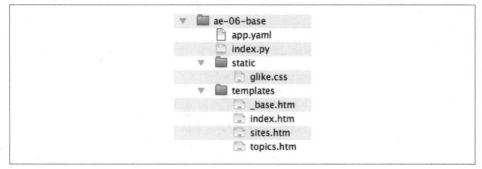

Figure 6-7. Using a base template

We include a template engine directive in the *_base.htm* template to indicate the beginning and end of the block that will be replaced by each template that uses (extends) *_base.htm*. The text "Replace this" will not appear in the resulting HTML after the render has been completed.

We do not need to make any change to the *index.py* code—the use of a base template is something that is handled completely in the `template.render()` call.

Conditional Processing Templates

Our application has several pages, and although we have moved most of the repeated text into a base file, there is one area in the *_base.htm* that needs to change between files. If we look at the pages, we see that as we move between pages, we want to have the navigation links colored differently to indicate which page we are currently looking at, as shown in Figure 6-8.

We make this change by using the `selected` class in the generated HTML. For example on the *topics.htm* file, we need the "Topics" link to be indicated as "selected":

```
<ul>
    <li><a href="sites.htm">Sites</a></li>
    <li><a href="topics.htm" class="selected">Topics</a></li>
</ul>
```

We need to generate this text differently on each page, and the generated text depends on the file we are rendering. The path indicates which page we are on, so when we are on the Topics page, the path is */topics.htm*.

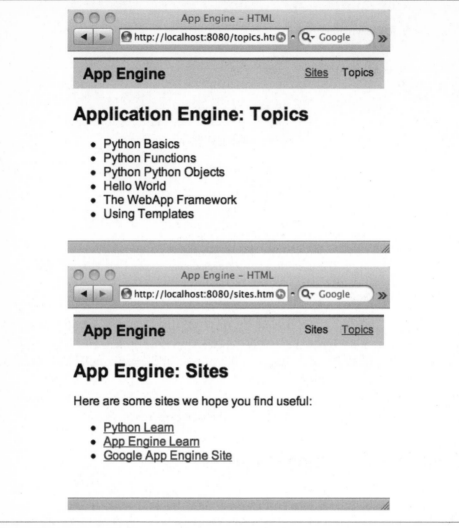

Figure 6-8. Navigation details

We make a small change to the handler to pass the current path into the render process as follows:

```
class MainHandler(webapp.RequestHandler):

    def get(self):
        path = self.request.path
        temp = os.path.join(
            os.path.dirname(__file__),
            'templates/' + path)
        if not os.path.isfile(temp):
            temp = os.path.join(
```

```
        os.path.dirname(__file__),
        'templates/index.htm')

    outstr = template.render(temp, { 'path': path })
    self.response.out.write(outstr)
```

Instead of passing an empty dictionary as the second parameter to `template.render()`, we give every template the current path in a variable named `'path'`.

With this change, the template code has access to the current path for the request. We then make the following change to the template:

```
<ul>
    <li><a href="sites.htm"
        {% ifequal path '/sites.htm' %}
            class="selected"
        {% endifequal %}
        >Sites</a></li>
    <li><a href="topics.htm"
        {% ifequal path '/topics.htm' %}
            class="selected"
        {% endifequal %}
        >Topics</a></li>
</ul>
```

This initially looks a bit complicated. At a high level, all it is doing is adding the text `class="selected"` to the anchor (`</a>`) tag when the current path matches */topic.htm* or */sites.htm*, respectively.

We are taking advantage of the fact that whitespace and end-lines do not matter in HTML. The generated HTML will look one of the following two ways:

```
<li><a href="topics.htm"
            class="selected"
        >Topics</a></li>
```

or

```
<li><a href="topics.htm"
        >Topics</a></li>
```

Although it looks a little choppy, it is valid HTML and our `class="selected"` appears when appropriate. Looking at the code in the template, we can examine the `ifequal` template directive:

```
{% ifequal path '/topics.htm' %}
        class="selected"
{% endifequal %}
```

The `ifequal` directive compares the contents of the `path` variable with the string */topics.htm* and conditionally includes the `class="selected"` in the generated output.

The combination of the two `ifequal` directives means that the links give us the properly generated navigation HTML based on which page is being generated. This is quite nice because now the entire navigation can be included in the _base.htm file, making the page templates very clean and simple:

```
{% extends "_base.htm" %}
{% block bodycontent %}
    <h2>App Engine: About</h2>
    <p>
    Welcome to the site dedicated to
    learning Google App Engine.
    We hope you find www.appenginelearn.com useful.
    </p>
{% endblock %}
```

With these changes, when we navigate to the Topics page, it looks as shown in Figure 6-9.

Figure 6-9. Conditional navigation display

The source code for the page looks like this:

```
<html xmlns="http://www.w3.org/1999/xhtml">
<head>
  <title>App Engine-HTML</title>
  <link href="/static/glike.css" rel="stylesheet"
        type="text/css" />
</head>
<body>
  <div id="header">
    <h1><a href="index.htm">App Engine</a></h1>
    <ul>
      <li><a href="sites.htm"

          >Sites</a></li>
      <li><a href="topics.htm"
```

```
                    class="selected"

                >Topics</a></li>
            </ul>
        </div>
        <div id="bodycontent">

            <h2>App Engine: Topics</h2>
            <ul>
                <li>Python Basics</li>
                <li>Python Functions</li>
                <li>Python Python Objects</li>
                <li>Hello World</li>
                <li>The WebApp Framework</li>
                <li>Using Templates</li>
            </ul>

        </div>
    </body>
</html>
```

There are some blank lines in the output where the `ifequal` and `endifequal` directives were found in the templates. You can alter your templates to remove these blanks lines, but it is probably not worth the effort. Having easily read templates is valuable.

This approach makes it very simple to add a new page or make a change across all pages. In general, when we can avoid repeating the same code over and over, our code is easier to maintain and modify.

Replacing More Than One Block in the Base Template

You may have noticed that all our pages have the same title. This is because we have the `<title>` tag in the _base.htm_ file. Because every page extends this page, we end up with the same title on every page.

You may not want this—you may want to change the title on some pages and not on other pages. We can do this by putting the title in its own block in _base.htm_ as follows, by making the following changes to the `<head>` section of _base.htm_:

```
<head>
    <title>
        {% block title %}App Engine - HTML{% endblock %}
    </title>
    <link href="/static/glike.css" rel="stylesheet"
          type="text/css" />
</head>
```

We use template directives to define the `title` block in our file. Notice that the template directives do not have to be on separate lines. In between the `block` and `endblock` directives, we place the text "App Engine—HTML". This is the text that will be placed

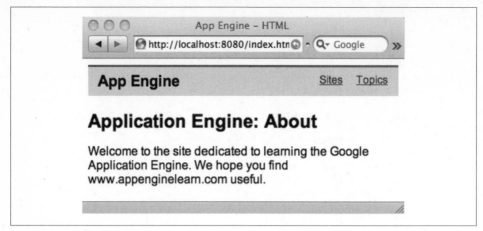

Figure 6-10. Rendered HTML page

in the block if the extending template does not provide text for a title block. We make no changes to our *index.htm* template, so this page renders as shown in Figure 6-10.

The title is "App Engine—HTML"—the default text. Then we make the following change to the *topics.htm* template:

```
{% extends "_base.htm" %}
{% block title %}
    App Engine - Topics
{% endblock %}
{% block bodycontent %}
      <h2>App Engine: Topics</h2>
      <ul>
        <li>Python Basics</li>
        <li>Python Functions</li>
        <li>Python Python Objects</li>
        <li>Hello World</li>
        <li>The WebApp Framework</li>
        <li>Using Templates</li>
      </ul>
{% endblock %}
```

In addition to providing text for the bodycontent block, we also provide text for the title block to override the default title text in *_base.htm*. With this change, the *topics.htm* page renders as shown in Figure 6-11.

Note that the title has indeed changed on the Topics page when *topics.htm* is rendered. By defining blocks in the *_base.htm* template with default text and optionally replacing that text in the template that extends the *_base.htm* template, we have great flexibility in how we generate our HTML without scattering repeated code throughout our application.

This process also makes adding a new page to our application much simpler and more straightforward.

Figure 6-11. Changing the title on a page

Extending Our Application

Now that you understand how to handle templates in general, we can start to build a real application. Our first improvement will be to add a simple screen to prompt for the user's account and password, as shown in Figure 6-12.

Figure 6-12. Login screen

For now, as we don't really have any user accounts, we will just pretend that all passwords are the word *secret*.

So far with this application, we have mostly been making HTTP GET requests as we navigate from one page to another. Now we will be handling POST requests as well. In a sense, this screen is somewhat like the number-guessing game—but instead, it's a password-guessing game.

We will make it so that our login page is at the URL */login*—we will be able to do a GET to the */login* URL to get the account/password form, and we can do a POST to this URL to submit the account and password for checking.

Because this login activity is a whole new chunk of work, we will make a new handler called LoginHandler and route the */login* URL to the LoginHandler.

The *app.yaml* file is pretty much unchanged, except for the application name:

```
application: ae-08-login
version: 1
runtime: python
api_version: 1
handlers:
- url: /static
  static_dir: static

- url: /.*
  script: index.py
```

We make several improvements to our *index.py* file:

```
import os
import logging
import wsgiref.handlers
from google.appengine.ext import webapp
from google.appengine.ext.webapp import template

def doRender(handler, tname='index.htm', values={}):
  temp = os.path.join(
      os.path.dirname(__file__),
      'templates/' + tname)
  if not os.path.isfile(temp):
    return False

  # Make a copy of the dictionary and add the path
  newval = dict(values)
  newval['path'] = handler.request.path

  outstr = template.render(temp, newval)
  handler.response.out.write(outstr)
  return True

class LoginHandler(webapp.RequestHandler):

  def get(self):
    doRender(self, 'loginscreen.htm')
```

```
    def post(self):
      acct = self.request.get('account')
      pw = self.request.get('password')

      if pw == '' or acct == '':
        doRender(
            self,
            'loginscreen.htm',
            {'error' : 'Please specify Acct and PW'} )
      elif pw == 'secret':
        doRender(self,'loggedin.htm',{ } )
      else:
        doRender(
            self,
            'loginscreen.htm',
            {'error' : 'Incorrect password'} )

  class MainHandler(webapp.RequestHandler):

    def get(self):
      path = self.request.path
      if doRender(self,path) :
        return
      doRender(self,'index.htm')

  def main():
    application = webapp.WSGIApplication([
        ('/login', LoginHandler),
        ('/.*', MainHandler)],
        debug=True)
    wsgiref.handlers.CGIHandler().run(application)

  if __name__ == '__main__':
    main()
```

The first change we make in *index.py* is to create a new function called doRender(), which is a reusable bit of code taken from MainHandler().

This new function takes three parameters: handler, a template name, and a dictionary called *values* to be passed into template.render(). The syntax of the function definition also shows how a function can provide default values for parameters if it is called without one or more parameters. In this definition, if the second parameter is omitted, it is assumed to be *index.htm*, and if the third parameter is omitted, *values* is assumed to be an empty dictionary.

The code in doRender() first checks to see whether the template file exists; if the file does not exist, the logical constant False is returned, to indicate that the render was unsuccessful.

If the template file exists, we make a copy of the dictionary and then add the value of handler.request.path to the dictionary so that all templates have access to the current document being requested.

The `template.render()` is called and the response is written out using `handler.response.out.write()`. The function finishes and returns `True` to indicate that a successful render was completed.

With this new helper function, we can simplify the `MainHandler` code that renders our templates as follows:

```
class MainHandler(webapp.RequestHandler):
  def get(self):
    if doRender(self,self.request.path) :
      return
    doRender(self,'index.htm')
```

When `MainHandler` receives a `GET` request, it tries to render the document that was requested by the browser. If this render succeeds (`True` is returned), we are all done and we use `return` to exit the `get()` method. If the first render fails, we render the *index.htm* template.

 The keywords `class` and `def` have very different purposes. When we use `class`, we are defining a pattern that we use to make instances/objects of type `MainHandler`—the value in parentheses (`webapp.RequestHandler`) is a "base class" which we are extending to create `MainHandler`. A function definition such as `doRender()` is simply a reusable bit of code that we give a name. The values in the parentheses on a function definition (handler, tname, and values) are the parameters to the function. In this program, we have a global function that can be used throughout the file and also methods that are part of the `MainHandler` class (i.e., `get()`and `post()`).

Now that we have our new `doRender()` function, we can add a new handler. First we make some changes to the URL routing in the `main()` code:

```
def main():
  application = webapp.WSGIApplication([
    ('/login', LoginHandler),
    ('/.*', MainHandler)],
    debug=True)
  wsgiref.handlers.CGIHandler().run(application)
```

We add a new routing rule to the list of routes. If the browser requests a path/document of `'/login'`, we route all of those requests to the `LoginHandler`. And all other paths, like *topics.htm*, fall through and are routed to `MainHandler`.

We need to define the new `LoginHandler` or our program will not run. We can start with a simple `LoginHandler` that just handles `GET` requests and renders the template *loginscreen.htm* as follows:

```
class LoginHandler(webapp.RequestHandler):

  def get(self):
    doRender(self, 'loginscreen.htm')
```

When our `LoginHandler` receives a `GET` request, it renders the *loginscreen.htm* template using our nifty `doRender()` function. We will come back and add the rest of the `LoginHandler` in a bit, but for now, let's take a look at our new template, called *loginscreen.htm*:

```
{% extends "_base.htm" %}
{% block bodycontent %}
  <h2>Please Log In</h2>
  <p>
  Please enter your id and password to log in to this site.
  </p>
  <form method="post" action="/login">
  Account: <input type="text" name="account"/> <br>
  Password: <input type="password" name="password"/> <br/>
  <input type="submit"/>
  <input type="submit" value="Cancel"
     onclick="window.location='/'; return false;"/>
  </form>
  </p>
  {% if error %}
   <p>
   {{ error }}
   </p>
  {% endif %}
{% endblock %}
```

Let's take a look at some of the new bits of this code.

First, we create a form with two text input fields named `account` and `password`. We use `type="password"` on the password field to tell the browser not to show the actual typed characters, but to instead display an asterisk (*) for each character.

We will submit the form data for this page using the `POST` method to the */login* URL when Submit is clicked:

```
<form method="post" action="/login">
```

In addition to the Submit button, we also create a Cancel button, using a little bit of JavaScript:

```
<input type="submit" value="Cancel"
       onclick="window.location='/'; return false;"/>
```

The JavaScript that runs when the Cancel button is clicked navigates our browser (*window.location*) back to the main url (/). The purpose of the `return false;` in the code snippet is to make sure that the form data is not submitted when the Cancel button is clicked. This JavaScript code is triggered when the `onclick` event happens (i.e., when the button is clicked).

In addition to the new button, we make provisions for printing an error message if the `error` variable has been passed into the template:

```
{% if error %}
<p>
{{ error }}
```

```
</p>
{% endif %}
```

This sequence checks to see whether we have a value for **error** and whether we have been passed a value; we add a bit of HTML to the page, which prints the error. This step allows us to detect an error in the Python code and send the user back to the *loginscreen.htm* file with an error message, so he will hopefully make the appropriate corrections and resubmit.

The next change we need to make is to the *_base.htm* file. We need to add a new navigation option so that our users can get to the */login* URL, so they can be presented with the login screen.

We make the following change to the navigation code in *_base.htm*:

```
<ul>
    <li><a href="sites.htm"
            {% ifequal path '/sites.htm' %}
                class="selected"
            {% endifequal %}
        >Sites</a></li>
    <li><a href="topics.htm"
            {% ifequal path '/topics.htm' %}
                class="selected"
            {% endifequal %}
        >Topics</a></li>
    <li><a href="/login"
          {% ifequal path '/login' %}
                class="selected"
          {% endifequal %}
        >Login</a></li>
</ul>
```

We add a new entry to our list of navigation options. When `Login` is clicked we send the user to the `/login` URL with a `GET` request. And we use the `ifequal` pattern checking the current path to determine is we should add the `class="selected"` to the link to color it differently.

With these changes in place, our main page and login page look like those in Figure 6-13.

We should test to confirm that clicking the Cancel button navigates back to the main page. We cannot test Submit because we have not yet written the code to handle `POST` requests in our `LoginHandler`.

The `post()` method in the `LoginHandler` class needs to take the `account` and `password` fields from the form and check to make sure that the user knows the secret password before she can log in. If she makes a mistake, we will send her an error message and let her retry.

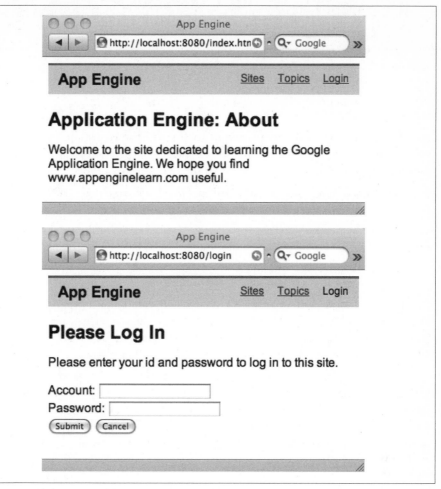

Figure 6-13. Application with login

Remember that for this program, the password is always the word *secret*. The complete LoginHandler is as follows:

```
class LoginHandler(webapp.RequestHandler):

    def get(self):
        doRender(self, 'loginscreen.htm')

    def post(self):
        acct = self.request.get('account')
        pw = self.request.get('password')
        logging.info('Checking account='+acct+' pw='+pw)

        if pw == '' or acct == '':
            doRender(
                self,
```

```
        'loginscreen.htm',
        {'error' : 'Please specify Acct and PW'} )
elif pw == "secret":
    doRender(self,'loggedin.htm',{ } )
else:
    doRender(
        self,
        'loginscreen.htm',
        {'error' : 'Incorrect password'} )
```

In the post() method for the LoginHandler, we first pull the account and password values from the incoming form data using self.request.get(). Then we do a series of if checks to see whether the user has entered the right information.

First, if either the account or password is blank, we send the user right back to *loginscreen.htm* with a helpful error message:

```
if pw == '' or acct == '':
    doRender(
        self,
        'loginscreen.htm',
        {'error' : 'Please specify Acct and PW'} )
```

Note that in order to make the Python code more readable, we break the doRender() line into several lines. If you are in the middle of a parameter list in parentheses (), Python allows you to break the line, in which case indentation is effectively ignored until the closing parenthesis of the function call is encountered.

If the account and password are not blank, we check to see whether the password matches *secret*. If so, we send the user to the *loggedin.htm* page with no error message. The *loggedin.htm* template is rather simple, showing how nice it is to be able to get all of your navigation from a *_base.htm* template with a single extends statement:

```
{% extends "_base.htm" %}
{% block bodycontent %}
    <p>
    Login successful.
    </p>
{% endblock %}
```

If the user did not have the correct password, we fall through to the else: statement and send him or her back to *loginscreen.htm*—again, with an appropriate error message:

```
else:
    doRender(
        self,
        'loginscreen.htm',
        {'error' : 'Incorrect password'} )
```

Once we have made all of these changes, our new login screen should be fully functional.

In order to add a new functionality to our application, take the following steps:

• Decide on the URL that you want to use for the new feature.

- Write a new handler—the handler can initially be simple and just handle a `GET` request that renders a new template.
- Add a routing entry in `main()` to send the URL to a new handler.
- Add new templates as needed.
- Update the *_base.htm* to add any new navigation that is needed.
- Build the rest of the handler code and test your new functionality.

Now that you have a good understanding of the act of adding a handler and a few templates, adding functionality to the application is pretty simple and can be accomplished with relatively few lines and little or no repetitive code.

Syntax Errors

By now, if you have been following along and implementing the code as we go, you have likely made some errors in your program and seen the "purple screen of death," as shown in Figure 6-14.

Figure 6-14. Syntax error

This can be a bit intimidating and is certainly hard to read. The most important rule when reading this screen is to generally ignore everything except the very last few lines of the screen, which are shown in Figure 6-15.

The message that it gives you may or may not describe your mistake. But it usually gives you some clues as to where to look for the error. In this example, the mistake was a missing comma on line 60 of my *index.py*.

If you make a mistake inside of a template, the error message is also pretty verbose and cryptic, as shown in Figure 6-16. Again, scroll to the bottom of the error message and work backward.

Figure 6-15. Syntax error detail

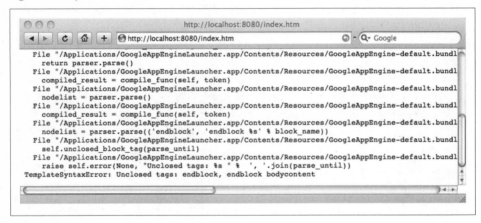

Figure 6-16. Template syntax error

In this example, we forgot to close a `{% block %}` tag, as follows:

```
{% extends "_base.htm" %}
{% block bodycontent %}
    <h2>App Engine: About</h2>
    <p>
    Welcome to the site dedicated to
    learning Google App Engine.
    We hope you find www.appenginelearn.com useful.
    </p>
```

Over time, the error messages will make a bit more sense to you. But in the meantime, the best defense is to write your programs and templates slowly and make sure to test them every time you make a few changes. So if something breaks, you can go back and look at the few changes that you have made since the program was last working.

More on Templates

This chapter has only scratched the surface of the template directives. The Google App Engine template library comes from the Django project (*http://www.django.org*). You can read more about the template language features at *http://www.djangoproject.com/documentation/0.96/templates/*.

Summary

Using templates and separating your View (HTML) from your Controller (Python) allows you to write increasingly larger programs without going crazy keeping track of details. Adopting and following patterns in your software development will make your applications more readable to you and to others.

Google App Engine provides a powerful template language that was adapted from the successful Django project, which allows text and blocks to be replaced, plus provides support for base templates and templates that extend those base templates.

Exercises

1. What is the main purpose for using templates to generate HTML instead of the `self.response.write` statement in Python?
2. What characters are used in templates to start and end a template directive?
3. Why is it a good idea to store your templates in the folder called *templates*?
4. Give an example of the template syntax needed to take a string generated in Python and embed it into the HTML output of a template.
5. What is the Python data structure (list, string, dictionary, integer) used to pass in the data to be substituted into the template? Why is this a good choice as a data structure to pass in the template material?
6. What does the `template.render()` method do?
7. What is the purpose of the Controller in the Model-View-Controller pattern?
8. A template is an example of which: Model, View, or Controller?
9. What is the purpose of the `extends` template directive? Why is "extends" a good mnemonic name for this particular function?
10. What is the primary purpose of placing some files in "static" areas and other files in "templates"?
11. How do you change the *app.yaml* file to indicate that a particular folder contains static material? What would your *app.yaml* file look like if you wanted to store static content in a folder named *barcelona*?

12. If a base template had a replaceable block named `capetown`, what syntax would you use in your main template to replace that block of text with "Welcome to Amsterdam!"?

13. What is the purpose of `class="selected"` in the list of navigation options in the example in this chapter.

14. In the following syntax from an App Engine template:

```
{% ifequal path '/topics.htm' %}
    class="selected"
{% endifequal %}
```

what is `path` and how do we set `path` in our Python code?

15. The following template has a syntax error. What would you do to fix the error?

```
{% ifequal path '/sites.htm' %}
        class="selected"
{% endifequal %}
>Sites</a></li>
<li><a href="topics.htm"
    {% ifequal path '/topics.htm' %}
            class="selected"
    {% endfequal %}
>Topics</a></li>
```

16. In your application, neither login nor logout are working. The instructor says that you have made a mistake in the following code. What is the mistake and how do you fix it?

```
application = webapp.WSGIApplication([
    ('/.*', MainHandler),
    ('/logout', LogoutHandler),
    ('/login', LoginHandler)],
    debug=True)
```

## CHAPTER 7

Cookies and Sessions

A common pattern in web applications is to maintain the *state* of an interaction with a particular user/browser by using a cookie stored in the user's browser that indexes a session on the server. The *session* is just a place to put data that persists across multiple request/response cycles. Each session has a key that is usually a large random number. The session contains small amounts of data indexed by a key, much like a Python dictionary object. The server stores the session key in a cookie on the user's browser so that the server can "find" the correct session in the server when it receives the next request from the browser.

HTTP Cookies

Cookies are part of the HTTP request/response cycle. When the server returns a page to the browser, it can include one or more cookies with the page. The web browser then retains those cookies (indexed by the domain name of the website). When a new GET or POST request is sent back to the server, the browser appends all the cookies for the domain name to the request and sends the cookies back to the server on every request, as shown in Figure 7-1. For more information, please also see *http://en.wikipe dia.org/wiki/HTTP_cookie*.

The content and names of the cookies are opaque to the browser. The browser keeps the cookies separate for each of the hosts that it is communicating with. In a way, the cookies belong to the server, even though they are stored in the browser.

Let's take a look at the data that is exchanged on the three interactions. First, the browser requests a web page using the following HTTP commands:

```
GET /index.htm HTTP/1.1
Accept: www/source
Accept: text/html
User-Agent: Lynx/2.4
```

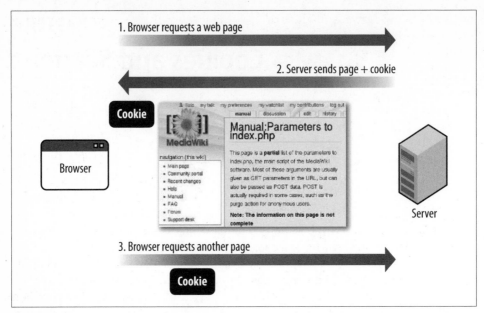

Figure 7-1. Browser cookie lifecycle

When the server wants to set a cookie, it is set as part of the HTTP response headers that precede the HTML document:

```
HTTP/1.1 200 OK
Content-type: text/html
Set-Cookie: sessid=123

<head> .. </head>
<body>
<h1>Welcome ....
```

Then, when the browser makes additional requests for pages from the same server, the browser sends back the cookie information as part of the HTTP headers of each succeeding request:

```
GET /index.htm HTTP/1.1
Accept: www/source
Accept: text/html
Cookie: sessid=123
User-Agent: Lynx/2.4
```

The cookie mechanism provides a limited amount of storage space, which the server can make use of, in each user's browser. Servers use cookies to mark each user's browser so that the server can identify which requests are coming from which browser.

The browser is very careful not to mix cookies from different servers. Each cookie is marked with the domain name of the server that set the cookie, and cookies are only sent back on requests destined for the server that initially set the cookie.

Because cookies are stored on the user's system, it is important to remember that the user may be able to modify the cookie. Most browsers do not allow the user to easily modify cookies, but if you install the Firefox Web Developer plug-in, it is trivial to view and/or modify any cookie in your browser.

Because users can change cookies, servers tend not to store information like "this user is logged in as *username*" in a cookie because it would be too easy for users to fake or modify a cookie, thus bypassing a system's security and appearing to be logged in as some other user.

So the general pattern is for the server to set a single cookie called the *session id* and then store any data that needs protecting on the server in an area called the *session*. The session cookie is used to look up the session object on the server and the session object on the server is used to store information such as the current logged-in user.

The session id is chosen as a very large random number, so it is nearly impossible to guess. Each time the user contacts the application, she is given a new session and a new large random number session id. So although users can manipulate cookies, unless they can figure out the session id of another user, they cannot fake logging in. If they play with their session cookie, the most they can do is get inadvertently logged out by corrupting their session cookie.

The server usually creates a session and sets the session cookie in the browser on the very first page returned to the browser. Then, when the user logs in, it usually ends up being a change to the session information rather than a change to the session cookie.

Sessions are used to store many bits of data that the server application wants to track for the duration of an interaction between the application and a user. The most obvious thing to store in a session is the username and other information about the current logged-in user. It is also common to store things like a subset of user preferences or possibly the contents of a shopping cart in the session. This chapter focuses on how the session supports logging in and logging out.

Logging In and Logging Out Using Sessions

We will continue to improve our ongoing example application by actually logging users in when they get the password right. We will make it so the navigation changes when the user is logged in. We will also add a feature to log the user out.

Before the user logs in, he will see a navigation interface with a Login button, and after he logs in, the button text changes to show Logout and shows the account name of the current logged-in user in parentheses.

The changes to the program will actually be very simple because we will install some prebuilt software that will add session support to our application. Once the session software is installed, we will add a few lines to use the session to indicate whether the user is logged in.

We will start with the previous example (*ae-08-login*), and after we make all the changes, we end up with *ae-09-session* from the sample applications that come with this book.

Installing the Simple Session Utility

Google Application Engine does not provide session capability, so we must add some utility code to our application. In Chapter 11, we will actually look at this code in detail as an example of the use of the memory cache.

The session utility code that supports the examples in this section can be downloaded as part of the online materials for this book (see the preface for the URL).

Download and unzip the file and place it in your application in a folder called *util*, as shown in Figure 7-2.

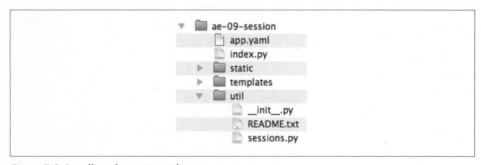

Figure 7-2. Installing the session utility

Then include the following line at the beginning of your Python program:

```
from util.sessions import Session
```

and you should be able to use the session capability throughout your application.

Using the Session to Mark Login and Logout

To access the session and log the user in when he or she provides the correct password, add the following code to the `LoginHandler()`:

```
class LoginHandler(webapp.RequestHandler):

    def get(self):
        doRender(self, 'loginscreen.htm')

    def post(self):
        self.session = Session()
        acct = self.request.get('account')
        pw = self.request.get('password')
        logging.info('Checking account='+acct+' pw='+pw)
```

```
        self.session.delete_item('username')

        if pw == '' or acct == '':
          doRender(self,'loginscreen.htm',
                {'error' : 'Please specify Acct and PW'} )
        elif pw == 'secret':
          self.session['username'] = acct
          doRender(self,'index.htm',{ } )
        else:
          doRender(self,'loginscreen.htm',
                {'error' : 'Incorrect password'} )
```

First, we must initialize the session using the `Session()` constructor. If the session already exists, the current session is retrieved; if no session exists, a session is created. Because the `Session()` call may set a cookie in the response when a new session is created, it is important to call `Session()` before any other output is produced.

Once we have the session, it operates much like a Python dictionary. We can set a key in the session using the following syntax:

```
        self.session['username'] = acct
```

A key can be any string; in this example, we use `'username'` as the key and the contents of the entry is the actual username (like "csev") of the logged-in user. When there is nothing stored in session under the `'username'` key, we assume that the user is not logged in.

To remove an entry from the session, we can again treat it like a Python dictionary. First, we check to see whether the key is in the dictionary, and if it is in the dictionary, we delete the entry using the built-in Python `del()` function.

```
        if 'username' in self.session:
            del self.session['username']
```

The session object that we are using for this program has a convenience method to automatically do this check and delete a key. It is called `delete_item()`:

```
        self.session.delete_item('username')
```

So the high-level result of the login process is that we end up with either the `'username'` entry in the session to contain the logged-in user's name or an empty `'username'` entry to indicate that no one is logged in.

To log the user out, we will create a new URL `'/logout'` and make a new handler called `LogoutHandler` to remove the `'username'` key from the session and log the user out.

First, we add a new route to the `main()` setup routine and route the `'/logout'` URL to the `LogoutHandler`:

```
        def main():
          application = webapp.WSGIApplication([
            ('/login', LoginHandler),
            ('/logout', LogoutHandler),
            ('/.*', MainHandler)],
```

```
        debug=True)
    wsgiref.handlers.CGIHandler().run(application)
```

The code for `LogoutHandler` is very basic:

```
class LogoutHandler(webapp.RequestHandler):

    def get(self):
        self.session = Session()
        self.session.delete_item('username')
        doRender(self, 'index.htm')
```

In the `get()` method, we retrieve the session and remove the `'username'` entry from the session.

Effectively, when there is a `'username'` value in session, we assume that the user is logged in, and when there is no `'username'` key in session, we assume that the user is not yet logged in.

Changing the User Interface for a Logged-In User

It is very common for a user interface to change based on whether you are logged in. Figure 7-3 shows our application before and after login.

When we are logged in, the Login link turns into a Logout link and shows the current logged-in user in parentheses. To make this happen, we can make a change to our _base.htm_ file, which contains our navigation:

```
        <li><a href="topics.htm"
            {% ifequal path '/topics.htm' %}
                class="selected"
            {% endifequal %}
            >Topics</a></li>
    {% if username %}
        <li><a href="/logout">Logout ({{username}})</a></li>
    {% else %}
        <li><a href="/login"
            {% ifequal path '/login' %}
                class="selected"
            {% endifequal %}
            >Login</a></li>
    {% endif %}
    </ul>
</div>
```

This simple if-then-else logic in the _base.htm_ template generates the Login link when `username` is empty and generates the Logout link when the user is logged in. Make sure to add `class="selected"` when on the "/login" page.

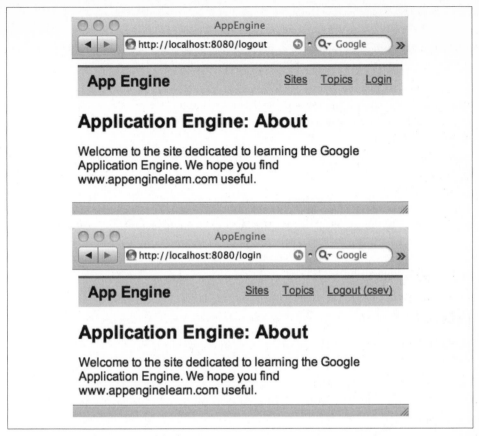

Figure 7-3. Navigation changed for login

In order to pass in the `username` variable to our templates, we will update our `doRender()` function to add the new variable to the dictionary, which we pass to the render process as follows:

```
def doRender(handler, tname = 'index.htm', values = { }):
  temp = os.path.join(
      os.path.dirname(__file__),
      'templates/' + tname)
  if not os.path.isfile(temp):
    return False

  # Make a copy of the dictionary
  newval = dict(values)
  newval['path'] = handler.request.path
  handler.session = Session()
  if 'username' in handler.session:
    newval['username'] = handler.session['username']

  outstr = template.render(temp, newval)
```

```
handler.response.out.write(outstr)
return True
```

We get the current session and then, if the user is logged in, we copy the username from the session into the dictionary, which we pass into the template.render() call.

This completes the changes to have our users actually log in when they provide the appropriate account and password. In the next chapter, we use the Google Datastore to create real user accounts with real passwords and allow the user to have some password other than *secret*.

Summary

This chapter covers cookies and sessions and how to use sessions in applications to associate data in the server with a particular browser across multiple request/response cycles. Sessions are used to track per-user data for the web application. A very common use of a session is to keep track of whether a user is logged in, as well as the identity of the currently logged-in user.

Exercises

1. What is the difference between a cookie and a session?
2. Why don't we store information like the current logged-in user's name or current bank balance in a cookie?
3. Why might it be OK to store a user's "shopping cart" in a cookie instead of a session?
4. Why might a web developer prefer to store data in a cookie instead of a session when the user is not yet logged in?
5. How are HTTP headers separated from the HTML document in an HTTP response?
6. What is the HTTP header that sets a cookie in an HTTP response?
7. What happens when a server sends out a response with one value for a cookie, and then in a later response, the same server sets the same cookie to a different value?
    a. The whole Internet crashes with an error of "non-unique cookie found."
    b. The old value of the cookie is unchanged.
    c. The new value of the cookie overwrites the old value of the cookie.
    d. The two values are concatenated together with two colon characters (::).
8. What header is used to send back cookie information to the server on an HTTP request (GET or POST)?

9. Assume that in three successive HTTP responses, the server sets cookie A to 10, cookie B to 100, and cookie C to "hello there." On the next GET request, which cookie is sent back with the HTTP request?

    a. No cookies are sent back because once the server attempts to set more than one cookie, the browser turns off cookies for the site.

    b. The C cookie is sent back because it is the most recent.

    c. The A cookie is sent back because it was the first.

    d. All three cookies are sent back.

    e. The Internet crashes with an error of "The Internet just ran out of cookie space."

10. What is the most common data stored in a session?

11. How does a website such as Flickr.com know who you are even after your laptop is restarted? What does this mean if your laptop is stolen?

12. What Python data structure is usually used to store session information (dictionary, list, string, or integer)? Why is this a good data structure for session information?

13. Why is it necessary to call Session() before any output is generated?

14. (Advanced) What if a user turns off cookies in her browser—how could we still have support for a session?

## CHAPTER 8

App Engine Datastore

When using Google App Engine, we do not have access to a traditional relational database such as Oracle, MySQL, or SQLite. Instead, we have access to the Google Datastore, which takes more of a hierarchical object-oriented storage approach. The Google Datastore is based on Google's Bigtable technology; go to *http://labs.google.com/papers/bigtable.html* for more information.

The focus of Bigtable and the Google Datastore is to achieve efficient application scalability within the Google cloud, given the dynamic and distributed nature of the Google production infrastructure.

For users who are familiar with relational databases, the Google Datastore will seem somewhat different. Beginning users may find that the Google Datastore is much simpler to get started with than a relational database would be. If you learn the App Engine Datastore first and then switch to relational databases, you might find relational databases a bit clunky compared to the App Engine Datastore.

The Google App Engine Datastore, much like with templates, uses syntax similar to the approach that Django uses to describe its Models.

We will explore basic use of the Datastore by modifying our application to allow users to create real accounts with real passwords and store those user accounts in the Datastore.

The Model-View-Controller Pattern

Now that we are adding some data storage to our application, it is time to revisit the Model-View-Controller (MVC) pattern.

To review, the MVC pattern breaks the code in a web application into three basic areas:

Model
    The persistent data that we keep in the datastore

View

The HTML, CSS, and so on that bring about the look and feel of the application (i.e., the templates and static files in our application)

Controller

The code that does the sequencing and decision making (i.e., the handlers in *index.py*)

The idea is to partition your application into these three areas and be disciplined about adding new functionality in the proper place.

We can look at how information flows from the browser to the controller, which makes use of the Model and/or View and then produces a response that it sends back to the browser, as shown in Figure 8-1.

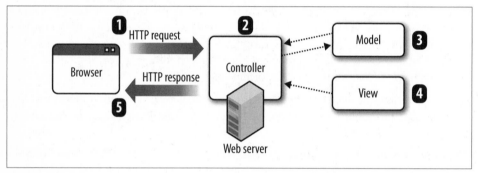

Figure 8-1. Model-View-Controller

The controller orchestrates all of the other activities. The controller receives the incoming HTTP request, handles the session, makes any Datastore changes, and then selects the view, renders the view, and sends back the HTTP response.

When the controller is working with the Model, sometime there is some new data from input that needs to be put into the Model, and sometimes there is some data that needs to be retrieved, even while processing a single HTTP request.

Defining Models

Before we can make new accounts, we need to define the data model for each User to be stored in the Datastore. To define the User model, we create a Python class that extends the db.Model class. We list the data elements that make up the object in the class. For each data element, we name the variable and specify its type. Add the following import statement to the beginning of *index.py*:

```
from google.appengine.ext import db
```

Then add a class that defines the User model in *index.py*. This is typically done at the beginning of the file, just after the import statements:

```
# A Model for a User
class User(db.Model):
  account = db.StringProperty()
  password = db.StringProperty()
  name = db.StringProperty()
```

This example is a User model with three string data elements (account, password, and name).

Adding a New Account Form

Now that we have model that we can use to store User accounts in the App Engine Datastore, we need a New Account screen so that users can create their accounts. Later, we will also add a feature to list all user accounts.

First, we need to add a New Account button so that the user can get to the new account screen from the login screen, as shown in Figure 8-2.

Figure 8-2. Adding a new account

We edit the *loginscreen.htm* template to add the New Account button and to use the onclick event of the button to run a bit of JavaScript to switch to the New Account screen at the */apply* URL as follows:

```
{% extends "_base.htm" %}
{% block bodycontent %}
    <h2>Please Log In</h2>
    <p>
    Please enter your id and password to log in to this site.
    </p>
```

```
<form method="post" action="/login">
Account: <input type="text" name="account"/> <br>
Password: <input type="password" name="password"/> <br/>
<input type="submit">
<input type="submit" value="Cancel"
   onclick="window.location='/'; return false;"/>
<input type="submit" value="New Account"
   onclick="window.location='/apply'; return false;"/>
</form>
</p>
{% if error %}
 <p>
{{ error }}
</p>
{% endif %}
{% endblock %}
```

The remainder of *loginscreen.htm* is unchanged from the previous example.

Adding a User Account

When the user clicks the New Account button, she will be routed to a screen designed for users to apply for a new account, as shown in Figure 8-3.

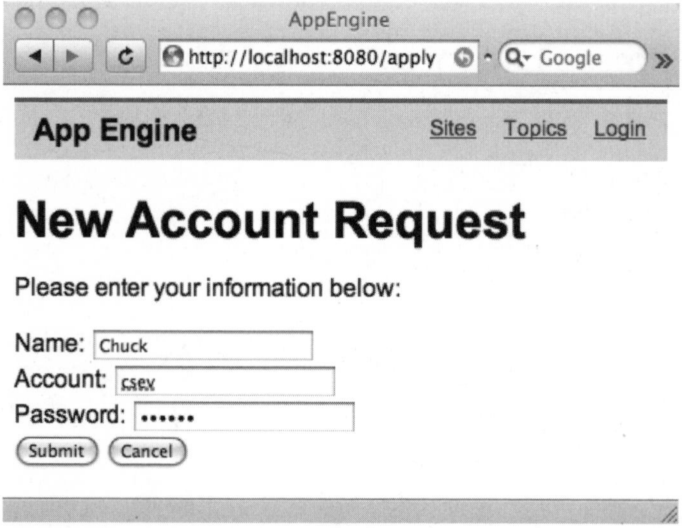

Figure 8-3. New account screen

We create a new template called *applyscreen.htm* to produce a form that takes three data values from the user and posts data to the */apply* URL. This code is very similar to the code used in *loginscreen.htm*:

```
{% extends "_base.htm" %}
{% block bodycontent %}
   <h1>New Account Request</h1>
   <p>
   Please enter your information below:
   </p>
   <form method="post" action="/apply">
   Name: <input type="text" name="name"/> <br/>
   Account: <input type="text" name="account"/> <br>
   Password: <input type="password" name="password"/> <br/>
   <input type="submit" />
   <input type="submit" value="Cancel"
     onclick="window.location='/'; return false;"/>
   </form>
   </p>
   {% if error %}
   <p>
   {{ error }}
   </p>
   {% endif %}
{% endblock %}
```

Once we have created the new view in *applyscreen.htm*, we need to modify the controller by adding a new handler to display the screen on a GET request and handle the new account data that comes in on a POST request.

To display the page, we add a new route to route to main()that routes the */apply* URL to the ApplyHandler:

```
def main():
   application = webapp.WSGIApplication([
       ('/login', LoginHandler),
       ('/logout', LogoutHandler),
       ('/apply', ApplyHandler),
       ('/.*', MainHandler)],
       debug=True)
   wsgiref.handlers.CGIHandler().run(application)
```

Then we add an ApplyHandler to our *index.py* to display *applyscreen.htm* as a response to a GET request and to handle the incoming new account request when a POST request is received:

```
class ApplyHandler(webapp.RequestHandler):

   def get(self):
     doRender(self, 'applyscreen.htm')

   def post(self):
     self.session = Session()
     name = self.request.get('name')
     acct = self.request.get('account')
     pw = self.request.get('password')
     logging.info('Adding account='+acct)

     if pw == '' or acct == '' or name == '':
```

```
        doRender(
            self,
            'applyscreen.htm',
            {'error' : 'Please fill in all fields'} )
        return

    # Check whether the user already exists
    que = db.Query(User)
    que = que.filter('account =',acct)
    results = que.fetch(limit=1)

    if len(results) > 0 :
        doRender(
            self,
            'applyscreen.htm',
            {'error' : 'Account Already Exists'} )
        return

    # Create the User object and log the user in
    newuser = User(name=name, account=acct, password=pw);
    newuser.put();

    self.session['username'] = acct
    doRender(self,'index.htm',{ })
```

Before we insert the object, we first run a query to determine whether the User already exists in the Datastore, by constructing a query and trying to retrieve the object.

db.Query(User) produces a generic query of the User objects; then we add a filter to the query that instructs the query to return only User objects whose account field matches the account value from the application form.

Then we call fetch() to retrieve the objects(s). As we are only wondering whether an object exists, we tell fetch() to limit the query to a single User object (limit=1). Because we are trying to add a new user, the normal case is that there are no matching User objects. If there is one or more User objects, the account already exists, so we return an error message to the user.

If the account does not exist in the Datastore, we construct a new User object with the three values that came in from the form, and use put() to store the new object in the Datastore.[*]

This is a simple example to get started. To be more robust, we should enclose the put() in a try/except block, in case there is a problem with inserting the object. Also there is a "race condition" whereby an object might get inserted during the very short time between when we do the check and when we actually insert the object.

---

[*] In a real application, you do not store the plain-text password. Typically, the password is encoded for storage in a database. This is why the administrators of systems can change your password to something new, but usually cannot look up your existing password.

Also, after the User object is successfully inserted, we also automatically log the user in by storing the account name into the session under the username key and rendering the main page (*index.htm*) as the HTTP response.

Looking Through the Datastore

Once you get the *apply.htm* screen working and you think that you have added a user to the Datastore, you can verify this by looking directly at the Datastore through the Google App Engine Development Console.

The Development Console allows you to manipulate the Datastore without writing an application. This feature is quite useful while you are developing your programs, as it allows you to make sure that things are working properly.

To navigate to the Development Console, use the following URL: *http://localhost:8080/_ah/admin/*. If you are using your application hosted on Google's appspot.com servers, only the designated administrators for the application can navigate to this page. When you are running as a developer on your local computer, there are no security checks to view the Development Console, as shown in Figure 8-4.

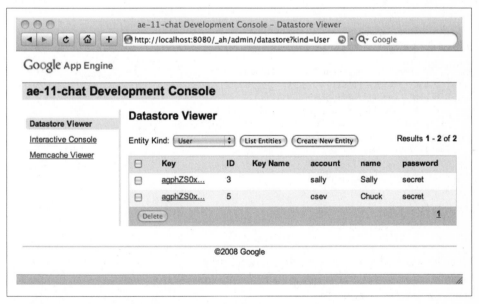

Figure 8-4. The Google App Engine Development Console

You can create, read, update, or delete instances of models in the Datastore using this interface. When you make changes in the Datastore using this interface, it is the same as if your program made the changes.

Logging In and Checking Accounts and Passwords

Now that we can insert our new User objects into the Datastore, we should retrieve them when the user tries to log in, to check whether the data on the login form matches the User data in the Datastore.

Make the following changes to the POST code in the LoginHandler to look up the user and the user's password in the Datastore:

```
Class LoginHandler(webapp.RequestHandler):

    def get(self):
        doRender(self, 'loginscreen.htm')

    def post(self):
        self.session = Session()
        acct = self.request.get('account')
        pw = self.request.get('password')
        logging.info('Checking account='+acct+' pw='+pw)

        self.session.delete_item('username')

        if pw == '' or acct == '':
            doRender(
                self,
                'loginscreen.htm',
                {'error' : 'Please specify Acct and PW'} )
            return

        # Check to see if our data is correct
        que = db.Query(User)
        que = que.filter('account =',acct)
        que = que.filter('password = ',pw)
        results = que.fetch(limit=1)

        if len(results) > 0 :
            self.session['username'] = acct
            doRender(self,'index.htm',{ } )
        else:
            doRender(
                self,
                'loginscreen.htm',
                {'error' : 'Incorrect password'} )
```

Once we verify that we have nonblank data, we construct a Query for the User model and then add filters to the query to look only for User objects that match *both* the account and password fields.

When we execute the query, we are hoping to get one result indicating that a User object exists that matches both the account and password. If a matching User object is found, we log the user in by setting the username key in the session; if no matching object is found, we return an error message.

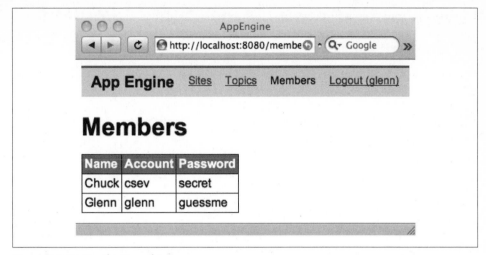

Figure 8-5. Listing the User objects

Retrieving and Displaying Many Objects

Next, we will add a feature to list all of the users who have created an account. This example will allow us to explore how to retrieve a list of Datastore objects and loop through those objects in the *memberscreen.htm* template.

To implement the new screen shown in Figure 8-5, first add a Members link to the *_base.htm* file that uses the URL */members*. We show the Members link only when the user is logged in:

```
<li><a href="topics.htm"
        {% ifequal path '/topics.htm' %}
            class="selected"
        {% endifequal %}
    >Topics</a></li>
{% if username %}
  <li><a href="/members"
        {% ifequal path '/members' %}
            class="selected"
        {% endifequal %}
    >Members</a></li>
{% endif %}
{% if username %}
  <li><a href="/login"
```

We add a corresponding `MembersHandler` controller as follows:

```
class MembersHandler(webapp.RequestHandler):

    def get(self):
        que = db.Query(User)
        user_list = que.fetch(limit=100)
        doRender(self, 'memberscreen.htm',
                    {'user_list': user_list})
```

We first construct a generic `Query` for the `User` model and then fetch the first hundred `User` objects and then pass the entire list of `User` objects to the *memberscreen.htm* template in the `user_list` render variable.

We also add a routing entry in `main()` to route the *members* URL to the `MembersHandler` as follows:

```
def main():
    application = webapp.WSGIApplication([
        ('/login', LoginHandler),
        ('/logout', LogoutHandler),
        ('/apply', ApplyHandler),
        ('/members', MembersHandler),
        ('/.*', MainHandler)],
        debug=True)
    wsgiref.handlers.CGIHandler().run(application)
```

Because each `User` object has a name, account, and password and we have many users to display, we will use an HTML table to display our member list. The rows of the table will be the users and the columns of the table will be the names, accounts, and passwords.

In the *memberscreen.htm* template, we use a `for` directive that loops through the list to generate the data rows in the HTML table:

```
{% extends "_base.htm" %}
{% block bodycontent %}
    <h1>Members</h1>
    <p>
    <table>
        <tr>
            <th>Name</th>
            <th>Account</th>
            <th>Password</th>
        </tr>
        {% for user in user_list %}
        <tr>
            <td>{{ user.name }}</td>
            <td>{{ user.account }}</td>
            <td>{{ user.password }}</td>
        </tr>
        {% endfor %}
    </table>
{% endblock %}
```

We construct a table and give it a header row. Then we use the template `for` command to loop through each `User` object in the `user_list` render variable and generate a table row for each of the elements in the list. Each row has three `td` entries for the name, account, and password.

When we complete these changes, our page shows a table with a header line and a data line for each of our two users, as shown in Figure 8-6.

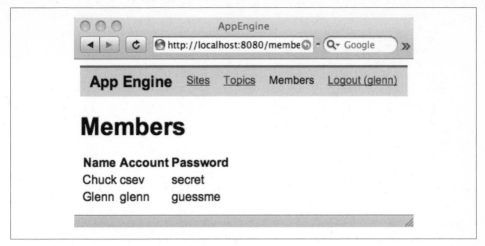

Figure 8-6. Member screen without CSS formatting

If you view the page source, you can see the generated HTML for the table:

```
<table>
    <tr>
        <th>Name</th>
        <th>Account</th>
        <th>Password</th>
    </tr>
    <tr>
        <td>Chuck</td>
        <td>csev</td>
        <td>secret</td>
    </tr>
    <tr>
        <td>Glenn</td>
        <td>glenn</td>
        <td>guessme</td>
    </tr>
</table>
```

The entire table is enclosed in a `<table>` .. `</table>` tag. Each table row is enclosed in a `<tr>` .. `</tr>` tag. The header row has column titles, which are enclosed in `<th>` .. `</th>` tags and the data rows have each data column enclosed in `<td>` .. `</td>` tags.

The structure for basic HTML tables is pretty straightforward and logical.

The default formatting of a table leaves something to be desired. Luckily, this is quite easy to fix by adding a bit of formatting to your */static/glike.css* to make the table render much more nicely:

```
table {
  border-collapse: collapse;
  border: 1px solid black;
}
```

```
th {
  text-align: left;
  border: 1px solid black;
  background: gray;
  color: white;
  padding: 0.2em;
}

td {
  border: 1px solid black;
  padding: 0.2em;
}
```

With these changes to the CSS, our Members page looks quite respectable, as you can
see in Figure 8-7.

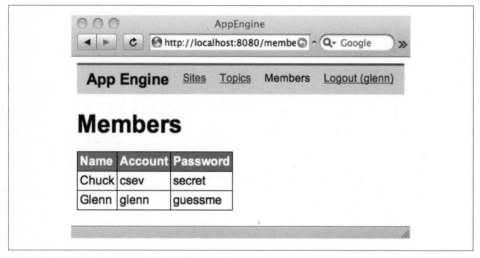

Figure 8-7. Member screen with table formatted using CSS

Now that we have modified our application to support a single Datastore model and
successfully stored User objects, we will now create another model for chat messages,
and link the ChatMessage objects to their corresponding User objects to record which
user posted each chat message.

Terminology: Different Types of Keys

Some terminology is necessary in order to describe relationships between models. The
term "keys" describes data in the models that we use to find and retrieve the right
instance of a model from the Datastore. The following terms are commonly used to
describe the different types of keys in relational databases. There are three types of keys
that we will describe:

Logical key
> What we use to look something up from the outside world; usually unique, for a model.

Primary key
> Some "random" number or string assigned by the database as the object is inserted. Primary keys are unique and opaque to the application.

Reference
> When we have a field in one model that points to the primary key of another model. A reference is also known as a *foreign key* in relational database terminology.

So far, you have seen an example of only one of these key types. The `account` field in the `User` model is the logical key for the `User` model. We use `account` in filters when we are taking input from the user forms (the "outside world") to look up the appropriate `User` object.

References Between Data Models

As our application gets more complicated, we will create multiple models. A very important part of building multiple models is how connections are made between models to define the relationships between the models. App Engine calls these connections *references* because we store a reference from one model instance to another model instance.

So let's add a multiuser chat feature to our example application. This feature will require a new model in which to store the `ChatMessage` objects. We will allow users to chat only when they are logged in, and we will record which user issued which chat message, as shown in Figure 8-8.

The data model for `ChatMessage` objects has a text variable for the message, a date variable that indicates when the message was posted, and a reference to the `User` object that posted the chat message. We could optionally store the user as a string value and store the account name ("csev" or "sally"), but a better practice is to add a reference linking each `ChatMessage` object to the corresponding `User` object.

Figure 8-8. Adding a chat feature

The following model shows how we represent a `Reference` in the `ChatMessage` model:

```
class ChatMessage(db.Model):
    user = db.ReferenceProperty()
    text = db.StringProperty()
    created = db.DateTimeProperty(auto_now=True)
```

The `ChatMessage` model includes a `user` property, which is indicated as a reference property. This model also includes a `DateTime` property that will be automatically supplied by the Datastore any time the object is updated.

Interactions Between Models

When we insert an object, the framework assigns a primary key to the object in the Datastore. Every object in the Datastore is assigned a unique key across all objects, regardless of the type of the model. When you store an object using `put()`, the key is returned to you when the `put()` is complete. If you have a variable that contains a object, you can retrieve its primary key using the `key()` method.

Take another look at the `User` model; you can see the logical key and the primary key for the model, as shown in Figure 8-9.

We do not need to indicate which of the fields is the logical key. App Engine watches our usage and essentially "figures out" which field (i.e., `account`) we are using to look up `User` objects. When App Engine notices that we are using one field more often than

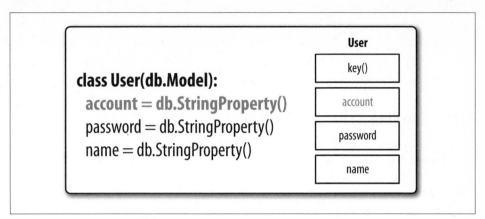

Figure 8-9. The user model and its primary key

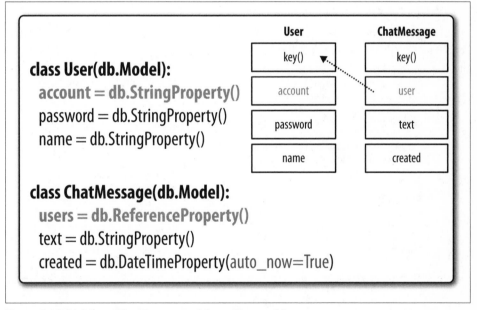

Figure 8-10. Linking a ChatMessage model to a User model

the others for lookups, the Datastore may build an index to make those lookups perform faster.

When we are going to set a reference property on one object, we need to use the primary key from the referenced object. As we build up these relationships, we create a linked network of objects, as shown in Figure 8-10.

This example shows an example of all three types of keys: (a) `account` is a logical key for the `User` model, (b) `key()` is the primary key for both models, and (c) `user` is a reference/foreign key to link a `ChatMessage` object to its corresponding `User` object.

As you build your data models and define links between them, it is often helpful to make diagrams like Figure 8-10 to keep your data model thinking organized.

Putting the Primary Key into Session

As we create new `ChatMessage` objects, we will need to have available the logged-in user's primary key to set the references in the `ChatMessage` objects before we put the objects into the Datastore. We accomplish this by storing the primary key of the currently logged-in user in the session, in addition to the account name, so the user's primary key is always available throughout the application.

We need to carefully go through and make sure that we add and remove the user key from each of the places that we add and remove the user name from the session. There are three places where we manipulate the session in this way.

We set up the session when the user logs into our application in the `post()` method of `LoginHandler`, so we make the following changes:

```
def post(self):
    self.session = Session()
    acct = self.request.get('account')
    pw = self.request.get('password')
    logging.info('Checking account='+acct+' pw='+pw)

    self.session.delete_item('username')
    self.session.delete_item('userkey')

    if pw == '' or acct == '':
      doRender(
          self,
          'loginscreen.htm',
          {'error' : 'Please specify Acct and PW'} )
      return

    que = db.Query(User)
    que = que.filter('account =',acct)
    que = que.filter('password = ',pw)

    results = que.fetch(limit=1)

    if len(results) > 0 :
      user = results[0]
      self.session['userkey'] = user.key()
      self.session['username'] = acct
      doRender(self,'index.htm',{ } )
    else:
      doRender(
          self,
```

```
'loginscreen.htm',
{'error' : 'Incorrect password'} )
```

Because our `User` object is being retrieved with a `fetch()` call, we grab the first result (i.e., `results[0]`) and get its primary key using `key()` and put the primary key into the session.

We also make a similar change to the `post()` method in `ApplyHandler`:

```
if len(results) > 0 :
  doRender(
      self,
      'applyscreen.htm',
      {'error' : 'Account Already Exists'} )
  return
# Create the User object and log the user in
newuser = User(name=name, account=acct, password=pw);
pkey = newuser.put();
self.session['username'] = acct
self.session['userkey'] = pkey
doRender(self,'index.htm',{ })
```

In this code, we are creating a new user; as we put the user in the store, the key for that particular user is returned to us from the `put()`, and we store the key in the session along with the account name of the user.

We also need to make sure to remove the `'userkey'` entry from the session when the user logs out, so we make the following change to `LogoutHandler`:

```
class LogoutHandler(webapp.RequestHandler):

  def get(self):
    self.session = Session()
    self.session.delete_item('username')
    self.session.delete_item('userkey')
    doRender(self, 'index.htm')
```

Once we have changed these three handlers to deal with both the `userkey` and `username`, the rest of the code can assume that if the user is logged in, the primary key for the corresponding `User` object is in the session under `'userkey'`.

Adding the Chat Feature

Now that we have the primary key of the logged-in user available, we can add our new chat feature. See Figure 8-11.

Figure 8-11. Chat feature

We need to add a new screen to our application, so we first create a new template called *chatscreen.htm*. It is a simple form with a chat message input area and a Submit button, which does a POST to the */chat* URL:

```
{% extends "_base.htm" %}
{% block bodycontent %}
    <h1>App Engine Chat</h1>
    <p>
    <form method="post" action="/chat">
    <input type="text" name="message" size="60"/>
    <input type="submit" name="Chat"/>
    </form>
    </p>
    {% if error %}
     <p>
     {{ error }}
     </p>
    {% endif %}
    {% for chat in chat_list %}
      <p>
        {{ chat.text }} ({{chat.user.account}})
        {{ chat.created|date:"D d M Y" }}
      </p>
    {% endfor %}
{% endblock %}
```

(At the end of the template is a `for` loop to print out the chat messages. We will describe the `for` syntax after we describe the `ChatHandler`.)

We build a new handler for the chat feature like this:

```
class ChatHandler(webapp.RequestHandler):

    # Retrieve the messages
    def get(self):
        que = db.Query(ChatMessage).order('-created');
        chat_list = que.fetch(limit=10)
        doRender(
            self,
            'chatscreen.htm',
            { 'chat_list': chat_list })
```

The template for this page (*chatscreen.htm*) needs a list of the chat messages to display. In the get() method, we use Query to retrieve to the most recent 10 chat messages and pass them to the *chatscreen.htm* template in the chat_list variable. We specify that the returned ChatMessage objects should be sorted in descending order by created date, so the most recent chat message appears first.

The variable chat_list is used by the for directive in the *chatscreen.htm* template to display the list of recent chat messages:

```
{% extends "_base.htm" %}
{% block bodycontent %}
    <h1>App Engine Chat</h1>
    <p>
    <form method="post" action="/chat">
    <input type="text" name="message" size="60"/>
    <input type="submit" name="Chat"/>
    </form>
    </p>
    {% if error %}
     <p>
     {{ error }}
     </p>
    {% endif %}
    {% for chat in chat_list %}
      <p>
        {{ chat.text }} ({{chat.user.account}})
        {{ chat.created|date:"D d M Y" }}
      </p>
    {% endfor %}
{% endblock %}
```

The for loop goes through chat_list; for each chat, it generates a paragraph that includes the chat.text, chat.user.account, and chat.created.

Note that the account name (csev) is in the account field in the User object that is referenced by the ChatMessage object. So chat.user.account can be thought of as "stepping through" the related User object to find the account name of the related User object.

The other bit of strange syntax in the previous example is changing the format of the date that is printed. The string |date:"D d M Y" formats the date value with the day of the week, day of the month, month, and year—it is formatted like "Thu 22 Nov 2008" when it is displayed. This syntax with the vertical bar is called a *filter*; it gives you the ability to control how you format the variables in the double braces. This example shows how you can format a date. Check out the Django documentation for examples of the other available filters.

The overall structure of the *chatscreen.htm* file is to show the form, then show any error messages, and then show the 10 most recent chat messages.

Continuing with the rest of the ChatHandler, the post() method is called when the user clicks the Submit button on the *chatscreen.htm* page:

```
class ChatHandler(webapp.RequestHandler):

  # Retrieve the messages
  def get(self):
    que = db.Query(ChatMessage).order('-created');
    chat_list = que.fetch(limit=10)
    doRender(
        self,
        'chatscreen.htm',
        { 'chat_list': chat_list })

  def post(self):
    self.session = Session()
    if not 'userkey' in self.session:
      doRender(
          self,
          'chatscreen.htm',
          {'error' : 'Must be logged in'} )
      return

    msg = self.request.get('message')
    if msg == '':
      doRender(
          self,
          'chat.htm',
          {'error' : 'Blank message ignored'} )
      return

    newchat = ChatMessage(user=self.session['userkey'], text=msg)
    newchat.put();
    self.get();
```

At the very start of the post() method, we check the session to make sure that we have a userkey value in the session. Because we are about to create and store a new ChatMessage object that depends on having the primary key of the currently logged-in user, we need to give the user an error if she is not currently logged in.

We also issue an error if the user clicks the Submit button without actually having entered a message.

Once we get past all of these checks, it is time to actually create the ChatMessage object and store it in the Datastore. We set the user attribute to the key of the currently logged-in user, which is retrieved from self.session['userkey']. The text attribute is set from the message field on the submitted form. Note that the created attribute is not explicitly set because the ChatMessage model definition specifies that created was to be set automatically.

By setting the user field to be the key of the currently logged-in user pulled from the session, we establish the relationship between the ChatMessage object and the related User object.

There is also one more clever trick in the post() method. At the end of the post(), after we have added the new ChatMessage object, we need to retrieve the 10 most recent chat messages and rerender the *chatscreen.htm* template. You'll see that this is exactly what the get() method does. So instead of rewriting this code, we call the get() method at the end of the post() method, as follows:

```
if msg == '':
  doRender(
      self,
      'chat.htm',
      {'error' : 'Blank message ignored'} )
  return
newchat = ChatMessage(user=self.session['userkey'], text=msg)
newchat.put();
self.get();
```

The self in self.get() refers to the currently executing instance of the ChatHandler. This is a simple pattern that allows the get() code to be reused at the end of a successful post() method.

By now, we should know the needed changes to main() to add the routing for the */chat* URL:

```
def main():
    application = webapp.WSGIApplication([
        ('/login', LoginHandler),
        ('/logout', LogoutHandler),
        ('/apply', ApplyHandler),
        ('/members', MembersHandler),
        ('/chat', ChatHandler),
        ('/.*', MainHandler)],
        debug=True)
    wsgiref.handlers.CGIHandler().run(application)
```

Also, we need to add the navigation link for the user to use the chat tool in *_base.htm*:

```
{% if username %}
  <li><a href="/chat"
        {% ifequal path '/chat' %}
            class="selected"
        {% endifequal %}
```

```
        >Chat</a></li>
    {% endif %}
```

Once we have made these changes, we should be able to launch and test our new chat feature.

Log in from two different browsers (such as Safari and Firefox) to be able to post messages from two accounts at the same time. To see new chat messages from the "other" user without posting a message, click on the Chat link in the navigation on your browser to do a GET on the */chat* URL to see the most up-to-date chat messages.

We will eliminate the need to refresh the screen to retrieve new messages and make the chat application more interactive using JavaScript and AJAX in the next chapter.

Summary

This chapter showed how we use the App Engine Datastore to store long-term data for our application. The Datastore is the equivalent of a relational database in most traditional web applications. There are some similarities and differences between a relational database, such as MySQL or Oracle, and the App Engine Datastore. The Datastore is particularly well suited for operation in a distributed, dynamic, and scalable environment such as Google App Engine.

Building models in Google App Engine is actually quite simple and is pretty intuitive. We define a model in Python and list the fields that we would like in the model and the types of our fields—App Engine takes care of the rest. There are no schemas or table structures that are needed to describe data, as are necessary when using a relational database for long-term storage.

You learned how to build and populate a single model and then how to build multiple models and make connections between multiple models using reference properties.

Exercises

1. What data was the Google Bigtable initially developed to store?
2. In the following code, what is the purpose of the string db.model?

```python
class User(db.Model):
    account = db.StringProperty()
    password = db.StringProperty()
    name = db.StringProperty()
```

3. Does the use of the word Model in the data description in Exercise 2 make sense in the context of the Model-View-Controller pattern? Why? What is the term that describes names that are easy to remember?
4. What does the following HTML code display in the browser? What happens when you click on the item? Does this generate an HTTP GET or POST request?

```
<input type="submit" value="Cancel"
    onclick="window.location='/'; return false;"/>
```

5. A fellow student in your class just added the `ApplyHandler` to his application and updated the URL routing as follows. No matter what he tries, you seem completely unable to get the navigation screen to display—even if you type in the URL by hand. The handler code looks fine. What did he do wrong and how should he fix it?

```
def main():
  application = webapp.WSGIApplication([
    ('/login', LoginHandler),
    ('/members', MembersHandler),
    ('/logout', LogoutHandler),
    ('/.*', MainHandler),
    ('/apply', ApplyHandler)],
    debug=True)
  wsgiref.handlers.CGIHandler().run(application)
```

6. In the following code, what are the three model field names and what are the variables that contain the input values that came in from the HTTP request variables?

```
newuser = User(name=name, account=acct, password=pw);
```

7. This code was included right before the application is about to create a new user account. What is the purpose of this code?

```
que = db.Query(User).filter('account =',acct)
results = que.fetch(limit=1)
```

8. What URL do you use to look through the Datastore by hand if your application is running locally and on port 8080?

9. In an HTML table, what is the tag for a "table header," which labels a column of data?

10. Why is it important to always style HTML tables in CSS?

11. What is the App Engine template directive to loop through a set of items?

12. List the three types of keys and give a definition for each.

13. How do you represent a foreign key in an App Engine data model? How do you set the key in your Python code?

14. What method call do you use to retrieve the primary key of an instance of a model?

15. If you are creating a new instance of a model, what method must be called on that new instance before the primary key is defined?

16. Draw a data model showing primary, logical, and foreign keys for a `Person` object and an `Address` object, for which each person has a single address.

17. (Advanced) Find and fix the security error in the `get()` method in the `ChatHandler()`. The reported bug is that users can see the chat messages without logging in by simply hand-navigating to the /chat URL. Reproduce the error and then fix the error.

CHAPTER 9

JavaScript, jQuery, and AJAX

In this chapter, we improve the interactivity of our application using some simple AJAX (Asynchronous JavaScript and XML) support to our application. AJAX allows us to update parts of the screen. Increasing use of AJAX allows web applications to approach the rich flexibility of Desktop applications.

If you look at the Chat screen, you'll see an area that changes with each screen refresh and an area that stays constant with each screen refresh, as shown in Figure 9-1.

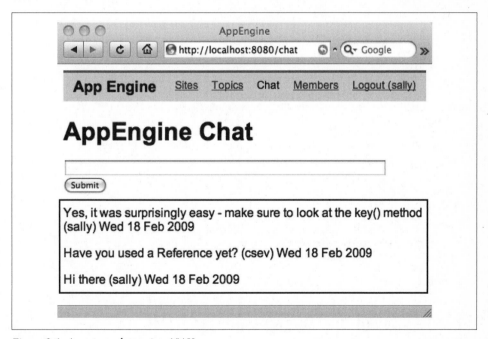

Figure 9-1. Area to update using AJAX

We will use AJAX to update the outlined area without updating the overall screen.

jQuery

AJAX has been evolving since Microsoft introduced the first form of AJAX (XMLHttpRequest) in 1999. In the early days, AJAX and JavaScript and the browsers' support for the Document Object Model (DOM) were very much in flux, and it took quite a bit of effort to keep one's AJAX code working across successive releases of many browsers.

As widely used applications such as Google Mail made increasing use of AJAX, browsers' support for AJAX improved over time. Also, libraries were produced that shielded the typical developer from cross-browser differences. These two trends together have made the use of AJAX relatively straightforward and something that can be integrated into a wide range of applications to improve the usability of those applications.

One of the more popular of these AJAX/JavaScript libraries is called jQuery, which is available from *http://jquery.com*. To add jQuery to your application, download the jQuery JavaScript code and install it in your */static* folder as shown in Figure 9-2.

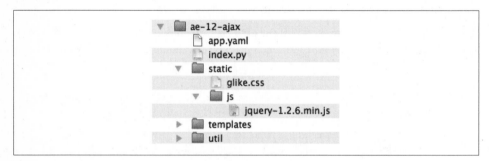

Figure 9-2. Adding the jQuery library to your application

Then edit your */templates/_base.htm* file to include the jQuery library:

```
<!DOCTYPE html PUBLIC "-//W3C//DTD XHTML 1.0 Strict//EN"
 "http://www.w3.org/TR/xhtml1/DTD/xhtml1-strict.dtd">
<html xmlns="http://www.w3.org/1999/xhtml">
 <head>
   <title>App Engine - HTML</title>
   <link href="/static/glike.css" rel="stylesheet" type="text/css" />
   <script type="text/javascript"
           src="/static/js/jquery-1.2.6.min.js"></script>
 </head>
 <body>
```

Create a View of the Chat Messages in HTML

Because we will be replacing a portion of our page, we need a URL that will generate an HTML fragment consisting of the chat messages. We don't want any header information or body tags—we just want a fragment of HTML.

Create a template in *messagelist.htm* that looks like this:

```
{% for chat in chat_list %}
  <p>
      {{ chat.text }} ({{ chat.user.account }})
      {{ chat.created|date:"D d M Y" }}
  </p>
{% endfor %}
```

This *messagelist.htm* template does not extend the *_base.htm* file. It will not generate the HTML for the header or navigation. This is simply the `for` loop that we used to display the chat messages in the *chatscreen.htm* template in the previous version of the program.

We also need to add a new route mapping the */messages* URL to our `MessagesHandler()`:

```
def main():
    application = webapp.WSGIApplication([
        ('/login', LoginHandler),
        ('/logout', LogoutHandler),
        ('/apply', ApplyHandler),
        ('/members', MembersHandler),
        ('/chat', ChatHandler),
        ('/messages', MessagesHandler),
        ('/.*', MainHandler)],
        debug=True)
    wsgiref.handlers.CGIHandler().run(application)
```

The code in the `MessagesHandler()` is very simple—it retrieves the messages from the Datastore and passes the message list into the *messagelist.htm* template:

```
class MessagesHandler(webapp.RequestHandler):

    def get(self):
      que = db.Query(ChatMessage).order('-created');
      chat_list = que.fetch(limit=100)
      doRender(self, 'messagelist.htm', {'chat_list': chat_list})
```

This code is moved from the `ChatHandler get()` method in the previous version of the program. Because the *chatscreen.htm* template no longer displays the list of messages, there is no need to retrieve the list of chat messages and place them in the render variables when rendering the *chatscreen.htm* template.

Removing the message retrieval code from the `ChatHandler` leaves the `get()` method, which is very simple:

```
class ChatHandler(webapp.RequestHandler):

    def get(self):
      doRender(self, 'chatscreen.htm')

    def post(self):
      self.session = Session()
      # ...
```

Once the `MessagesHandler()` and routing for the */messages* URL is in place, we can navigate to the */messages* URL and see our HTML fragment. Make sure that you have logged in and have a few chat messages in the Datastore. You should see something similar to Figure 9-3.

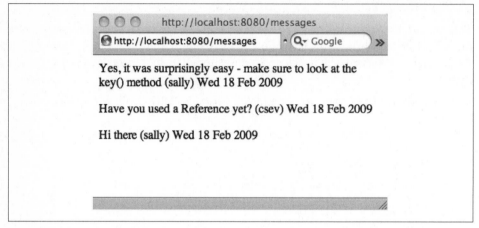

Figure 9-3. Looking at the HTML used by AJAX

Remember that as this is an HTML fragment and does not extend *_base.htm*, the chat messages render with no header, navigation, or anything beyond the HTML fragment that contains the messages.[*]

We can view the source of the generated message list page to verify this:

```
<p>
    Yes, it was surprisingly easy - make sure
    to look at the key() method (sally)
    Wed 18 Feb 2009
</p>
<p>
    Have you used a Reference yet? (csev)
    Wed 18 Feb 2009
</p>
<p>
    Hi there (sally)
    Wed 18 Feb 2009
</p>
```

It is simply an HTML fragment. Now we will edit *chatscreen.htm* and add the Java-Script/AJAX code to replace the contents of a `<div>` with our newly minted HTML fragment.

---

[*] Technically the term for this is not AJAX (Asynchronous JavaScript and XML); when we retrieve HTML fragments and use them directly, it is called AHAH (Asynchronous HTML and HTTP).

Asynchronously Updating a <div> Using AJAX

In this section, we show you how to do one of the simplest AJAX operations using the jQuery library: periodically replace the contents of a named `<div>` with data retrieved from a URL.

We modify the *chatscreen.htm* file to remove the code that displayed the list of chat messages and replace it with a named `<div>` and some JavaScript/AJAX/jQuery code:

```
{% extends "_base.htm" %}
{% block bodycontent %}
    <h1>App Engine Chat</h1>
    <p>
    <form method="post" action="/chat">
    <input type="text" name="message" size="60"/>
    <input type="submit" name="Chat"/>
    </form>
    </p>
    {% ifnotequal error None %}
     <p>
     {{ error }}
     </p>
    {% endifnotequal %}
    <div id="chatcontent">
        Loading...
    </div>
<script>
function updateMsg() {
  $.ajax({
    url: "/messages",
    cache: false,
    success: function(html){
      $("#chatcontent").html(html);
    }
  });
    setTimeout('updateMsg()', 4000);
}
updateMsg();
</script>
{% endblock %}
```

There are two important sections to this code. The first section:

```
<div id="chatcontent">
        Loading...
</div>
```

defines a `div` tag that indicates where in the document to place our HTML fragment. We give the `div` tag a CSS `id` and include some default text that will show up in the browser until the HTML fragment is successfully retrieved. Another common approach is to put an animated GIF image that appears to rotate in the `div`—this image then displays until the `div` is replaced.

The second bit of code is some jQuery and JavaScript. At first glance, it looks a little complex, but it is actually pretty simple and easily adapted to many similar uses:

```
<script>
function updateMsg() {
  $.ajax({
    url: "/messages",
    cache: false,
    success: function(html){
      $("#chatcontent").html(html);
    }
  });
  setTimeout('updateMsg()', 4000);
}
updateMsg();
</script>
```

This JavaScript code creates a JavaScript function called `updateMsg`. In the `updateMsg` function, we make a jQuery AJAX call to retrieve the HTML fragment at */messages*. Once jQuery has received the fragment (`success:`) we use the fragment to replace the HTML contents of the `chatcontent` `<div>`.

After the text is retrieved and placed in the `chatcontent` div, we set a timer to call ourselves back every four seconds (4,000 milliseconds).

Once this is complete and you navigate to the */chat* page, you should see the same page that you saw in the previous application (Figure 9-4).

Figure 9-4. Our completed AJAX chat

The difference is that now the bottom half is being retrieved using AJAX. You may even see the "Loading..." message flash for a moment when the page first draws and before the chat messages are retrieved via AJAX and the div is replaced.

And more importantly, if you open two browsers (i.e., Safari and Firefox) and log in as two different users at the same time, you can actually chat; within four seconds, both windows will asynchronously update and show new messages—even if you are halfway through typing your next message.

If you watch the log for a while, you can see the browser requesting the /messages URL repeatedly every four seconds through AJAX, as shown in Figure 9-5.

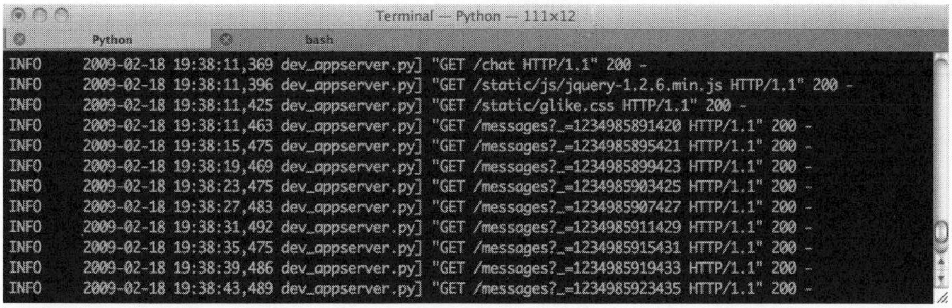

Figure 9-5. Watching AJAX requests in the log

The jQuery library automatically appends a timestamp to the URL to make sure that the browser does not mistakenly cache the URL (thanks, jQuery).

Summary

This chapter explained how to use some simple AJAX and JavaScript to independently update an area of the page instead of the entire page. In addition, we can update a portion of the page in the background using a timer to simulate the appearance of pushed information.

This approach allows us to enhance the usability of our application and make it seem more desktop-like—it is a very simple use of AJAX and JavaScript and only scratches the surface of the usefulness of these technologies for your web application.

Exercises

1. What is the primary value of using the jQuery library instead of writing your own JavaScript?
2. What company created the innovation by which the browser could make HTTP requests from within JavaScript?

3. Why don't we extend the base template in the *messagelist.htm* template?

4. How do websites make the spinning "Loading" image appear while AJAX requests are being processed?

5. What does the following code accomplish?

```
setTimeout('updateMsg()', 4000);
```

6. When you monitor the log while the AJAX chat is running, you see many messages of this form:

```
GET /messages?_=1235418059929 HTTP/1.1
```

What is the purpose of the long random number at the end of the URL?

7. What HTML attribute is typically used to identify areas within the HTML that can be replaced in AJAX? Why is this a good attribute to use for this purpose?

8. (Advanced) Your application has a bug, in that users can manually navigate to the */messages* URL and see messages even when they are not logged in. Reproduce the problem, figure out why it occurs, and then fix the problem in the code and verify that your corrected version indeed works (make sure that users cannot see messages until they have logged in).

## CHAPTER 10

Running Your Application on the Google Infrastructure

Noah Botimer

This chapter describes how to move from local development to hosting your application on the App Engine infrastructure. It covers the fundamentals of establishing an App Engine account, monitoring their health in the Application Console (this is what I call the page which is the collection of things like Dashboard, Logs, Data Viewer, and so on), and managing versions of your applications.

Application Engine Accounts

Google makes a basic level of App Engine service available to anyone at no charge. If your application exceeds the limits for bandwidth, storage, or computation on your free accounts, you can upgrade to a pay plan and scale your application as far as you like.

All that is required to get started is a Google account and the ability to receive an SMS (text) activation message.

To set up your App Engine account, start by visiting the App Engine developer's site: *http://appengine.google.com*. If you do not already have a Google account, you can create one there with an existing email address or create a Gmail account here (which will allow you to log into the Application Console): *http://mail.google.com*.

To create your first application, you will be required to verify your account by mobile phone. You will receive an SMS message with a verification code; enter the code during the application process. After verifying your account, you will be allowed to create applications to be hosted on Google's servers.

Creating an Application on App Engine

Each application is given a hostname on appspot.com, like tsugiproject.appspot.com, which corresponds to the `application` field from *app.yaml*. This is called the Application Identifier; it may not be changed for an application. Currently, accounts are limited to 10 applications. Google does not yet allow applications to be deleted, so you should take care to not use up all your applications.

Creating a new application is simple. From the Application Console, click the "Create an Application" button. You will need to specify a few basic items to finish creating your app:

- The Application Identifier (App ID), which must be unique and not already in use.
- The Application Title, which will be displayed in places like the login screen.
- (Optional) The authentication mode, which, if your application uses the Users API, will decide whether your application is available to the public (those with Google accounts), or restricted to a specific Google Apps domain.

In this sample, we are creating an application to house the AJAX chat program from the book.

In Figure 10-1, we have chosen an available Application Identifier (*ae-12-ajax*), given the application a title, and left the authentication settings at the defaults. After clicking Save, we get the success page, when the application is created.

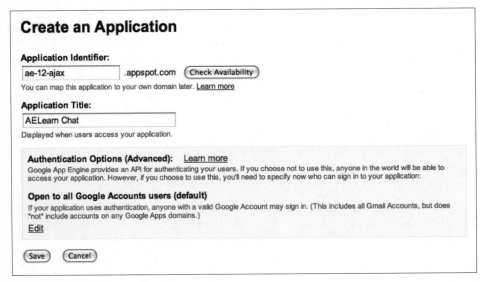

Figure 10-1. Creating a new application

At this point, the application is registered, but there is nothing uploaded.

Uploading Your Application

After ensuring that the Application Identifier is correct in *app.yaml*, we can upload our application:

```
application: ae-12-ajax
version: 1
runtime: python
api_version: 1
```

We use *appcfg.py* to upload applications to App Engine. The simplest form is to use the update command with the directory of your application. You will be prompted for your account information. After entering your email address and password (which will not be shown), everything will be uploaded in one step:

```
golabki:~/Desktop/appeng botimer$ ls
ae-12-ajax
golabki:~/Desktop/appeng botimer$ appcfg.py update ae-12-ajax/
Email: noahbotimer@gmail.com
Password for noahbotimer@gmail.com:
Saving authentication cookies to /Users/botimer/.appcfg_cookies
Scanning files on local disk.
Initiating update.
Cloning 2 static files.
Cloning 12 application files.
Uploading 12 files.
Closing update.
Uploading index definitions.
golabki:~/Desktop/appeng botimer$
```

You may notice that the *appcfg.py* script saves authentication cookies, which allows you to issue repeated commands without logging in each time. You can use the --no-cookies option to disable this behavior if you prefer.

Testing Your Application

Once *appcfg.py* finishes uploading and you are returned to the command prompt, the application will be live. You can verify that your application is up and running by simply visiting it in your browser at *http://ae-12-ajax.appspot.com*. Figure 10-2 shows the application running at *appspot.com*.

You can continue to run your local version of your application with the SDK and use update when you are ready to upload changes. If you don't change the version number in *app.yaml*, your changes will be made live immediately. When you are developing your application and are not formally in production, it is good practice to leave the version number unchanged when you upload new versions.

Figure 10-2. Our application on Google's infrastructure

Logs, Statistics, and Other Features

You can view the Application Console for your application at *http://appengine.google* *.com*, logging in with your Google Account, and selecting your application.

Within the Application Console, you may view various types of logging, usage, and administrative data. The Dashboard page presents an overview, including charts showing request traffic, bandwidth and CPU usage, and errors over time. You can also track which parts of your application are responsible for the most load. Figure 10-3 shows a snapshot of our personal code review app's Dashboard after just a few requests.

As your application is used over time, the Dashboard can help you tune performance and locate possible bugs. You can also use the Logs and Admin Logs to keep find more information on application and management events, respectively.

In addition to the information about your code and application events, the Data Viewer page provides diagnostics and direct access to your Datastore entities and indexes. From the Data Viewer, you can browse entities and issue Datastore queries to examine your production data, as shown in Figure 10-4.

If you have done the wise thing and added logging messages to your application, they will come in handy when you're trying to understand what is going on in your application when it is running on appspot.com. The Logs page looks somewhat different than the log that you watch when running applications on your desktop.

You have the ability to search and filter the log messages to help deal with the potential mountain of log messages, as shown in Figure 10-5.

You can see the message for creating the new session as well as the message indicating that a new account was created.

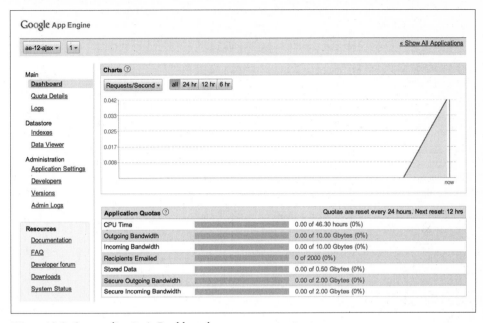

Figure 10-3. Our application's Dashboard

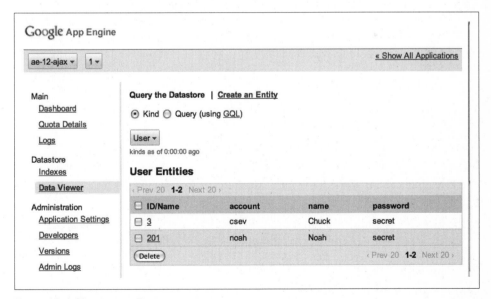

Figure 10-4. Viewing our Datastore

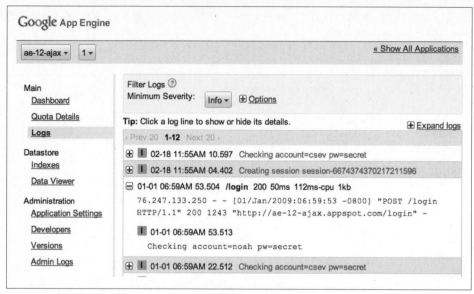

Figure 10-5. Viewing the logs for our application

Uploading New Versions

When developing an application that people actively use, it is important that changes are "pushed" to the users only when they are tested and ready for deployment. App Engine allows you to upload multiple versions of your application and activate them when ready or to roll them back if needed. If we make some changes to our application and want to test them out on App Engine but do not want to affect other users, we can modify the `version` field in *app.yaml*:

```
application: ae-12-ajax
version: 2
runtime: python
api_version: 1
```

After the number is changed, all we have to do is issue another update with *appcfg.py*. When the upload is finished, the new version will not be the default for your regular users, so their experience will not be disrupted. Visiting the Application Console and selecting Versions will show all of the active versions of your app, as shown in Figure 10-6.

In the Live URI column, you can retrieve a direct link to any version of the application to test it. When you are comfortable that your users should be served a given version by default, you can select it and click Make Default.

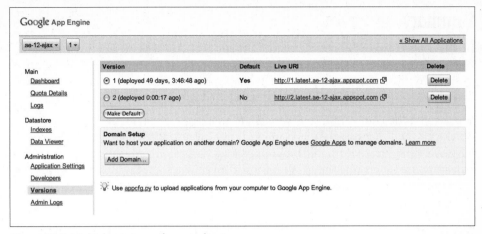

Figure 10-6. Multiple versions of our application

Collaboration on Applications

When working on some projects, it is important for multiple people to be able to upload updates to your application on App Engine. It is very easy to allow this. From the Application Console Developers page, you can invite other Google accounts, which will let them collaborate on the application. Here is the screen where the current developers are listed; you can send an invitation to a colleague (Figure 10-7).

Figure 10-7. Adding collaborators to our application

Summary

In this chapter, we explored the basics of managing App Engine applications on the Google infrastructure at appspot.com. We walked through the steps of setting up an account. With an account in place, we looked at how applications can easily be added and maintained with *appcfg.py* and the web-based Application Console.

We covered the core administrative tasks of uploading apps, managing versions and developers, and checking the diagnostics of applications. With these fundamentals, we have everything ready to publish our apps and start taking advantage of the Google infrastructure for hosting them. We have also given you some familiarity with the core components needed to allow experimentation with more advanced features.

Exercises

1. How does Google verify your identity when you apply to use Google's App Engine?
2. If you were to create an application named "hazcheez" and upload your application to *appspot.com*, what would the URL for your application be?
3. What is the relationship between the application identifier in your *app.yaml* file and the application identifier in Google's hosting environment?
4. How do you add more developers to the team that is supporting the production environment for your production application?

## CHAPTER 11

Memory Cache

When Google examined the usability of the Google Search service, it found that one of the factors that most influences the usability of a web application is speed. Users prefer web applications that are faster to equivalent applications that are slower. Over the years, Google has learned how to make web applications run fast, even when millions of users are accessing those applications. One approach to increasing the speed of a web application is to use a distributed memory cache for storage, instead of retrieving commonly used data from disk.

When you put information into the Datastore, your information is stored permanently and is stored somewhere in the cloud on disks and backed up and maintained even when your application is not in use.

The memory cache is spread across the memory of all the instances of your application in the cloud (Figure 11-1). It is also possible to have dedicated memory cache servers. Because the memory cache is "temporary," it does not have to be stored on disk or backed up. This makes the memory cache much faster then the Datastore.

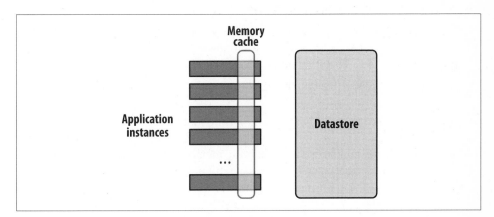

Figure 11-1. The memory cache and Datastore

The memory cache is based on a product called "memcached," which provides a high-speed distributed cache in a number of languages. The memcached software uses the network to keep all of the copies of the data in sync. When the data is updated in one of the servers, those updates are communicated to all of the other servers participating in the memory cache: *http://www.danga.com/memcached/*.

As a user of Google App Engine, you do not have to worry about how the memory cache works internally. All you have to know is how to use the memory cache. And you must know the rules of the memory cache in order to use it properly.

The Rules of Memory Cache

The most basic rule of the memory cache is that nothing in the memory cache is guaranteed. The memory cache gives you its best effort to give your data back to you when requested. When you put data in the cache, you indicate how long you would like to keep the data in the cache. You could, for example, ask that your data be stored for an hour (3,600 seconds). However, if your application instances run low on memory, they might throw away your data in a few seconds to free up some memory.

This setup may seem at first to make the memory cache pretty much useless. However, if your application is not running low on memory, the likelihood that the memory cache will lose your data is very small. This permission to lose data once in a great while is what makes the memory cache so blazingly fast. It also means that for really precious data, you cannot simply store a copy in the memory cache. You must also keep a copy of the data in the Datastore.

It turns out that there is often a great deal of data in a scalable web application for which we will happily accept the compromise of the memory cache. There are many data elements that can be reconstructed if their contents are lost once in a while. Also, there is data such as "number of currently logged-in users" that does not have to be perfect.

The other rules of memory cache are as follows:

- There is one memory cache shared across your application instances. If you store data on one instance, it is available to all instances. If you delete data from one instance, it is deleted from all instances.
- The memory cache operates like a gigantic distributed Python dictionary. Each item in the cache has a unique key.
- Each item in the cache has an expiration time that can range from a few seconds up to a month. You can omit the lifetime and the cache will keep the object as long as it can. The typical lifetime of data in the memory cache is somewhere between 10 seconds and several hours. You can extend the lifetime by replacing the object in the cache and specifying a new lifetime.

Put into the memory cache items that make sense there. Its size is not infinite, so you should put items in the memory cache that are moderately small with a good chance of being reused.

Using the Memory Cache

Using the memory cache is pretty straightforward. You treat it like a really large Python dictionary. Here is a very simple program that demonstrates the use of the memory cache:

```
from google.appengine.api import memcache

x = memcache.get("1234")
if x is None:
    print "Nothing found in key 1234"
else:
  print "Found key 1234"
  print x

x = memcache.get("7890")
if x is None:
    print "Nothing found in key 7890"
else:
  print "Found key 7890"
  print x

y = { 'a': 'hello', 'b': 'world' }
memcache.add("7890", y, 3600)

x = memcache.get("7890")
if x is None:
    print "Nothing found in key 7890"
else:
  print "Found key 7890"
  print x

z = { 'l': 'more', 'n': 'stuff' }
memcache.replace("7890", y, 3600)
print "7890 replaced"
```

Note that the values in curly braces are Python dictionary constants. These constants consist of a set of keys and values that make up the dictionary.

The first time you run the program, the output will be as follows:

```
Nothing found in key 1234
Nothing found in key 7890
Found key 7890
{'a': 'hello', 'b': 'world'}
7890 replaced
```

If you then run the program again a moment later, the output will be as follows:

```
Nothing found in key 1234
Found key 7890
{'a': 'hello', 'b': 'world'}
Found key 7890
{'a': 'hello', 'b': 'world'}
```

The second time the program runs, the data stored at key 7890 is still there from the previous execution. The memory cache is persistent until your application is restarted, the entries expire, you explicitly clear the cache, or your application starts running low on memory.

Using the Application Console to Examine Memory Cache

You are probably wondering about where your memory cache data is going. Perhaps you might run a bit of Python code in App Engine without writing a bunch of HTML, an *index.py*, some templates, an *app.yaml*, and some URL routing code.

There is a nice application console that lets you interact with your running application as long as you are an administrator for the application. The application console is available at the following URL: *http://localhost:8080/_ah/admin*.

In Figure 11-2, the interactive console is used to run a snippet of code *within* your running application. When this code runs, it is equivalent to having the code run in your *index.py* file. If the code executed in the interactive console makes changes to the memory cache, it is really changed.

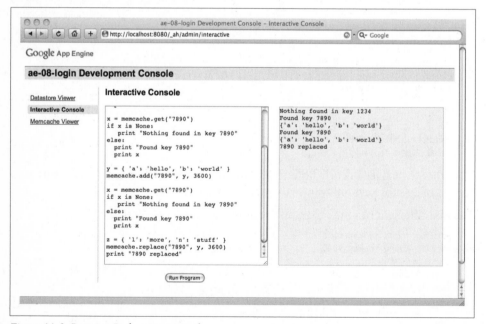

Figure 11-2. Running Python interactively

The application console has a Datastore viewer and a memory cache viewer. For now, let's take a look at the memory cache viewer, as shown in Figure 11-3.

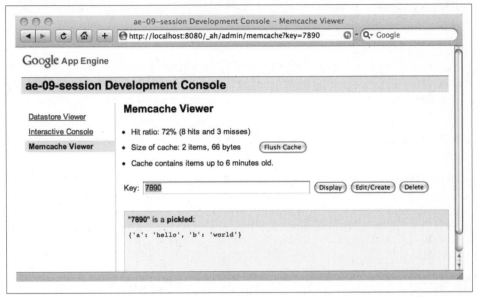

Figure 11-3. Retrieving data from the memory cache

Using the memory cache viewer, we can look up a cache entry using the key. We must know the key in advance because we cannot look at all keys. The viewer also tells us something about the nature and performance of the cache. In Figure 11-3, we have one item in the cache taking 66 bytes and our hit rate is 72%.

The *hit rate* measures how many times we issue a `get()` request to the cache and find an item (hit) and how many times we do a `get()` and do not find an item (miss). You can use the hit rate to get a sense of how often your data stored in the cache is being reused. The general desired pattern is to put something in the cache and use it several times to save from re-retrieving it from a slower source.

> In Figure 11-3, the word "pickled" means that the data in the memory cache is not exactly a Python dictionary. The data is a specially converted dictionary object suitable for transport over the network. When data is placed in the memory cache it is *pickled*, and when it is pulled back out it is *unpickled*. Other languages such as Java would refer to pickling and unpickling as *serialization* and *deserialization*, respectively.

Using a Memory Cache in Your Application

One common use of the memory cache might be for a multiperson RSS reader to cache a copy of the results of a RSS feed retrieval, so that the first user accessing the feed sees the delay of actually retrieving the feed into your application. Users who request the same RSS feed over the next few minutes are given the feed results stored in the cache (a hit).

The URL of the RSS feed is a natural key for the cache entry that holds the results of the RSS feed retrieval.

After some time period expires, the RSS results "age out," and when the next user asks for the feed, the application checks the cache; because the data is no longer there (a cache miss) the RSS feed is once again actually retrieved and placed in the cache.

Proper use of the memory cache can greatly improve the performance of your application, improve the user experience for the application, and greatly reduce the amount of resources that are consumed by the application.

Another common use of the memory cache is to prerender entire pages that are used repeatedly and serve those pages out of the memory cache instead of constructing the pages dynamically on every request. The cached copy is regenerated as appropriate, so users see new data and do not notice that the copy they're seeing might be a few minutes old.

Building a Session Store Using Memory Cache

We have already used the session object earlier in the book. At that point, we simply downloaded and used the code. Now we will look at the implementation of the session object that we used in Chapter 7 to examine how to use the App Engine memory cache, how to read and set cookies, as well as take a deeper look at how Python supports object-oriented programming.

Although this session object implementation will work for our simple developer applications and would work well for a simple, low-volume App Engine project, it is not a good idea to use this particular implementation for a highly scalable application.

Because our only storage mechanism in this implementation for session data is the memory cache, if our application ran low on memory, our sessions would start disappearing. When a session disappears, our user is unceremoniously logged out from the application. Even worse is that the session system would immediately create a new session and store it in the memory cache, which would further exacerbate the "low memory" problem.

This session implementation would scale to a certain number of users. When too many users use the application at the same time, the application would run low on memory and this session implementation would start failing and thrashing. But our purpose here is to both understand memory cache and sessions, so a nice simple implementation that works 99.9999% of the time suits our purposes at this point.

If you are interested in a scalable and robust session implementation, you can check the Internet for free session implementations. The following project provides an implementation of sessions that uses both the memory cache and the Datastore: *http: //code.google.com/p/gaeutilities/*.

This appengine utilities implementation of the session object has the same name as the session object in this chapter, so it should be relatively simple to swap out the session implementation used in this chapter with a more robust and scalable session implementation.

Our `Session` class is all about dictionaries. The memory cache is a large distributed dictionary, and each of the sessions is simply a dictionary of keyword/value pairs. The `Session` class makes use of cookies in the browser. The overall flow is as follows:

- When we receive an incoming HTTP request, we check to see whether there is a session cookie set on the incoming request.
- If there is no session cookie on the request, we make a new session, picking a large random number as the session ID. Then we create the session and store it in the memory cache with a key like `'sess-12345'` and set the cookie on the outgoing HTTP response.
- If there is a session cookie on the incoming request, we try to retrieve the session from the memory cache using the key from the cookie (i.e., `'sess-12345'`). If the matching session is in the memory cache, we use that session.
- If there is a session cookie but no corresponding session in the memory cache, we assume that something is wrong and make a new session, picking a new random number, storing the session in the memory cache, and setting the new session ID as a cookie in the outbound request.

The rest of the `Session` class is to provide methods to allow our calling user to make use of the session object we have returned.

When we used the session object in our application, the first thing we did was access the session using the following line:

```
class LogoutHandler(webapp.RequestHandler):

  def get(self):
    self.session = Session()
    self.session.delete_item('username')
    doRender(self, 'index.htm')
```

This line is creating a new session object from the `Session` class and storing it in the variable `self.session`.

Within the `Session` class, at the moment when the session object is being created, it calls a special method in the class called the "constructor." Within the class, the constructor is defined as the method named __init__().

Much of the work of the `Session` class is done in the constructor (__init__() method) for the class.

There are three code paths through this constructor: (a) we have a cookie and a session, (b) we have a cookie but no matching session, and (c) we have no cookie set. In paths (b) and (c) we make a new session, store it in the cache, and set the cookie.

The first step is to retrieve the cookie information from the headers in the incoming request using os.environ.get(). Then we parse the cookie headers using the Cookie.SimpleCookie class and check for the session cookie:

```
import Cookie

class Session(object):

    def __init__(self):
        self.sid = None
        self.key = None
        self.session = None
        string_cookie = os.environ.get('HTTP_COOKIE', '')
        self.cookie = Cookie.SimpleCookie()
        self.cookie.load(string_cookie)

        # check for existing cookie
        if self.cookie.get(COOKIE_NAME):
            self.sid = self.cookie[COOKIE_NAME].value
            self.key = 'session-' + self.sid
            try:
                self.session = memcache.get(self.key)
            except:
                self.session = None
            if self.session is None:
                logging.info('Invalidating session '+self.sid)
                self.sid = None
                self.key = None

        # Make a new session and set the cookie
        if self.session is None:
            self.sid = str(random.random())[5:]
            self.key = 'session-' + self.sid
            logging.info('Creating session '+self.key);
            self.session = dict()
            memcache.add(self.key, self.session, 3600)

            self.cookie[COOKIE_NAME] = self.sid
            self.cookie[COOKIE_NAME]['path'] = DEFAULT_COOKIE_PATH
            # Send the Cookie header to the browser
            print self.cookie
```

If the session cookie is present, we try to load the existing session from the memory cache. If we find a matching session in the memory cache, we use this as our session. If there is no session in the memory cache that matches the cookie value, we create a new session.

To create a new session, choose a large random number to use as the new session key. Create an empty Python dictionary and then store the empty dictionary in the memory cache using the new session key.

The final step of creating the session is to set the session cookie on the outbound HTTP response. The line `print self.cookie` actually prints out an HTTP response header that looks as follows:

```
Set-Cookie: appengine-simple-session-sid=921288672590409739; Path=/
```

As long as this line comes out before any of the body of the response, browsers will see this as a header line and set the cookie appropriately. This is why it is important to initialize the session before any response output has been sent to the browser.

In this section of code from our application, we create or load the session as the first line of the `post` method in the `LoginHandler()`:

```
class LoginHandler(webapp.RequestHandler):

    def post(self):
        self.session = Session()
        acct = self.request.get('account')
        pw = self.request.get('password')
        logging.info('Checking account='+acct+' pw='+pw)
```

After the `__init__` method, we define a method, so that any time we change the local copy of the dictionary (`self.session`), we also replace the copy in the memory cache:

```
    # Private method to update the cache on modification
    def _update_cache(self):
        memcache.replace(self.key, self.session, 3600)
```

We provide a convenience method called `delete_item()`, which checks to see whether a key is in the session before trying to do a delete (and risking a traceback):

```
    # Convenient delete with no error method
    def delete_item(self, keyname):
        if keyname in self.session:
            del self.session[keyname]
            self._update_cache()
```

The remainder of the `Session` class is a set of utility methods to allow the user to treat the session object as a dictionary object. For example, this method lets us call `get()` on the session object:

```
    # Support the dictionary get() method
    def get(self, keyname, default=None):
        if keyname in self.session:
            return self.session[key]
        return default
```

Another aspect of Python support for object-oriented programming is allowing a class to add methods to support certain syntactic patterns. For example, our session object can support the square bracket lookup operation, as follows:

```
    x = session['username']
```

Python sees this syntax and transforms it into the following code:

```
    __getitem__(session, 'username')
```

Because we want to support this syntax in our session object, we add the following method to our class:

```
# x = session[keyname]
def __getitem__(self, keyname):
    if keyname in self.session:
        return self.session[keyname]
    raise KeyError(str(keyname))
```

You can look through the source code of the *sessions.py* to see how we provide these methods so that our session object supports all the operations of a dictionary object and our end user can use our session object as if it were a Python dictionary.

Sessions and Memory Cache

We can take a look at how the session works and how the cookie is established and how they work together by watching the application log and the application console. First, we start with no application running and all browsers closed.

Start up your *ae-09-session* application and watch the console output. Then open your browser and navigate to *http://localhost:8080*. The console will show that the session has been created and show us the key used by the session (see Figure 11-4).

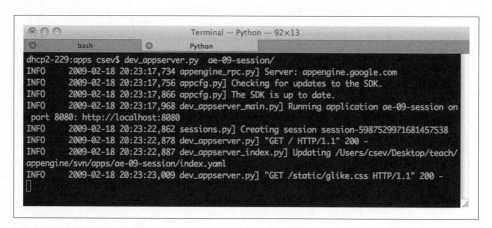

Figure 11-4. Creating sessions

Navigate to the Application Console at *http://localhost:8080/_ah/admin/*. Select the memory cache viewer, enter the key for your session from the log, and retrieve the session from the memory cache. It will appear as shown in Figure 11-5.

After we have successfully logged in, Figure 11-6 shows that we now have data in the session under the key `'username'` because we have successfully completed the login step.

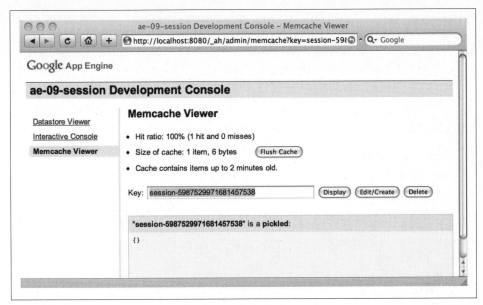

Figure 11-5. A session in the memory cache (not logged in)

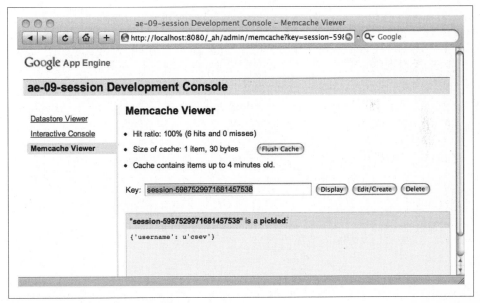

Figure 11-6. A session after login has been completed

Summary

In this chapter, we covered the App Engine memory cache capability and implemented a simple session object using the memory cache. We also looked more deeply into Python's support for object-oriented programming.

Exercises

1. What is the main purpose of the App Engine memory cache?
   a. Making your application blazingly fast
   b. Reducing the amount of Google resources that you use
   c. Increasing the number of simultaneous users that you support
   d. Reducing your costs
   e. All the above

2. If the memory cache is so great, why don't we just use it for all of our applications' data storage needs?

3. Why is storing session data (the example used in this chapter) a particularly bad use of memory cache?

4. Some applications actually cache their own HTML output for certain pages in order to save the effort of regenerating those pages from the Datastore. Give an example of a page for which caching the page contents (or most of the page contents) might be very effective.

5. Why is the memory cache significantly faster than the Datastore?

6. What must you always keep in mind when placing your application data in the memory cache?

7. What data structure in Python is most similar to the memory cache (integer, string, dictionary, list)? Why is this a good data structure for the memory cache?

Installing and Running Google App Engine on Windows XP

This appendix describes the installation of the Google App Engine Software Development Kit (SDK) under Windows XP and running a simple "Hello, world" application.

The App Engine SDK allows you to run Google App Engine Applications on your local computer. It simulates the runtime environment of the Google App Engine infrastructure.

Download and Install

Download the appropriate install package for the Google App Engine SDK from *http://code.google.com/appengine/downloads.html*, as shown in Figure A-1.

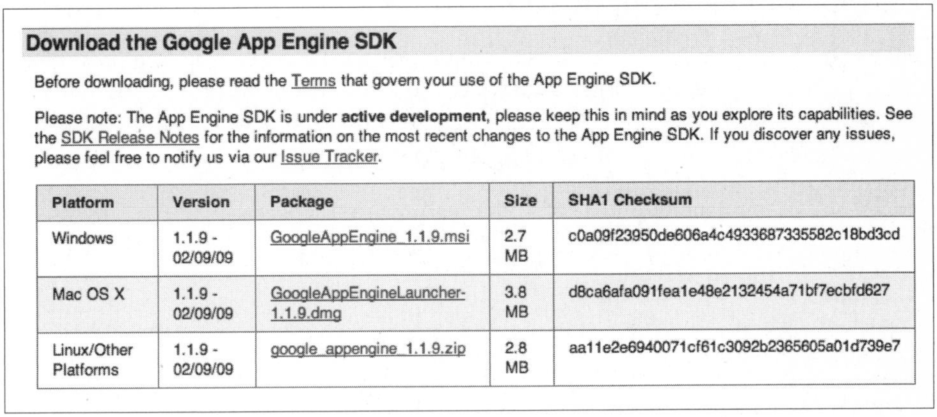

Download the Google App Engine SDK

Before downloading, please read the Terms that govern your use of the App Engine SDK.

Please note: The App Engine SDK is under **active development**, please keep this in mind as you explore its capabilities. See the SDK Release Notes for the information on the most recent changes to the App Engine SDK. If you discover any issues, please feel free to notify us via our Issue Tracker.

Platform	Version	Package	Size	SHA1 Checksum
Windows	1.1.9 - 02/09/09	GoogleAppEngine_1.1.9.msi	2.7 MB	c0a09f23950de606a4c4933687335582c18bd3cd
Mac OS X	1.1.9 - 02/09/09	GoogleAppEngineLauncher-1.1.9.dmg	3.8 MB	d8ca6afa091fea1e48e2132454a71bf7ecbfd627
Linux/Other Platforms	1.1.9 - 02/09/09	google_appengine_1.1.9.zip	2.8 MB	aa11e2e6940071cf61c3092b2365605a01d739e7

Figure A-1. Downloading Google Application Engine

Download the Windows installer and double-click on the GoogleApplicationEngine installer; the setup wizard will launch, as shown in Figure A-2.

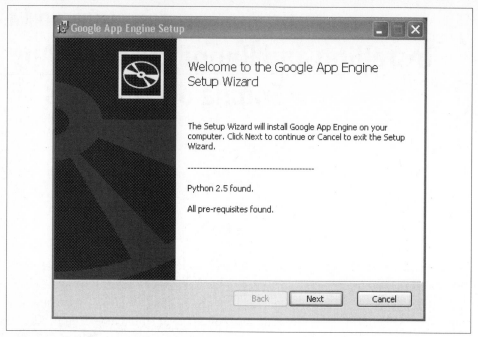

Figure A-2. Installing Google App Engine

Click through the installation wizard, which should install App Engine. If you do not have Python 2.5, it will install Python 2.5 as well. Once the install is complete, you can discard the downloaded installer.

Making Your First Application

Let's create a simple application. Make a folder for your Google App Engine applications. For this example, we'll use a folder called *apps* on the desktop: *C:\Documents and Settings\csev\Desktop\apps*. Make a subfolder in within *apps* called *ae-01-trivial*: *C:\ Documents and Settings \csev\Desktop\apps\ae-01-trivial*.

Using a text editor such as jEdit (*http://www.jedit.org*), create a file called *app.yaml* in the *ae-01-trivial* folder, with the following contents:

```
application: ae-01-trivial
version: 1
runtime: python
api_version: 1

handlers:
- url: /.*
  script: index.py
```

If you are looking at a PDF copy of this book, please do not copy and paste these lines into your text editor; you might end up with strange characters. Just type them into your editor.

Then create a file in the *ae-01-trivial* folder called *index.py*, with three lines of Python:

```
print 'Content-Type: text/plain'
print ''
print 'Hello there Jim'
```

Then start the Command Prompt program by clicking the Windows icon in the lower left and typing Command in the Start Search box. When it selects the Command Prompt item, press Enter to start the Command Prompt. Use the cd command to navigate into the *apps* directory, as shown in Figure A-3.

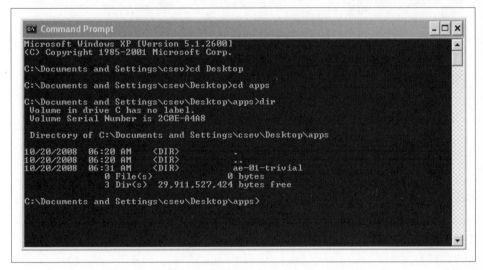

Figure A-3. Navigating to the application directory

Then start the Google App Engine Web Server and run your application using the following command:

```
\Program Files\Google\google_appengine\dev_appserver.py ae-01-trivial
```

You can save some typing by using the following sequence, pressing the Tab key as indicated (these are just shown to make it easier): \ProTAB \GoTAB\goTAB\devTAB. It works because when you type part of a filename or folder name and press the Tab key, Windows completes the name for you to save you some typing. It makes more sense after you've tried it for a bit.

Once App Engine starts your application, you will be asked if you want App Engine to check for updates (type **y**) and then, after a few messages, the server will start up, as shown in Figure A-4.

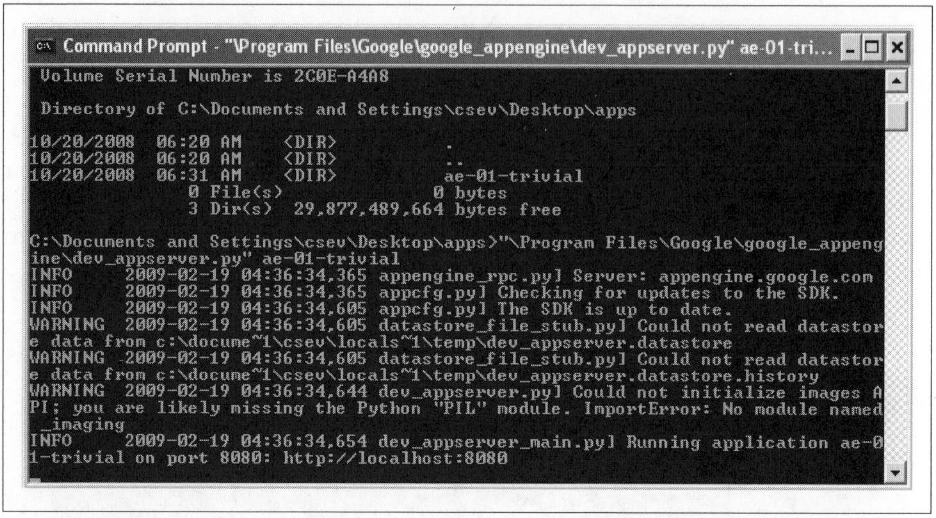

Figure A-4. Starting the application server

The last line tells you which port your application is running on and what URL you should use to access your application. In this case, our application is at *http://localhost: 8080*.

Paste *http://localhost:8080* into your browser, and you should see your application, as shown in Figure A-5.

Just for fun, edit *index.py* to change the name Jim to your own name and refresh the page in the browser to verify your updates.

Dealing with Errors

With two files to edit, there are two general categories of errors that you may encounter. The first common error is making a mistake in your *app.yaml* file. If you make a mistake in the *app.yaml* file, App Engine will not start, and you will see an error on the command line, as shown in Figure A-6.

In this instance, the mistake is an incorrect indentation in the last line in the *app.yaml* (line 8).

When you make a mistake in the *app.yaml* file, you must the fix the mistake and attempt to start the application again.

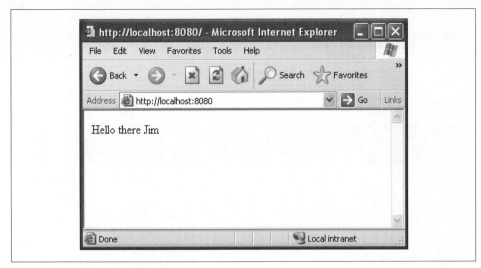

Figure A-5. Your Google application

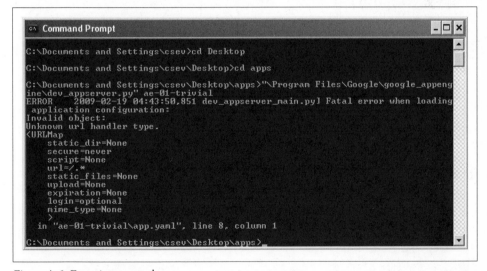

Figure A-6. Error in app.yaml

The second type of error is in the *index.py* file. If you make a syntax error in the *index.py* file, the error will appear in your browser. The error will make it look like everything has gone wrong, as shown in Figure A-7.

Do not be alarmed. Ignore most of the output and scroll to the very bottom of the error output. The error that you need to see is likely to be the very last line of the output. In this case, there was a Python syntax error on the first line of our one-line application, as shown in Figure A-8.

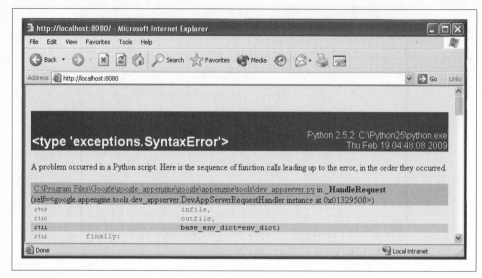

Figure A-7. Syntax error

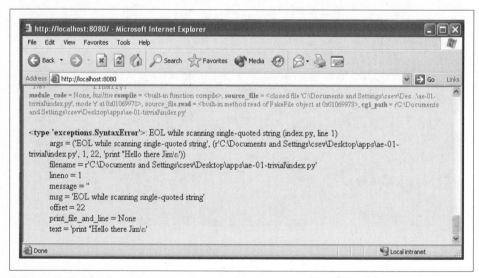

Figure A-8. Finding the syntax error

See also *http://en.wikipedia.org/wiki/Stack_trace* for more information.

If you make a mistake in a file like *index.py*, you can just fix the file and refresh the page in your browser. There is no need to restart the server.

Shutting Down the Server

To shut down the server, go into the window where you started the server and close the window to abort the server. When the server is shut down, you will notice that navigating to *http://localhost:8080* will fail because there is no software running on and listening to port 8080.

Installing and Running Google App Engine on Windows Vista

This appendix describes the installation of the Google App Engine Software Development Kit (SDK) under Windows Vista and running a simple "Hello, world" application. The App Engine SDK allows you to run Google App Engine Applications on your local computer. It simulates the runtime environment of the Google App Engine infrastructure.

Download and Install

Download the appropriate Google App Engine SDK install package from *http://code .google.com/appengine/downloads.html* as shown in Figure B-1.

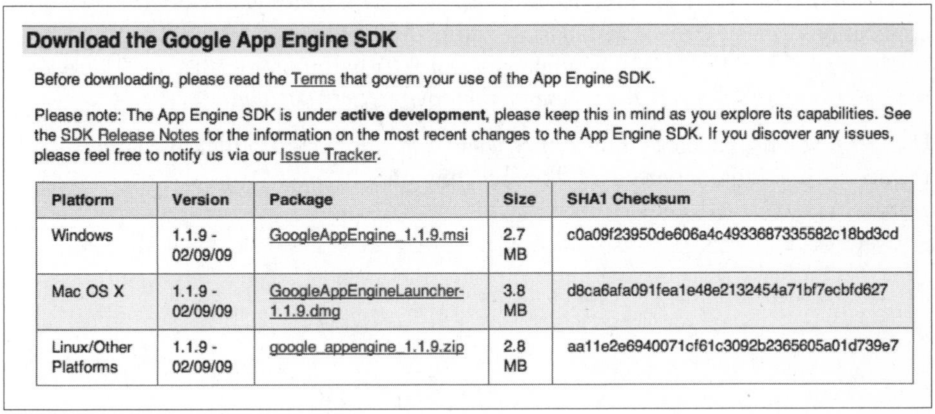

Download the Google App Engine SDK

Before downloading, please read the Terms that govern your use of the App Engine SDK.

Please note: The App Engine SDK is under **active development**, please keep this in mind as you explore its capabilities. See the SDK Release Notes for the information on the most recent changes to the App Engine SDK. If you discover any issues, please feel free to notify us via our Issue Tracker.

Platform	Version	Package	Size	SHA1 Checksum
Windows	1.1.9 - 02/09/09	GoogleAppEngine_1.1.9.msi	2.7 MB	c0a09f23950de606a4c4933687335582c18bd3cd
Mac OS X	1.1.9 - 02/09/09	GoogleAppEngineLauncher-1.1.9.dmg	3.8 MB	d8ca6afa091fea1e48e2132454a71bf7ecbfd627
Linux/Other Platforms	1.1.9 - 02/09/09	google_appengine_1.1.9.zip	2.8 MB	aa11e2e6940071cf61c3092b2365605a01d739e7

Figure B-1. Downloading Google Application Engine

Download the Windows installer, double-click on the GoogleApplicationEngine installer, and accept any security warning dialog boxes that pop up.

Click through the installation wizard, as shown in Figure B-2, and it will install App Engine. If you do not have Python 2.5, it will install Python 2.5 as well.

Figure B-2. Installing Google Application Engine

Once the install is complete, you can discard the downloaded installer.

Making Your First Application

Now you need to create a simple application. Make a folder for your Google App Engine applications. This example installation will be put into a desktop folder called *apps*: *C:\Users\csev\Desktop\apps*. Then make a subfolder within *apps* called *ae-01-trivial*— the path to this folder is *C:\Users\csev\Desktop\apps\ae-01-trivial*.

Using a text editor such as jEdit (*http://www.jedit.org*), create a file called *app.yaml* in the *ae-01-trivial* folder with the following contents:

```
application: ae-01-trivial
version: 1
runtime: python
api_version: 1

handlers:
- url: /.*
  script: index.py
```

 If you are reading a PDF version of this book, please do not copy and paste these lines into your text editor—you might end up with strange characters. Instead, just type them into your editor.

Create a file in the *ae-01-trivial* folder called *index.py* with three lines of Python:

```
print 'Content-Type: text/plain'
print ''
print 'Hello there Chuck'
```

Then start the Command Prompt program by clicking the Windows icon in the lower-left and typing Command in the Start Search box. When the Command Prompt item is highlighted, press Enter to start the Command Prompt.

Then use the cd command to navigate into the *apps* directory, as shown in Figure B-3.

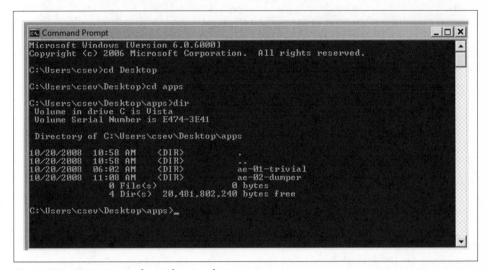

Figure B-3. Navigating to the application directory

Start the Google App Engine Web Server and run your application using this command:

```
"\Program Files\Google\google_appengine\dev_appserver.py" ae-01-trivial
```

Once App Engine starts with your application, you will be asked if you want App Engine to check for updates (type y) and then, after a few messages, the server will start up, as shown in Figure B-4.

The last line tells you which port your application is running on and what URL you should use to access your application. In this case, our application is at *http://localhost: 8080*. Paste *http://localhost:8080* into your browser, and you should see your application, as shown in Figure B-5.

Just for fun, edit *index.py* to change the name Chuck to your own name and refresh the browser to verify your updates.

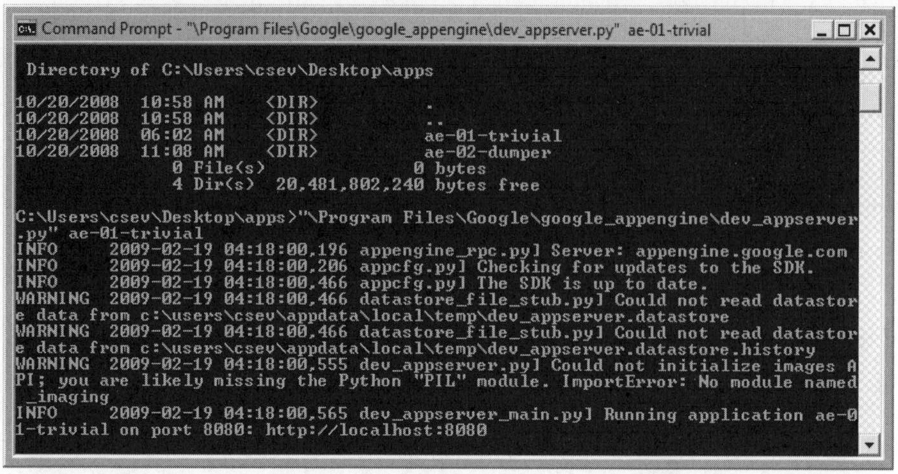

Figure B-4. Starting the application server

Figure B-5. Your Google application

Dealing with Errors

With two files to edit, there are two general categories of errors that you may encounter. If you make a mistake in the *app.yaml* file, App Engine will not start, and you will see an error, as shown in Figure B-6.

In this instance, the mistake was an incorrect indentation in the last line in the *app.yaml* (line 8).

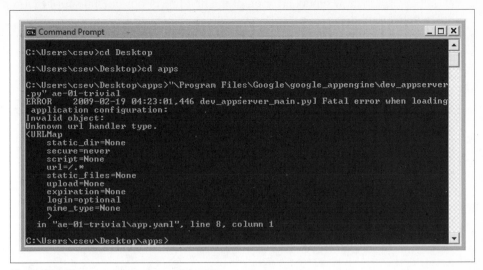

Figure B-6. Error in app.yaml

When you make a mistake in the *app.yaml* file, you must the fix the mistake and attempt to start the application again.

If you make a syntax error in the *index.py* file, the error will appear in your browser. The error looks bad, as if everything has gone completely wrong, as shown in Figure B-7.

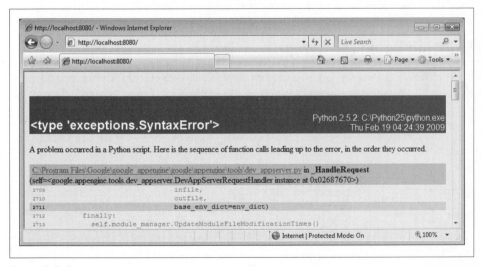

Figure B-7. Syntax error

Do not be alarmed! Ignore most of the output and scroll to the very bottom of the error output. The error that you need to see is likely to be the very last line of the output. In this case I made a Python syntax error on of the first line of our one-line application, as shown in Figure B-8.

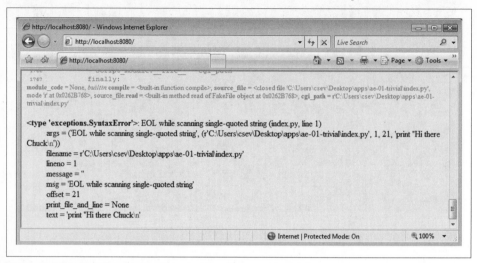

Figure B-8. Finding the syntax error

See also *http://en.wikipedia.org/wiki/Stack_trace* for more information.

If you make a mistake in a file like *index.py*, you can just fix the file and refresh your browser. There is no need to restart the server.

Shutting Down the Server

To shut down the server, go into the window where you started the server and close the window to abort the server. When the server is shut down, you will notice that navigating to *http://localhost:8080* will fail because there is no software running on and listening to port 8080.

Installing and Running Google App Engine on a Macintosh System

This appendix describes the installation of the Google App Engine Software Development Kit (SDK) on a Macintosh and running a simple "Hello, world" application.

The App Engine SDK allows you to run Google App Engine Applications on your local computer. It simulates the runtime environment of the Google App Engine infrastructure.

Download and Install

Download the appropriate install package for the Google App Engine SDK from *http://code.google.com/appengine/downloads.html*, as shown in Figure C-1.

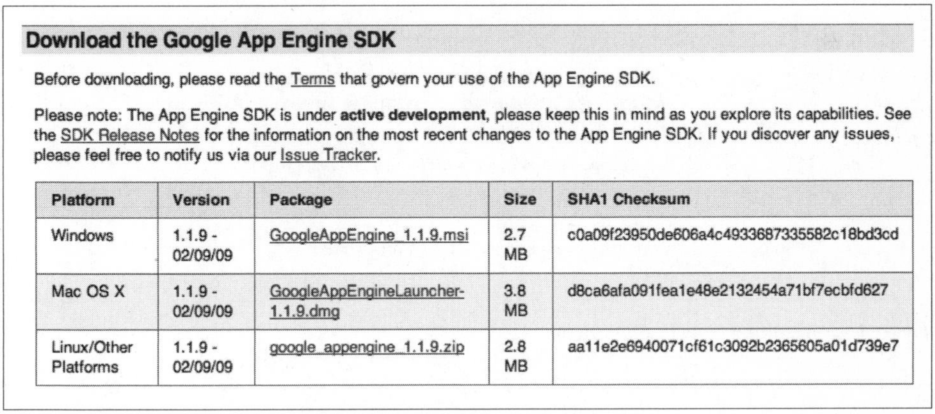

Download the Google App Engine SDK

Before downloading, please read the Terms that govern your use of the App Engine SDK.

Please note: The App Engine SDK is under **active development**, please keep this in mind as you explore its capabilities. See the SDK Release Notes for the information on the most recent changes to the App Engine SDK. If you discover any issues, please feel free to notify us via our Issue Tracker.

Platform	Version	Package	Size	SHA1 Checksum
Windows	1.1.9 - 02/09/09	GoogleAppEngine_1.1.9.msi	2.7 MB	c0a09f23950de606a4c4933687335582c18bd3cd
Mac OS X	1.1.9 - 02/09/09	GoogleAppEngineLauncher-1.1.9.dmg	3.8 MB	d8ca6afa091fea1e48e2132454a71bf7ecbfd627
Linux/Other Platforms	1.1.9 - 02/09/09	google_appengine_1.1.9.zip	2.8 MB	aa11e2e6940071cf61c3092b2365605a01d739e7

Figure C-1. Downloading Google Application Engine

Download the Mac OS X installer. It should automatically mount as a virtual drive (Figure C-2).

Figure C-2. The App Engine Installer

Drag the GoogleAppEngineLauncher to the *Applications* folder on your hard drive. This step copies Google App Engine and installs it as an application on your system. Once this is done, you can eject the virtual drive.

Navigate to the */Applications* folder on your main disk, find the AppEngineLauncher icon, and launch it. You may need to scroll to the bottom of your screen to see the App Engine icon.

Click Accept or Open in any dialog box that asks whether it is OK to launch, as shown in Figure C-3.

Figure C-3. Installing Google App Engine

When the Engine launches for the first time, it asks if you want to make Command Symlinks, as shown in Figure C-4.

Figure C-4. Making symbolic links

Click OK. This step will allow you to run App Engine from the command line later. You will have to type an administrator password to make the links.

At this point, you can actually close the App Engine Launcher—you will run the application from the command-line interface (the Terminal application) instead of using the Launcher user interface.

Making Your First Application

Now you need to create a simple application. We could use the graphical launcher to make our application, but instead we will do it by hand to give you a better sense of what is going on.

Make a folder for your Google App Engine applications. I am going to name the folder on my Macintosh Desktop *apps*. The path to this folder is: */Users/csev/Desktop/apps*—obviously your path will use your account name instead of mine. Then make a subfolder in within *apps* called *ae-01-trivial*: */Users/csev/Desktop/apps/ae-01-trivial*.

Create a file called *app.yaml* in the *ae-01-trivial* folder with the following contents:

```
application: ae-01-trivial
version: 1
runtime: python
api_version: 1

handlers:
- url: /.*
  script: index.py
```

If you are looking at a PDF copy of this book, please do not copy and paste these lines into your text editor. You might end up with strange characters. Just type them into your editor.

Then create a file in the *ae-01-trivial* folder called *index.py*, with three lines of Python:

```
print 'Content-Type: text/plain'
print ''
print 'Hello there Chuck'
```

Then start the Terminal program, which can be found under Applications→Utilities→ Terminal. Use the `cd` command to navigate to the *apps* directory, as shown in Figure C-5.

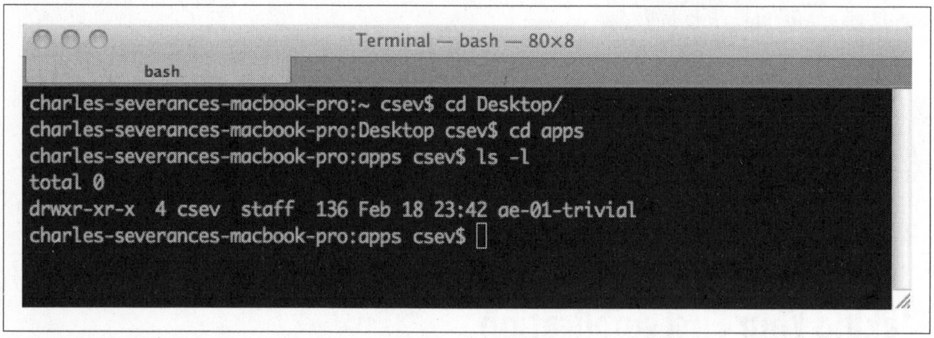

```
 ● ● ●                    Terminal — bash — 80×8
      bash
charles-severances-macbook-pro:~ csev$ cd Desktop/
charles-severances-macbook-pro:Desktop csev$ cd apps
charles-severances-macbook-pro:apps csev$ ls -l
total 0
drwxr-xr-x  4 csev  staff  136 Feb 18 23:42 ae-01-trivial
charles-severances-macbook-pro:apps csev$ []
```

Figure C-5. Navigating to the apps directory

When you are in the *apps* directory, start the Google App Engine Web Server and run your application using the following command:

```
/usr/local/bin/dev_appserver.py ae-01-trivial
```

You will be asked if you want App Engine to check for updates (type y); after a few messages, the server will start up, as shown in Figure C-6.

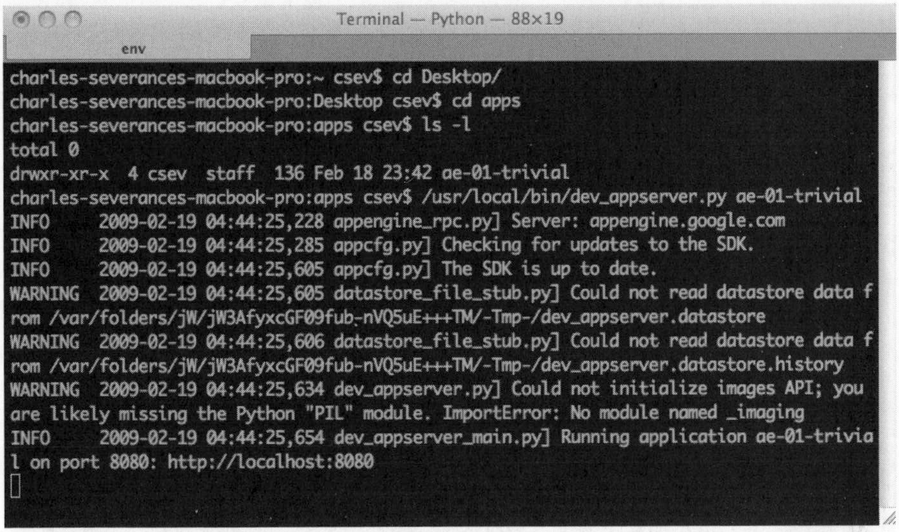

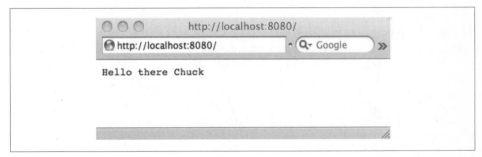

Terminal — Python — 88×19
env
charles-severances-macbook-pro:~ csev$ cd Desktop/
charles-severances-macbook-pro:Desktop csev$ cd apps
charles-severances-macbook-pro:apps csev$ ls -l
total 0
drwxr-xr-x 4 csev staff 136 Feb 18 23:42 ae-01-trivial
charles-severances-macbook-pro:apps csev$ /usr/local/bin/dev_appserver.py ae-01-trivial
INFO   2009-02-19 04:44:25,228 appengine_rpc.py] Server: appengine.google.com
INFO   2009-02-19 04:44:25,285 appcfg.py] Checking for updates to the SDK.
INFO   2009-02-19 04:44:25,605 appcfg.py] The SDK is up to date.
WARNING 2009-02-19 04:44:25,605 datastore_file_stub.py] Could not read datastore data f
rom /var/folders/jW/jW3AfyxcGF09fub-nVQ5uE+++TM/-Tmp-/dev_appserver.datastore
WARNING 2009-02-19 04:44:25,606 datastore_file_stub.py] Could not read datastore data f
rom /var/folders/jW/jW3AfyxcGF09fub-nVQ5uE+++TM/-Tmp-/dev_appserver.datastore.history
WARNING 2009-02-19 04:44:25,634 dev_appserver.py] Could not initialize images API; you
are likely missing the Python "PIL" module. ImportError: No module named _imaging
INFO   2009-02-19 04:44:25,654 dev_appserver_main.py] Running application ae-01-trivia
l on port 8080: http://localhost:8080

Figure C-6. Starting the application server

The last line tells you which port your application is running on and what URL you should use to access your application; in this case, our application is at *http://localhost:8080*.

Paste *http://localhost:8080* into your browser and you should see your application, as shown in Figure C-7.

http://localhost:8080/
http://localhost:8080/
Google
Hello there Chuck

Figure C-7. Your Google application

Just for fun, edit the *index.py* to change the name "Chuck" to your own name and refresh the page in the browser to verify your updates.

Dealing with Errors

With two files to edit, there are two general categories of errors that you may encounter. The first common error is making a mistake in your *app.yaml* file. If you make a mistake on the *app.yaml* file, App Engine will not start, and you will see an error as shown in Figure C-8.

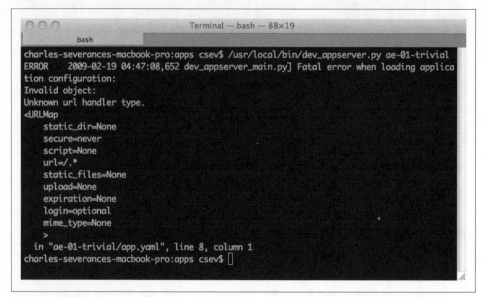

Figure C-8. Error in app.yaml

In this instance, the mistake is an incorrectly indented final line in the *app.yaml* (line 8).

When you make a mistake in the *app.yaml* file, you must the fix the mistake and attempt to start the application again.

The second type of error is in the *index.py* file. If you make a syntax error in the *index.py* file, the error will appear in your browser. The error looks terrible and looks like everything went wrong, as shown in Figure C-9.

Do not be alarmed! Ignore most of the output and scroll to the very bottom of the error output. The error you need to see is likely to be the very last line of the output—in this case, I made a Python syntax error on the first and only line of our one-line *index.py* file, as shown in Figure C-10.

See also *http://en.wikipedia.org/wiki/Stack_trace* for more information.

If you make a mistake in a file like *index.py*, you can just fix the file and refresh your browser—there is no need to restart the server.

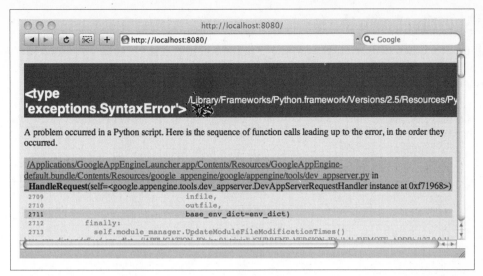

Figure C-9. Syntax error

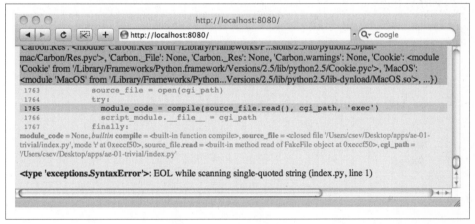

Figure C-10. Finding the syntax error

Shutting Down the Server

To shut down the server, go into the window where you started the server and press Ctrl-C to abort the server. You should see a message that says something like "Server interrupted by user, terminating" and the server will shut down. You can start it back up using the `dev_appserver.py` command again. When the server is shut down, navigating to *http://localhost:8080* will fail because there is no software running on and listening to port 8080.

Installing and Running Google App Engine on a Linux System

Marc Alier and Jordi Piguillem Poch

This appendix describes the installation of the Google App Engine Software Development Kit (SDK) on Linux, plus how to run a simple "Hello, world" application.

The App Engine SDK allows you to run Google App Engine Applications on your local computer. It simulates the runtime environment of the Google App Engine infrastructure.

Checking for Python

Google App Engine needs the Python interpreter to work on your system. Python comes usually preinstalled on most Linux distributions. To check whether Python is installed, open a Terminal window and type **python** to execute the Python interpreter:

```
python
Python 2.5.2 (r252:60911, Feb 22 2008, 07:57:53)
...
```

The first line will show you the version of Python running on your system. Type **exit()** to return to the command line.

If Python is not installed or you have a version other than 2.5.x, you will need to download this version (2.5) of Python from *http://python.org*. Check to see whether there is a package containing Python 2.5 for your Linux distribution.

Download and Install

Download the Google App Engine SDK from *http://code.google.com/appengine/down loads.html*; download the appropriate install package, as shown in Figure D-1.

Download the Google App Engine SDK

Before downloading, please read the Terms that govern your use of the App Engine SDK.

Please note: The App Engine SDK is under **active development**, please keep this in mind as you explore its capabilities. See the SDK Release Notes for the information on the most recent changes to the App Engine SDK. If you discover any issues, please feel free to notify us via our Issue Tracker.

Platform	Version	Package	Size	SHA1 Checksum
Windows	1.1.9 - 02/09/09	GoogleAppEngine_1.1.9.msi	2.7 MB	c0a09f23950de606a4c4933687335582c18bd3cd
Mac OS X	1.1.9 - 02/09/09	GoogleAppEngineLauncher-1.1.9.dmg	3.8 MB	d8ca6afa091fea1e48e2132454a71bf7ecbfd627
Linux/Other Platforms	1.1.9 - 02/09/09	google_appengine_1.1.9.zip	2.8 MB	aa11e2e6940071cf61c3092b2365605a01d739e7

Figure D-1. Downloading Google Application Engine

In this case, you must download the Linux package onto your computer's desktop, as shown in Figure D-2.

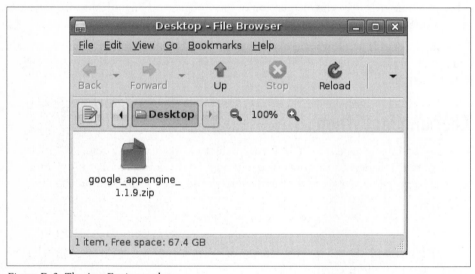

Figure D-2. The App Engine package

Decompress the downloaded file. In Figure D-3, we are using File Roller to unzip the file.

Figure D-4 shows how you can also use the built-in `unzip` command-line tool in the Terminal application. Here we are uncompressing *google_appengine_1.1.9.zip* (the SDK) to our desktop folder.

Once you have completed the unzipping process, you will get a folder named *google_appengine* that contains all the files necessary to develop your applications, as shown in Figure D-5.

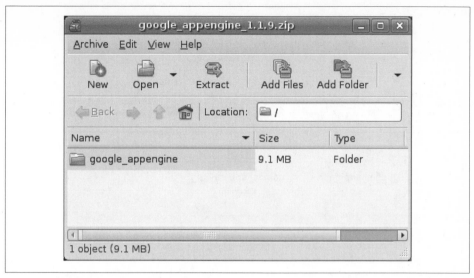

Figure D-3. Unzipping the file using File Roller

Figure D-4. Unzipping the file using Terminal

The last step is to include the path to Google App Engine scripts into the system's PATH variable to launch its applications from a terminal using the command:

```
export PATH=$PATH:/home/computer_name/Desktop/google_appengine/
```

Substitute your username instead of *computer_name*.

The **export** command will work only during your current session. Check your Linux distribution manual to see which file (such as *.bashrc_login*) you can edit to add this

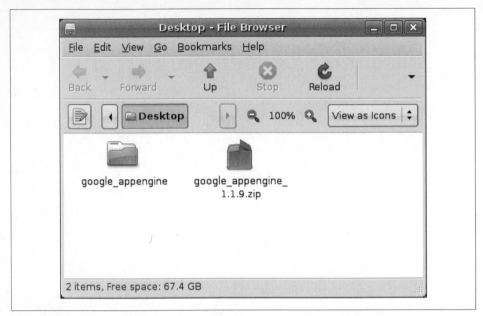

Figure D-5. Unzipped content

command so that the PATH variable is set properly in each new terminal window that is opened.

We will use this window for the remainder of the steps in this process. If you start a new window, type the previous PATH command once in each new window until you edit your login script to make the path change automatic.

Making Your First Application

Make a folder for your Google App Engine applications. I am going to put the folder on my desktop and call it *apps*. The path to this folder is */home/pigui/Desktop/apps*. Then make a subfolder in within *apps* called *ae-01-trivial*. The path to this folder would be */home/pigui/Desktop/apps/ae-01-trivial*.

Create a file called *app.yaml* in the *ae-01-trivial* folder with the following contents:

```
application: ae-01-trivial
version: 1
runtime: python
api_version: 1

handlers:
- url: /.*
  script: index.py
```

If you are looking at a PDF copy of this book, please do not copy and paste these lines into your text editor. You might end up with strange characters. Just type them into your editor.

Then create a file in the *ae-01-trivial* folder called *index.py*, with three lines of Python:

```
print 'Content-Type: text/plain'
print ''
print 'Hello there Chuck'
```

Using the Terminal, navigate to the *apps* directory, start the Google App Engine Web Server, and run your application using the following command:

```
dev_appserver.py ae-01-trivial
```

You will be asked if you want App Engine to check for updates (type y). After a few messages, the server will start up, as shown in Figure D-6.

Figure D-6. Starting the application server

The last line tells you which port your application is running on and what URL you should use to access your application. In this case, our application is at *http://localhost: 8080*. Paste *http://localhost:8080* into your browser, and you should see your application, as shown in Figure D-7.

Just for fun, edit the *index.py* to change the name "Chuck" to your own name, and refresh the page in your browser to verify your updates.

Dealing with Errors

With two files to edit, there are two general categories of errors that you may encounter. The first common error is making a mistake in your *app.yaml* file. If you make a mistake

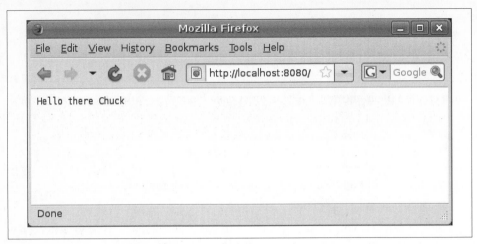

Figure D-7. Your Google application

on the *app.yaml* file, App Engine will not start, and you will see an error as shown in Figure D-8.

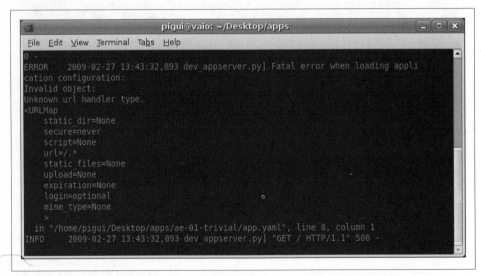

Figure D-8. Error in app.yaml

In this instance, the mistake is an incorrect indentation of the final line in *app.yaml* (line 8).

When you make a mistake in the *app.yaml* file, you must the fix the mistake and attempt to start the application again.

If you make a syntax error in the *index.py* file, the error will appear in your browser. The error looks terrible, like everything went wrong, as shown in Figure D-9.

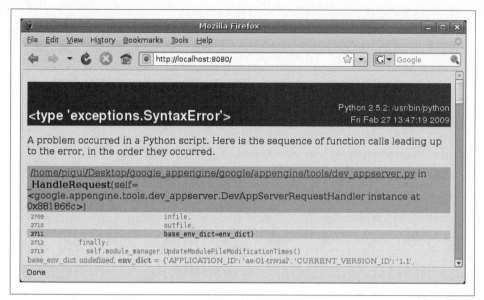

Figure D-9. Syntax error

Do not be alarmed! Ignore most of the output and scroll to the very bottom of the error output. The error that you need to see is likely to be the very last line of the output. In this case, I made a Python syntax error on the first line of our one-line application, as shown in Figure D-10.

See also *http://en.wikipedia.org/wiki/Stack_trace* for more information.

If you make a mistake in a file like *index.py*, you can fix the file and refresh the page in your browser. There is no need to restart the server.

Shutting Down the Server

To shut down the server, go into the window where you started the server and press Ctrl-C to abort the server. You should see a message that says something like "Server interrupted by user, terminating," and the server will shut down. You can start it back up by using the `dev_appserver.py` command again. When the server is shut down, you will notice that navigating to *http://localhost:8080* will fail because there is no software running on and listening to port 8080.

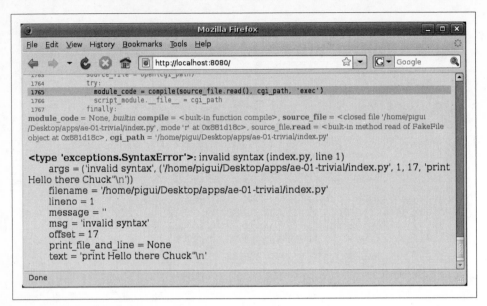

Figure D-10. Finding the syntax error

Index

We'd like to hear your suggestions for improving our indexes. Send email to *index@oreilly.com*.

About the Author

Charles Severance is a Clinical Assistant Professor in the School of Information at the University of Michigan and works with the IMS Global Learning Consortium as the IMS Developer Network Coordinator. He is also the author of *High Performance Computing*, Second Edition (O'Reilly). His home page is *http://www.dr-chuck.com*.

Colophon

The animal on the cover of *Using Google App Engine* is a great gray shrike (*Lanius excubitor*). The great gray shrike is found in Europe and Asia, and in North America, in Canada and Alaska. It is approximately 22–26 cm long, with a white belly, and it is pearlish-gray on top. It has black wings, a black tail, and a characteristic black stripe running through its eye. A solitary bird, it can usually be found sitting alone atop a bush or post scanning the ground for prey, which includes everything from insects to mice and other birds. It uses its feet to capture smaller prey such as bees or flies, but it has to impale larger prey on a sharp object, such as a thorn; once the prey is secure, the great gray shrike can use its strong hooked bill to devour it.

The cover image is from the Dover Pictorial Archive. The cover font is Adobe ITC Garamond. The text font is Linotype Birka; the heading font is Adobe Myriad Condensed; and the code font is LucasFont's TheSansMonoCondensed.

Related Titles from O'Reilly

Web Applications

Ambient Findability

Developing Feeds with RSS & Atom

Don't Click on the Blue E!: Switching to Firefox

Dreamweaver 8: The Missing Manual

eBay Hacks, 2nd Edition

eBay: The Missing Manual

Firefox Hacks

Flash 8: The Missing Manual

Google Hacks, *3rd Edition*

Google Pocket Guide

Google Advertising Tools

Google: The Missing Manual, *2nd Edition*

Greasemonkey Hacks

Internet Annoyances

Mapping Hacks

Online Investing Hacks

Podcasting Hacks

Skype Hacks

Talk is Cheap: Switching to Internet Telephones

Using Moodle, *2nd Edition*

Visualizing Data

Web Mapping Illustrated

Web 2.0 Design Patterns

Windows PowerShell: The Definitive Guide

Yahoo! Hacks